Versions of Hollywood Crime Cinema

Versions of Hollywood Crime Cinema
Studies in Ford, Wilder, Coppola, Scorsese and others

Carl Freedman

intellect Bristol, UK / Chicago, USA

First published in the UK in 2013 by
Intellect, The Mill, Parnall Road, Fishponds, Bristol, BS16 3JG, UK

First published in the USA in 2013 by
Intellect, The University of Chicago Press, 1427 E. 60th Street,
Chicago, IL 60637, USA

A catalogue record for this book is available from the
British Library.

Cover designer: Ellen Thomas
Copy-editor: MPS Technologies
Index: Lyn Greenwood
Production manager: Jelena Stanovnik
Typesetting: Planman Technologies

ISBN 978-1-84150-724-8

Printed and bound by Hobbs, UK

For Annette, always

Table of Contents

Acknowledgments

Because I have been watching and discussing movies for quite a long time—specifically, ever since I went to see *Westward Ho, the Wagons!* (William Beaudine, 1956) at the age of five—I cannot possibly hope to list all, or even most, of the people who have made a significant contribution to my understanding of cinema or to my work as a film critic. But I will try to particularize the most important debts of which I am consciously aware.

First, there are several editors to whom I am especially grateful. Most of the chapters of this volume were originally published, in earlier form, in the splendid journal *Film International*. Its editor, Daniel Lindvall, has done more than any other single individual to nurture and support my work in film criticism, and my debt to him is immense—truly a case of "without whom this book could never have been written". Two other chapters were first published, also in somewhat different form, in two anthologies: *Red Planets: Marxism and Science Fiction* (Pluto Press, 2009), edited by Mark Bould and China Miéville, and *Neo-Noir* (Wallflower Press, 2009), edited by Mark Bould, Kathrina Glitre, and Greg Tuck. Mark Bould and Greg Tuck were the editors who worked specifically with me on my contributions, which are clearly superior to what they would have been without editorial assistance. Finally, I must name my editor at Intellect, Jelena Stanovnik, whose help, enthusiasm, and support have been indispensable; not the least of her valuable services was the recruiting of two anonymous readers, who themselves made many large and small suggestions that helped to improve the book.

Another (and somewhat overlapping) group of individuals from whom I have learned much is composed of the friends with whom I have discussed film over the years and decades—in person, by correspondence, and, especially during recent years, in a great many discussion-threads on Facebook. With apologies to the many whom I will inevitably neglect to name, I must list Andrew Banecker, Brad Bankston, Zachary Bellino, Rick Blackwood, Keith Booker, Mark Bould, Sonia Brand-Fisher, Joseph Brown, Andrew M. Butler, Rich Cooper, Corey Creekmur, Istvan Csicsery-Ronay Jr., Chip Delany, Jason Dupuy, Jean Freedman, Jonathan Freedman, Rosa Freedman, Carl Gardner, Martin Gosserand, Dan Hassler-Forest, Jonathan Haynes, Jerod Ra'Del Hollyfield, Chris Kendrick, Mari Kornhauser, Rob Latham, Daniel Lindvall, Paul March-Russell, John Margeson, Katharine Mason, Pat McGee, Kristopher Mecholsky, Solimar Otero, Peter Y. Paik, Jerome Peltier, Stephen Peltier,

Sarah Pierce, John Rieder, Blake Robinson, Umberto Rossi, Barry Schwabsky, Steve Shaviro, Zoran Samardzija, Greg Tuck, Maxie Wells, Deborah Wilson, and Beth Younger.

Still another group of people from whom I have learned are the students at Louisiana State University with whom I have watched and discussed movies in my various film courses in the English Department and in the Honors College. These students are among the most lively and capable whom I have encountered in a teaching career that has lasted nearly 35 years so far; and I can only hope that the courses have been as valuable for them as for me. The list that follows is even further from being comprehensive than the one in the paragraph immediately above; but among the most important names to be mentioned are those of Christian Alch, Rachel Berard, James Buckley, Cole Connelly, Linda Cross, Cal Gunasingha, Alex Hotard, Jared Hromadka, Mikelle Humble, Rian Johnson, Mary-Claire Kanya, Lori King, Erica Laroux, Alexander Leder, Chris Lockwood, Sarah Masson, Liz Neuner, Garrett Ordner, Kittu Pannu, Stephen Peltier, Sarah Platt, and Anson Trahan.

My greatest debt in all things is to my wife Annette. She watched these movies with me, in some cases multiple times, even though many are by no means among her own personal favorites. In fact, I rather despair of ever convincing her of the merits of John Wayne's acting, of Martin Scorsese's directing, or of the entire genre of film noir. Nonetheless, her invariably intelligent and witty comments about these films have been quite important to me even (or perhaps especially) when I disagreed with them. Still more important to me is her absolute and imperishable love.

Introduction

T his book is intended as a kind of sequel to the one that I published in 2002 titled *The Incomplete Projects: Marxism, Modernity, and the Politics of Culture*.[1] I do not mean that a familiarity with the earlier book is the least bit necessary in order to understand and appreciate this one. The current volume is designed to be completely free-standing and fully intelligible on its own. But the two books are closely connected in my own mind, and to give some account of the earlier volume may be a good way to begin explaining what I am trying to do in this one.

Marxism, the "middle realm," and film

The Incomplete Projects is divided into two parts: a theoretical exposition and defense titled "Marxism Today" and a series of applications called "Case Studies in the Politics and Ideology of Culture". I consider "Marxism Today" to be the essential statement of the theoretical assumptions and principles that underlie not only the volume in which it appears but also the current volume and, indeed, all of my books and articles.[2] In it, I offer a synoptic outline of the Marxist critique of political economy found in the work of Marx himself and his successors; and I offer a defense of this critique as still necessarily forming what Sartre called the "untranscendable horizon" of all serious analysis in the human sciences. Marxism, I maintain, remains the privileged method for the understanding of capitalism and capitalist civilization: its obsolescence will begin only when the fundamental capitalist processes—primitive accumulation; the wage-relation; the production, extraction, and realization of surplus-value—are themselves transcended and begin to figure in human consciousness as bad historical memories, like slaveholding and feudalism. In addition to the exposition of Marxist economic theory, I also provide, in "Marxism Today," some reflections on the application of the Marxist method to the understanding of politics and, especially, of culture.

In the current volume, my continuing exploration of Marxist theory is at some points explicit. Examples include the discussion of primitive accumulation in the chapter on the *Godfather* films; the thesis that Marxism must be understood as both inflationary and deflationary that is expounded in the first chapter of the section on film noir; and the argument about imperialism in the penultimate chapter of the book. In addition, in the second of the two chapters about the John Wayne Western, I propose some theoretical reflections in a field—gender studies—that lies slightly outside Marxism proper but is congruent with it and must, I would argue, ultimately be integrated with it. On the whole, however, this volume is more concerned with detailed film criticism than with general theorizing. One cannot always be explaining and defending one's fundamental presuppositions, and the Marxism of this volume is most often mainly implicit. The reader who desires a more comprehensive and systematic justification of my methodological viewpoint than can be found in this volume is referred to "Marxism Today".

In the concluding pages of "Marxism Today," in the course of a discussion of Marxism and cultural analysis, I propose a generally unrecognized sector of cultural production as particularly interesting and fruitful for Marxist (and other) attention: namely, what I call the "middle" realm of modern culture. I construct this concept by way of *de*constructing what seems to me a relatively shallow binary opposition often assumed in the (Marxist and other) study of cultural production since about the First World War. The increasingly conventional assumption seems to be that culture bifurcates around the time that the guns of August 1914 bring to a close the "long" nineteenth century inaugurated by the French Revolution and the Napoleonic wars. Culture, it is held, splits into high modernism (and later "postmodernism"), on the one hand, and mass culture on the other. The former—typified by Joyce, say, in literature, or by Schoenberg in music—is generally accounted as representing the most valuable aesthetic achievements of the modern age: but achievements attained at the cost of leaving behind much or most of the culture-consuming public that in the previous century had thrilled to the work of a Dickens or a Beethoven. What now succeed in attracting a large audience are new, utterly massified forms of culture, typically regarded as aesthetically degraded and of almost no interest of the sort traditionally attracted by humane letters and the fine arts. By synecdoche, modern culture, in this understanding, is either *Ulysses* (1922) or the supermarket tabloids.

The surely most obvious yet infrequently discussed problem with this scheme is simply that it leaves out so much of modern culture. By the "middle" realm (not, I should acknowledge, a term that seems to me particularly felicitous but one that is perhaps, for the time being, almost inevitable given the dominance of the opposition between "high" modernism and "low" mass culture), I designate a huge number of cultural artifacts that justly attract a great deal of serious critical attention and yet also manage to find an audience far beyond the elite and often essentially academic precincts to which Joycean modernism and kindred varieties of cultural production are normally confined. The wide audience for major art that is often nostalgically celebrated in backward looks at Shakespeare or Balzac has, I argue, never, in fact, ceased to exist. In the case histories that follow "Marxism Today" in *The Incomplete Projects*, I examine a variety of important works from the "middle" realm. Though the majority of them are literary—novels by authors such as Dashiell Hammett, Robert Penn Warren, George Orwell, and Philip K. Dick—I also consider films and television series. Indeed, I suggest, in "Marxism Today," that cinema may well be considered a privileged instance of the "middle" realm.

The chapters that follow in this volume may, then, be considered as a second series of case histories allied to those that occupy the latter part of *The Incomplete Projects*. Here, however, all the works under consideration are films (plus one television series that bears an especially strong, though complex and in some ways contradictory, relationship to film). Film, it seems inarguable to me, has by far the longest and aesthetically richest history of all the uniquely modern art forms; and its history is very nearly at one with that of the modern itself. Though the origins of cinema are found in the late nineteenth century—that is, just a bit after French Impressionism in painting, which is generally regarded as perhaps the first and certainly one of the most important early instances of aesthetic modernism—most of its earliest masterpieces, like Griffith's *The Birth of a Nation* (1915), Chaplin's *The Gold Rush* (1925), or Keaton's *The General* (1926), come later, after the fateful year of 1914. To be sure, in its trajectory from its early phase onward, film undergoes numerous technical and other alterations; the innovation of synchronized sound in the 1920s, popularized by Warner Brothers with *The Jazz Singer* (Alan Crosland, 1927), almost certainly remains the most important. Nonetheless, the history of film as an aesthetic mode enjoys a substantial continuity that extends to the current day and that reaches back to Griffith and Chaplin—indeed, as Martin Scorsese has reminded us in his recent movie *Hugo* (2011), even back to Georges Méliès, the pioneering French filmmaker who produced significant short films before the turn of the twentieth century. Film, as a well-known critical sociologist has designated it, is "*the* art form of late capitalism" (emphasis added).[3]

Furthermore, film, more than any other art form in the modern age, bridges the gap—or, to be more precise, encompasses what is only *sometimes* a gap in modern cultural production, distribution, and consumption—between critical and popular success. Though full academic respectability for film studies arrived only relatively late in the twentieth century, it built on an extensive tradition of serious film criticism and theory that can be traced back to such major figures as Walter Benjamin (1892–1940), Sergei Eisenstein (1898–1948), Siegfried Kracauer (1889–1966), and various others. At the same time, film has managed to win a popularity that is close to universal. There are plenty of people who dislike reading novels or looking at paintings; still more who almost never read poetry; and even a fair number who have little interest in listening to music. But one hardly ever meets a person who doesn't at all enjoy the movies. One might, indeed, argue that one can find, *within* the production and reception of film, a bifurcation similar to that often assumed between high modernism and mass culture more generally. Here the binary opposition would probably be between European "art" cinema (the names of Bergman and Fellini remain perhaps the most iconic in this regard) and Hollywood's summer blockbusters. Yet this opposition, like the larger one of which it is a specialized instance, collapses from its inability to cover such a staggering amount of material. Nearly all the films analyzed in detail in the pages to follow—works by Hollywood directors like Ford, Hawks, Wilder, Kubrick, Coppola, and Scorsese—surely belong to the "middle" realm of modern cultural activity.[4]

It may well be, however, that film's standing as the most central art form of late capitalism is currently faced by a challenge that will ultimately prove to be successful. For most of its existence, television has been widely regarded as a degraded poor relation of the cinema—bearing, that is, a relation with regard to film similar to that which film had borne with regard to such older forms as the stage drama and the novel, and to that which the novel itself had still earlier borne with regard to poetry. The popular term for the television set—"idiot box"—in a way says it all. But this consensus is far weaker today than it once was, and there is some reason to think that it may be on the verge of being decisively overthrown.

Two closely related developments seem crucial here. In the first place, an awareness appears to be dawning that television—and especially the dramatic television series—does, in fact, possess a considerable history of aesthetically significant work. Within the English-speaking world,[5] one would first of all point especially (though by no means only) to such BBC series as have flourished from the 1970s onward as *Upstairs Downstairs* (1970–1975)—which I have analyzed in some detail in *The Incomplete Projects*—and *I, Claudius* (1976); and, more recently, to the best work done since the 1990s on American premium cable channels, especially HBO, typified above all, perhaps, by *The Sopranos* (1999–2007) and *The Wire* (2002–2008). Furthermore, and in the second place, the aesthetic achievements of television have grown increasingly impressive in a relative way—compared to those of film—as well as in an absolute way. As Hollywood cinema has declined from its most golden of all ages—the 1970s, distinguished by such stellar figures as Coppola and Scorsese—HBO and similar venues have often welcomed major innovative work from talents (such as David Chase of *The Sopranos* and David Simon of *The Wire*) that once would probably have expressed themselves more naturally in film. Today many of the finest writers and directors are finding television a more congenial creative environment than the Hollywood film studios; and today one might search long at the suburban multiplex before finding viewing as rewarding as Terence Winter's *Boardwalk Empire* (2010–present) on HBO or Neil Jordan's *The Borgias* (2011–present) on Showtime. If, as I strongly suspect, television is now in process of superseding film as the art form of late capitalism, the chapter in this volume on *The Sopranos* may be taken as a response to this development.

On crime films—and on crime

The film criticism in this volume focuses not on a miscellaneous selection of movies, but on major representatives of what I take to be the three major genres of the crime film: the mob movie, film noir, and the Western. To be sure, the Western is not always thought of as a kind of crime film in quite the same way that the mob movie and film noir are, but this omission strikes me as bizarre. Nearly all films usually categorized as Westerns present life not simply in the Old West—that is, American territory west of the Mississippi river during the decades immediately following the Civil War—but in the *Wild* West: and the "wildness" is precisely a function of the fact that the official forces of law and order are generally portrayed as exercising only a tenuous hold (at most) on the organization of society, in which crime, and especially violent crime, is therefore commonplace. Bank-robbing is an especially frequent motif in the Western, but the crime that figures most prominently is the same as that which is of central concern in the mob movie and in film noir: namely, murder, the most serious crime of all.

There are, of course, important differences among the three genres. The Western takes for its setting an entire society in which crime flourishes, yet is fought against (frequently by the protagonists of these films), while the mob movie tends to concentrate on a subculture of organized crime that is represented as embedded within a larger and mainly law-abiding society—though the legitimacy of this larger society is something rigorously questioned by most of the greatest mob movies. Film noir most often (though certainly not always) deals with crimes committed by individuals who are not regarded as habitual or "natural" criminals; but the environment of noir is generally represented (often by nonverbal means like dim lighting and sharp diagonal camera angles) as somehow conducive to crime, even if not exactly criminal in the straightforward way that the Wild West and, still more, the Mafia are. There are, to be sure, both individual crime films and entire kinds of crime cinema that do not necessarily fit neatly within the three genres I am concerned with. The police procedural is an obvious example, though this genre has probably flourished more on television than in the movies. Then too, there is the heist film. It may overlap with film noir, with the mob movie, *or* with the Western, but may also be largely independent of all three (Quentin Tarantino's *Reservoir Dogs* [1992] is an instance, though a small criminal organization does figure there). There are also important crime films—like Clint Eastwood's *Mystic River* (2003)—that seem essentially *sui generis*. Still, it seems to me that the mob movie, film noir, and the Western constitute the most ample and significant genres of crime cinema, and among them encompass the majority of noteworthy crime films.

If, however, we look beyond crime cinema in the sense of films to whose action crime is absolutely central, as is the case with the three genres under examination in this book, to films in which crime is simply important, then something of the total significance of crime cinema to cinema as a whole begins to become apparent. For, with the exception of the romantic comedy (and even here crime occasionally plays a nontrivial role), most major kinds of cinema frequently feature crime as an important presence, even if not necessarily a central and defining one.

Horror cinema, for example, is not a genre of crime cinema in the way that film noir or the Western are, yet often represents lawbreaking fairly prominently. Stanley Kubrick's *The Shining* (1980), one of the supreme masterworks of the genre, is, after all, about a man who murders a hotel cook and attempts to murder his own wife and child—quite obviously a criminal situation. Science fiction is still further removed from crime cinema in the strongest sense, but is by no means as innocent of crime as might initially be thought. Consider Don Siegel's *Invasion of the Body Snatchers* (1956), remade under the same title by Phil Kaufman in 1978 and as *Body Snatchers* by Abel Ferrara in 1993. The central action of "body snatching"—one of the more durable themes in science-fiction film and television—is in fact a crime: though of course the science-fictional point is that it is a new and strange sort of crime, one to which the ordinary forces of law and order are completely inadequate. In the cinema of social realism, by contrast, crime often figures in a much more straightforward way. To pick a few varied examples: *The Grapes of Wrath* (John Ford, 1940) is largely about the crimes committed against a family of impoverished internal migrants, often by those officially charged with *preventing* crime. *12 Angry Men* (Sidney Lumet, 1957) represents the deliberations of a jury during a murder trial. *Inherit the Wind* (Stanley Kramer, 1960) is a legal drama that explores the implications of criminalizing the teaching of science. Clint Eastwood's *Changeling* (2008) has serial child-murder at the center of its plot, but more prominently portrays lawbreaking by the police.

The war movie is an especially interesting genre in this context. War can be understood as a situation in which actions that would normally be criminal—paradigmatically the killing of another human being—are decriminalized, and even officially redefined as meritorious, by the military and political context. Yet the great war films are mostly *anti*-war films, so it is probably more appropriate to put the matter the other way around, so to speak, and to say that the war movie tends to see war as the greatest crime of all. In the war movie, we might say, crime is completely detached from its relationship of contrast (however deeply problematic) with law-abiding society and becomes the entirety of the filmic environment. Francis Coppola, maker of the *Godfather* trilogy (1972–1990)—arguably the greatest single achievement in the entirety of crime cinema—also directed *Apocalypse Now* (1979), one of the major war films; and a line of dialogue from the latter expresses the ambiguities of war and crime with brilliant succinctness. As Captain Willard (Martin Sheen) sets out on his quest to find Colonel Kurtz (Marlon Brando)—who has been charged with murder by his military superiors—Willard informs the viewer, in voice-over narration, "Charging a man with murder in this place [i.e., Vietnam during the American war] was like handing out speeding tickets at the Indy 500".

Of course, the prevalence of crime in cinema—and not only in crime cinema in the core sense with which this book is concerned—expresses the prevalence of crime in society at large. No developed society without crime is known to have existed, and none seems feasible under the actually existing socio-economic conditions of today. At the beginning of *The Scarlet Letter* (1850), Nathaniel Hawthorne's narrator ruefully notes that, however high the utopian hopes cherished by the founders of a new society, it is invariably found necessary to set aside some portion of available land for a prison. The point here—and it is one with which Hawthorne's novel is thoroughly and self-consciously conversant—is not just that crime is empirically widespread, on the movie screen and in the larger world beyond. It is also that by establishing the category of crime—by drawing an ostensibly bright line between the lawful and the criminal, however thin, blurry, or even effectively meaningless the line may in practice become in many concrete situations—society offers its own perhaps most consequential self-definition. Crime is "everywhere" in the sense that no part of the social fabric is untouched by the socially normative opposition between the criminal and the legitimate.

To be sure, society to some degree defines itself in all of its significant activities—in the gods (if any) that it worships; in the entertainments that it enjoys; in the structures of political leadership that it builds; in its familial patterns; in its preferred military tactics. Yet the definition of the criminal is an aspect of societal self-definition that is more fundamental, at least in some ways, than perhaps any other. For, here, society declares not simply what it makes possible or available but what it strictly *forbids*. This is not to deny the well-known Foucauldian point that social power operates not only by forbidding or repression but also affirmatively, in the constitution of subjectivity itself. Still less is it to deny that—as many of the great crime films, perhaps especially, as we will see, the *Godfather* trilogy, are themselves concerned to show—the act of social forbidding that constitutes criminal prohibition is often a deeply hypocritical one. But it does seem clear that by such prohibitions society, as it were, nails its colors to the mast in an especially explicit and emphatic way. Accordingly, films in which the transgressing of the criminal prohibition is central tend to openly invite the interrogation of social relations: an invitation extended by nearly every movie discussed in detail in this volume. Crime films especially (though of course not uniquely) demand interest in what I call, in *The Incomplete Projects*, the politics and ideology of culture.[6]

SECTION I

Gangsterism and Capitalism: The Mob Movie and After

The supplement of Coppola: Primitive accumulation and the *Godfather* trilogy

The concept of primitive accumulation

Volume One of Marx's *Capital* (1867) is in a certain way structured rather like the Victorian melodramatic novels with which it was contemporary, and of which Marx himself was an avid consumer. In most of the book—from Part One through Part Seven—Marx describes the typical functioning of the capitalist mode of production: "how money is transformed into capital; how surplus-value is made through capital, and how more capital is made from surplus-value," to quote his own summary.[7] As even this extremely brief account suggests, the process is essentially circular: or, more precisely, cyclical, since the circuits of the system tend to expand in scope, as more capital generates more surplus-value and more surplus-value generates more capital. The capitalist accumulation of capital thus presupposes such accumulation—it presupposes *itself*—on a lower, more restricted level. Accordingly, the theoretical model constructed by Marx (before Part Eight of Volume One) appears to beg an unavoidable question: how does the capitalist mode of production *begin* in the first place? If capitalism requires an accumulation of capital, then the accumulation produced *by* capitalism cannot possibly be that which enables the rise *of* capitalism. So how does capitalism originally emerge from the dying economies of feudal Europe? Logically, there must be some earlier capital accumulation *not* produced by capitalism itself. It is this that Marx, in the title of the first chapter of Part Eight, designates the "secret" of primitive accumulation.[8] Unmentioned throughout the book up to this point, it now appears at the end to explain a condition of possibility of everything that has been described before—just as, for example, the surprising secret of Pip's wealth, which makes possible so much of the action of Dickens's *Great Expectations* (1861), is not revealed until relatively late in the novel.

Marx sometimes describes the surprising secret he has discovered as "*so-called* primitive accumulation" (emphasis added). For, in some ways, it is not really an accumulation at all, at least insofar as that term connotes a smooth, routine, essentially peaceful operation. Primitive accumulation is, on the contrary, a process of staggering disruption, fraud, theft, and violence, one that is, in Marx's words, "written in the annals of mankind in letters of blood and fire" (p. 875). Within Europe, it was accomplished primarily by the forcible dispossession of the peasantry: the unilateral usurpation of their ancient feudal rights, the forcible seizure and privatization of their common lands, and, in addition, the forcible seizure and privatization of traditional state and church domains and of various kinds of feudal and clan property—all of which were transformed into modern, bourgeois private property.

The peasant producers were left with nothing: that is, with no land and no rights save the right, as newly "free" wage-laborers, to sell their labor-power to the bosses of a newly capitalist agriculture (and, later, of course, of capitalist industry as well). The enclosure movement in sixteenth-century England, against which Thomas More, for one, protested so bitterly at the time, is today probably the best-known example of this process.

In leaving the discussion of primitive accumulation to the end of his book, Marx is, in a way, mimicking and satirizing the psychology of capitalism itself. For primitive accumulation remains, throughout the capitalist era, the secret that must be repressed, the thing that must not be spoken of. The system that holds the right of property and the right of "free" contract (paradigmatically the contract between worker and capitalist) to be sacred naturally tends to discourage memory of the fact that this very system is based on massive theft of property and wholesale violation of established rights by naked force. Capitalism inevitably disinclines us to recall that capital, as Marx puts it, comes into the world "dripping from head to toe, from every pore, with blood and dirt" (p. 926).

Nor, indeed, was the foundational bloodiness of capitalism confined only, or even mainly, to Europe. Capital accumulation in the European metropolis could never have reached the level that made the "take-off" of the capitalist mode of production possible without the massive appropriation of non-European wealth: through the systematic thievery organized by Europe's rising empires in East Asia and South Asia, through the genocidal "discovery" and exploitation of the New World, and through the large-scale and frequently lethal kidnapping of black Africans into slavery. In Marx's own words:

> The discovery of gold and silver in America, the extirpation, enslavement and entombment in mines of the indigenous population of that continent, the beginnings of the conquest and plunder of India, and the conversion of Africa into a preserve for the commercial hunting of blackskins, are all things which characterize the dawn of the era of capitalist production. These idyllic proceedings are the chief moments of primitive accumulation. (p. 915)

One of the most frequent mistakes made in discussions of capitalism today is the assumption that "globalization" is a recent development. Throughout *Capital*, Marx makes clear that the world market has *always* been the most ultimately powerful determinant in capitalist production, circulation, and exchange. But in the discussion of primitive accumulation, it is evident that capitalism has been a global enterprise not only from the beginning but even, so to speak, from *before* the beginning. The violent plunder that produced sufficient capital accumulation to allow for capitalist take-off in Europe spanned every inhabited continent of the globe (except Australia, whose murderous "discovery" came later). Taken together, the various foundational moments of primitive accumulation may well constitute the largest and most violent crime against humanity in all of history.

If *accumulation*, with its tranquil and mundane connotations, thus seems a misleading term for such an enterprise, the force of "so-called" applies also to *primitive*, the other term in Marx's phrase, "so-called primitive accumulation." For *primitive* might be taken to suggest that the force and thievery of primitive accumulation, however appalling, exist decisively and exclusively in the past. We might be tempted to assume that primitive accumulation is a fact about the history of capitalism but not about capitalism as an ongoing mode of production today. It is, indeed, true that primitive accumulation is heterogeneous to the deliberately simplified model of "pure" capitalism that Marx constructs from Part One through Part Seven of Volume One of *Capital*. Yet as this model is fleshed out and complicated in the succeeding parts of Marx's multi-volume "critique of political economy"—and also in important work by such later scholars as Ernest Mandel and David Harvey—it becomes evident that primitive accumulation never really ends. If it is imagined as the series of explosions that started the motor of capitalist production, then, though these explosions may sometimes partially subside during the "normal" running of the engine, they are never completely extinguished. The model proposed in Volume One suggests that, in principle, capitalism could function without continuing theft and violence, just as it could, in principle, function without ever lowering wages below the true exchange-value of the workers' labor-power, and without ever raising prices above the exchange-value of the commodities offered for sale. But the actual history of capitalism shows that the system does not, in fact, operate without these things.

Examples of the continuing of so-called primitive accumulation are various. Some, which take distinctively modern (or "postmodern") forms, concern new kinds and degrees of intellectual property: for instance, the current tendency to extend copyright far beyond the lifetimes of the original authors, thus transforming elements of a commonly held cultural heritage into bourgeois private property. An even more striking instance of much the same process takes place when medical and pharmaceutical companies manage to patent knowledge of the active ingredients of herbal and other traditional medicines, or knowledge of single genes used in diagnostic procedures, thereby privatizing even humanity's biological heritage.

In other cases, primitive accumulation operates today in ways that have in fact existed for centuries but whose full significance has not been widely recognized until fairly recently. An example would be the environmental devastation caused by many capitalist enterprises. When rivers are poisoned by industrial waste, or when lethal gases escape into the atmosphere from a manufacturing plant, commonly held and indispensably vital resources—clean air, potable water, and the like—are being stolen by capitalists in order to generate greater profit from the surplus-value being produced. The attendant physical violence, in the form (for instance) of cancers and other diseases induced in the surrounding population, can be massive.

In still other cases, primitive accumulation functions today in forms that would have been immediately recognizable to the Marx of Part Eight of Volume One of *Capital*. The privatization of fishing rights today in what had for centuries been common fishing waters off parts of the coast of Africa is, for example, a precise parallel to the enclosure movement in Tudor England. But one need not go to the margins of the world capitalist system in order to find the fraud and force of primitive accumulation at their most unvarnished. One might go to New York City, the economic capital of the world's dominant power, to find functioning sweatshops where—in absolute violation of the supposedly "free" contract between employer and employee—workers (usually undocumented immigrants speaking little or no English) are forcibly held in virtual slavery and subjected to super-exploitation that exhausts them to (or beyond) their physical limits.

Primitive accumulation, then, far from existing as a one-off historical moment at the dawn of capitalism, might be understood as capitalism's *supplement* in the sense given that term by Jacques Derrida. One of the key concepts of Derridean deconstruction, supplementarity appears in Derrida's crucial early work *Of Grammatology* (1967) as a process that has haunted Western thought almost from the beginning but that has rarely been understood clearly. Briefly put, a supplement, for Derrida, is something that appears to be secondary and heterogeneous to something else; and the latter is normally understood to be prior and more "natural". Yet the supplement turns out, upon closer examination, not only to be far more important and complex than was initially supposed but even to be integral to that which it was initially supposed merely to "supplement" in the colloquial sense.

The best-known example is doubtless that "dangerous supplement," masturbation. Masturbation is usually thought to be a degraded, secondary sexual practice, decisively inferior to sexual intercourse, and tolerable, if at all, only as a "supplement" (in the colloquial sense) to sexual intercourse when the latter is for one reason or another unavailable. In his analysis of Rousseau's account of his own masturbatory practices in *The Confessions*, Derrida shows, however, that the matter is a good deal more complicated. As Rousseau makes clear, masturbation, with its attendant fantasies, possesses its own vast realm of sexual pleasure. For it allows Rousseau to enjoy, in imagination, a countless number of women, whose beauty and willingness are limited only by Rousseau's own imaginative capacity— and all without the tiresome need for seduction. What is even more important, however, is that the processes of imagination and symbolic representation in masturbatory fantasy constitute an indispensable dimension of sexual intercourse itself, indeed of all sexual experience whatever: "[I]t has never been possible to desire that[sexual] presence 'in person', before this play of substitution and this symbolic experience of auto-affection. The thing itself does not appear outside of the symbolic system that does not exist without the possibility of auto-affection".[9] In this sense, auto-eroticism is integral to all erotic experience.

There are many other instances of supplementarity. One of the most crucial instances for Derrida is writing. Though written language may appear to be secondary and inferior to the spoken language that it seems to represent (as Plato maintains in the *Phaedrus*), it not only has immense richness and complexity of its own that are not simply derivative of speech, but, even beyond that, forms (in literate cultures) some of the conditions of possibility of speech itself. Furthermore, since the signs of spoken language are themselves supplemental of the referents for which they stand, it follows that "writing is the supplement *par excellence* since it marks the point where the supplement proposes itself as supplement of the supplement, sign of a sign, *taking the place of* a speech already significant" (p. 281; emphasis in original).

Yet another example of supplementarity is the category of being itself, as Derrida analyzes it in one of his most important essays, "The Supplement of Copula: Philosophy *before* Linguistics" (in *Margins of Philosophy* [1972]). The philosophic concept of being may appear to be—and has been argued to be—a mere derivative of the grammatical copula: that is, a supplement, in the ordinary sense, of the linguistic function of the linking or copulative verb. But Derrida maintains that the philosophic category is in certain ways *prior* to the linguistic one—that being is not wholly dependent on the verb *to be*—and supports his argument in part by reference to languages in which being is inscribed despite the grammatical lack of any copulative verb.

Masturbation, writing, being: I hope that the (admittedly brief) presentation of these examples of supplementarity has been sufficient to give some concreteness to the fundamental theoretical premise of this chapter—that primitive accumulation is usefully understood in Marxist economic theory as a supplement, in the Derridean sense, of "normal" capitalism. From the most widely shared and common-sense coigns of vantage, primitive accumulation appears to be as secondary to the normal functioning of generalized commodity production—to the routine capitalist processes of the production, extraction, and realization of surplus-value—as masturbation is to normal sexuality. Primitive accumulation is, it may first appear, a special case of value creation, sharply distinct from genuinely typical capitalist practices. Yet a more careful reading of the history of capitalism shows that primitive accumulation, with all its violence and fraud, is actually indispensable to the entire capitalist mode of production: and not only as a foundational moment during the sixteenth and seventeenth centuries but as the repressed yet continual "shadow," so to speak, of the whole capitalist project, up to the current day. Pro-capitalist ideology may repress awareness of the importance of primitive accumulation to capitalism, just as many modes of understanding sexuality may prefer to exclude masturbation from the category of authentic or "legitimate" sexual practices. But such repression can never be completely successful (as Freud knew), and there will always be signs (if we bother to read them) by which primitive accumulation makes its reality known.

It is the central argument of this chapter that such signs are abundant in Francis Ford Coppola's *Godfather* trilogy (1972–1990), which, if the three films are counted as parts of one magnum opus, seems to me to rank, at least arguably, as the richest and most ambitious masterwork in the entirety of Hollywood cinema. I propose to examine it, more specifically, as the most interesting and important cinematic presentation of primitive accumulation that the American film industry has produced. I do not mean to *substitute* primitive accumulation for all the more obvious and more frequently discussed themes of the trilogy: organized crime, family, religion, ethnicity, the American experience in general, the American immigrant experience in particular, and the relations between America and Europe—among others. I will rather argue that such undeniably crucial motifs can be understood more fully if we co-ordinate them with the supplementarity of primitive accumulation that haunts—in progressively less allegorical forms—the *Godfather* films from the first scene of *The Godfather* (1972) to the final scene of *The Godfather, Part III* (1990; hereafter referred to as *The Godfather III*). I have to consider—to indulge for a moment in the kind of word play that Marx enjoyed no less, perhaps, than Derrida—not the supplement of copula but the supplement of Coppola.

The Godfather begins

The first words uttered in *The Godfather* are "I believe in America".[10] It is an audacious opening scene in several respects. The initial line is spoken over a completely dark screen. Then the light comes up to reveal, in extreme close-up, the speaker: a homely, nondescript middle-aged man who (as we will soon learn) is the undertaker Bonasera (Salvatore Corsitto). As the camera gradually zooms out from close-up to middle distance, Bonasera continues to talk, though it remains unclear for a brief while to whom he is speaking. He tells the story of his beautiful daughter, who had acquired a boyfriend, one not, as Bonasera is careful to make clear, of Italian background. While out on a drive with her boyfriend and another male friend, she found that she was expected to provide sexual favors to both boys; and, when she refused, they beat her viciously, disfiguring her for life ("Now she will never be beautiful again," sobs Bonasera). Her father, "like a good American," duly reported the crime to the police, and the boys were arrested, indicted, tried, and convicted; but the judge suspended the sentence. "Suspended the sentence!" says the undertaker in incredulity and disgust that the judge could have punished such a vile crime so lightly. Now he has come to the local crime boss, Don Vito Corleone, for justice. After some preliminary conversation between Bonasera and Corleone during which the camera remains behind the Don's right shoulder, the viewpoint of the shot reverses, and reveals, in a sumptuously lit medium close-up, Marlon Brando, in his greatest role. Don Corleone chides and humiliates Bonasera for never having sought his friendship before. But he does finally agree to see to it that the two boys will be made to suffer (though not killed, as he judges that too harsh a punishment, since the undertaker's daughter is still alive). Throughout most of the scene, Brando has been gently caressing a small cat that is squirming and playing in his lap.

Given the centrality of Bonasera and his story to this opening scene, the first-time viewer might well suppose, at this point, that the undertaker is to be one of the principal characters of *The Godfather* and that the story of his daughter and her attackers is to become one of the film's main narrative strands. This is not the case. In the nearly three hours (actually 175 minutes) of the film, Bonasera makes only one more, quite brief appearance, and the daughter and the attackers are never heard of again. It is, nonetheless, a sound cinematic strategy that leads Coppola to begin *The Godfather* as he does. For it is part and parcel of the film's epic sweep that some of its major concerns can be introduced with a scene that is, at most, tangential to the main action. Precisely because the scene is of little intrinsic narrative significance, it helps to highlight how omnipresent and thematically important are the motifs that it introduces.

The most foregrounded of these motifs, the one announced in the first line of dialogue, is the theme of America and, more narrowly, the ambiguities of the American immigrant's lifeworld. In his second line, Bonasera (whose first name is never mentioned in the film but is significantly given as Amerigo in Mario Puzo's 1969 novel, *The Godfather*, on which the film is based) adds, "America has made my fortune". The commercial society of the United States has enabled him to become an evidently prosperous small businessman (he is wearing a well-tailored suit), whereas he would, perhaps, have been doing well to avoid starvation back in Italy. His belief in America has led him to raise his daughter "in the American fashion," allowing her more freedom than would have been considered proper in the old country, and trusting, at first, to the institutionalized American system of law and justice. When this system fails him, he must turn to a much older and more personal kind of authority, one that derives from the almost pre-capitalist regime of rural Sicily that will be explored in some detail in *The Godfather, Part II* (1974; hereafter referred to as *The Godfather II*). When Don Corleone chastises the undertaker, he does so not only for Bonasera's prior aloofness to him personally but also for the naïve overinvestment in his adopted land that has led Bonasera to trust the American police and the American courts in the first place. "You found paradise in America," says the Don sarcastically.

Yet there is a certain unconscious irony in Don Corleone's sarcasm. It is, after all, he himself who has more triumphantly "found paradise in America" (after rising from beginnings that one would guess, in this film, to be unpromising and that are clearly shown, in *The Godfather II*, to be, indeed, about as unpromising as can easily be imagined). Amerigo Bonasera is a relatively affluent petty-bourgeois, but Vito Corleone is a member of the real ruling class: a man of immense wealth and power, who famously keeps judges and politicians in his pocket, and who, as we will soon see, is capable of winning a battle of wills against one of the richest, most influential, and most determined studio bosses in Hollywood. Nonetheless, as an Italian immigrant, Don Corleone remains, like Bonasera, only ambiguously American. One suspects that the non-Italian boyfriend of Bonasera's daughter has walked free at least in part because of a more unequivocally American identity (and, in Puzo's novel, the judge, indeed, explicitly says that he is extending lenience partly because of the defendants' "fine families,"[11] a phrase that in context almost certainly connotes a WASP—i.e., white Anglo-Saxon Protestant—background). Likewise, though Vito can afford to put on a spectacular wedding celebration for his daughter on the grounds of his luxurious mansion—several outdoor scenes of the wedding immediately follow the indoor scene with Bonasera in the Don's study—he must submit to the presence of FBI agents who mar the festivities by snooping around and writing down the license-plate numbers of the guests' cars. True enough, the FBI's interest is due to Don Corleone's being a crime boss rather than an Italian immigrant as such. But, of course, it was his ethnicity and impoverished immigrant status that led him to exercise his skills of leadership and entrepreneurialism in the Mafia rather than, say, in such (then) WASP near-monopolies and "legitimate" enterprises as Wall Street or the CIA.[12]

This ambiguity in the identity of the Italian Catholic immigrant—nominally American and yet not American in the strongest, most unqualified sense—interlocks with an even more important ambiguity concerning the nature of crime itself. What, really, *is* crime? Or, to put the question another way, what is the relation between the law and the justice that the law is meant to serve? Once again, the opening scene with the Don and Bonasera is exemplary. The judge who allows the attackers of Bonasera's daughter to go free is almost certainly acting within the letter of the law. But the viewer must agree that the suspended sentence is far from just. Even more ironically, in order to seek the justice that the law has denied, the undertaker must go to a *crime* boss. Though Don Corleone's power derives from illegal enterprises, his response to Bonasera—as he decides on corporal but not capital punishment for the two attackers—arguably displays not only a certain moral order but also quasi-judicial sobriety, restraint, and moderation.

The ambiguity that thus complicates any conventional axiological dichotomy between lawfulness and crime is intensified further after Don Corleone dismisses Bonasera and summons another supplicant into his study (there is quite a parade of them, all taking advantage of the Sicilian custom that prohibits one from refusing any favor on the day that one's daughter is married). This is another successful petty-bourgeois, the baker Nazorine (Vito Scotti), who, like Bonasera, also has a daughter. The US immigration authorities are planning to deport his assistant Enzo (Gabriele Torrei), whom Nazorine wishes to keep in America so that he can marry Nazorine's daughter and, presumably, eventually take over the family business. The Don promises to take care of things, and, after Nazorine and Enzo exit, tells Tom Hagen (Robert Duvall), his *consigliere* and adoptive son, to turn the matter over to "a Jew congressman in another district," evidently one of the numerous office-holders who do the Don's bidding. This is the first of many references to the Godfather's political connections; and it presents us with the irony of a professional lawbreaker who not only gives orders to professional lawmakers but who at least sometimes, as in the case of Enzo, does so in order to accomplish something right and just, if perhaps not strictly legal. In addition, the overt reference to the unnamed congressman's Jewishness obliquely announces that the theme of ethnicity is not restricted exclusively to Italian immigrants. The Las Vegas casino owner Moe Greene (Alex Rocco) constitutes a minor Jewish presence in the film; and, in *The Godfather II*, Hyman Roth (Lee Strasberg)—a powerful Mafia financier based on Meyer Lansky, as Greene is based on Bugsy Siegel—constitutes a major one. Moreover, Tom Hagen's Irish background is given some importance as well (though less than in Puzo's novel). The comparative marginalization, in WASP-dominated America, of more recent arrivals of non-WASP ethnicity, is of course unjust according to the universalistic Jeffersonian principles on which the United States is officially founded; and so the resulting uncertainty as to whether Italian and Jewish—and even Irish—immigrants are "truly" American is integral to the larger indeterminacy that renders hopelessly fuzzy the officially clear-cut categories of law, justice, and criminality.

It is, then, here, in the opening scenes of *The Godfather* in Vito's study, that primitive accumulation makes its first and most deeply allegorical appearance. For primitive accumulation is, after all, the crucial term of any deconstruction of the binary opposition between legality and criminality as understood in bourgeois society. Capitalist legality attempts to draw an absolutely clear iron line between itself and the criminality to which it opposes itself, so that the legitimacy of private property and the right of contract can be grounded as securely as possible. But the attempt never quite succeeds—the line is always, in fact, a permeable membrane—because capitalist legality is itself based (in its origins but also, as we have seen, to some degree as an ongoing enterprise) on massive crime, on the unilateral abrogation of property and contractual rights as well as on brute physical force. Such is the intrinsic instability—the potential moral, conceptual, and physical anarchy—that afflicts the fundamental presuppositions of capitalist society. And Don Corleone enacts this instability, this tissue of ambiguities, in the calm and shadowy luxury of his study, whose furnishings—the large wooden desk, the Persian carpet, the leather-lined chairs—all bespeak affluent bourgeois solidity even though, or rather precisely *because*, they are all the fruits of crime.

The complexity of the Don's *modus operandi*—the variation in the multiple ways that the line between crime and law is being constantly blurred—is nicely illustrated by the difference between the case of the baker and that of the mortician, both of which we see him resolve in the film's opening minutes. In the case of Nazorine and Enzo, Vito works, so to speak, "within the system". He will instruct the Jewish congressman (through Tom Hagen) to intervene on Enzo's behalf with the immigration authorities. Though the congressman's solicitude to Don Corleone is doubtless based, at least in large part, on the latter's generous campaign contributions, it seems probable that the provable facts of the matter would be insufficient to sustain a criminal prosecution for bribery—though of course the relationship between the Don and the congressman *is* one of bribery in any true sense of the word. In the case of Bonasera, by contrast, the Don acts decisively outside the law, dispatching (through several layers of intermediaries) professional thugs to commit assault and battery, and thereby engaging in just the kind of naked physical violence that is the clearest mark of primitive accumulation. But the viewer will perhaps forgive Bonasera for thinking that Don Corleone has indeed provided him with justice and therefore represents a higher sort of law.

Demystifying some legends of a fall

I have concentrated closely on the earliest scenes of *The Godfather* partly because I wish to contest—or at least severely to qualify—the conventional reading that sees the trilogy, and even the first film in itself, as narrating a *fall*, one that is most readily understood as the apparent moral decline from Vito Corleone to his successor and youngest son, Michael (Al Pacino). There is, to be sure, a striking change in Michael himself. At the beginning, he is an affable Ivy Leaguer and a Marine war hero returned home, who attends his sister's wedding in the company of his sweet, quintessentially WASP fiancée Kay Adams (Diane Keaton). In conversation with Kay, he makes clear, to her and to the viewer, that he wants nothing to do with his family's criminal empire. By the end of the film, however, he is an intense steely-eyed murderer, and will remain one throughout *The Godfather II* (Michael in the final installment of the trilogy is more relaxed and affable, though not at heart less murderous). It is also true that Vito (to no small extent because of Brando's staggeringly brilliant performance) maintains a more aesthetically attractive persona than any of his sons can manage. He unfailingly projects gravitas and dignity, never, for instance, losing his temper as Don Michael frequently does. His dealings with Bonasera and Nazorine may seem to exude the protective paternal strength and beneficence implied by the appellation, "Godfather," and in any case are unmatched by Michael, who, after *he* becomes the Godfather, is never seen attending to the needs of humble supplicants. Vito's reliable concern for his family is, on some level, genuine enough: "A man who doesn't spend time with his family can never be a real man," as he says in a rather "ethnic" and un-WASP expression of authentic masculinity. The contrast is clear with the way that Michael not only ultimately fails to hold his own marriage to Kay together, but also, more spectacularly, with the way he has his brother-in-law Carlo (Gianni Russo) murdered at the end of the film (and after Vito's death): an act that is, as it were, halfway to the sin of Cain, and that is doubled at the end of *The Godfather II*, when Michael goes all the way and has his actual brother Fredo (John Cazale) killed too.

Admittedly, then, *The Godfather* does, to some degree, tempt us with a nostalgia for the traditional (almost pre-modern) paternalistic family values—in which the demand for absolute obedience to the father is coupled with the absolute guarantee by him of stability and security—that Vito so strikingly incarnates, and that Michael, who tries to exact the demand while failing to provide the guarantee, so strikingly does not. But the film also demystifies such nostalgia, and the demystification begins with the film's early scenes, where Vito is at his most impressive. Even, for example, if one chooses not to think about what the "justice" that the Don provides to Bonasera would look like when it is actually taking place, it is not possible to avert one's eyes from the details of another of Vito's favors to a dependent. A more prominent supplicant than Nazorine or Bonasera, and one whose problem requires more elaborate fixing, Johnny Fontane (Al Martino)—Vito's godson and a popular singer and actor based on Frank Sinatra—needs help landing a part in a movie that could revive his flagging career almost overnight. After conventional negotiations fail, Don Corleone's more strenuous methods of persuasion are imaged in what is perhaps the film's single most widely remembered scene: the scene where the Hollywood studio boss Jack Woltz (John Marley) awakes alone in his immense mansion (which contains many tangible signs of wealth and luxury on which the camera lingers) to find, amid the silken bed sheets, the bleeding severed head of his prized, and extremely expensive, racehorse.

True, Woltz is not a particularly sympathetic character, especially after he has admitted that Johnny would be perfect for the role but that he intends to withhold it anyway because of a personal grudge. Nonetheless, the image of a beautiful, innocent animal hideously slaughtered in order to make a negotiating point indelibly marks for the viewer the violence and deep evil on which Don Corleone's benefactions are based. Of course, the Don is thousands of miles away when the deed is done. But his hands-off approach, like the impeccably courteous and soft-spoken way that his representative Tom Hagen speaks to Woltz (despite Woltz's own insults and bluster), only highlights how repellent what the Godfather stands for truly is when you see it up close.

The grotesque image of the severed head is unforgettable not only because of its considerable intrinsic power but also because, as the first overt representation of physical violence in the film, it amounts to a stand-in, by synecdoche, for much that follows. Just as the violence of sixteenth-century primitive accumulation recurs as a "dangerous supplement" throughout the further development of capitalism, so the violence on which Vito Corleone's success is based can never really end (the specific foundational act of violence will be dramatized in *The Godfather II*). Ultimately, it strikes even his own family, for whose safety and welfare his entire enterprise has been intended. The wedding of Vito's daughter Connie (Talia Shire) provides some brightly lit scenes of joy and celebration early in the film. But Vito's role as a crime boss contributes in several complex ways to the quick degeneration of Connie's marriage into a nightmare of physical and emotional abuse, setting her on the path to become the unhappily promiscuous playgirl of *The Godfather II*. Vito's line of work leads even more directly to the machine-gunning of his beloved oldest son and heir apparent Santino (or "Sonny," played by James Caan) in the deeply shocking scene at the toll plaza: one of the most graphically violent scenes in American cinematic history to that point (though the death scene at the end of Arthur Penn's *Bonnie and Clyde* [1967] provided a precedent and almost certainly a direct influence).

Even Vito himself is not immune to the violence on which his enterprise depends. Rejecting the advice of both Tom and Sonny, Vito decides against going into the heroin business with the narcotics pusher Sollozzo (Al Lettieri): *not*, as it is often misremembered, because of the slightest moral qualm but—as Vito himself goes out of his way to make clear—exclusively because of the prudential consideration that his all-important political connections might not survive the stigma of dealing in hard drugs. The result is that he is shot down by Sollozzo's thugs. He survives the attack, barely, but never regains his old health and strength, and is forced by his weakened condition into retirement from his position as the Don. It is pure poetic justice, a textbook illustration of what proverbially happens to him who lives by the sword—or, in this case, the gun.

Despite, then, the strikingly different kinds of affect that Brando and Pacino project, it is difficult to see the passage from Don Vito to Don Michael as any sort of fundamental moral decline. The cycle of, and dependence on, violence begins with Vito; and Michael does nothing that Vito has not made possible. Beyond such strictly moral considerations, however, a more sophisticated way of reading the *Godfather* films as the narrative of a fall is suggested in the concluding pages of Fredric Jameson's contribution to the inaugural issue of *Social Text*: pages that contain one of the earliest important treatments of the films and that have certainly been highly influential on much, perhaps most, serious *Godfather* criticism since.[13] Jameson argues that the structure of *The Godfather* is essentially mythic. The film projects a myth of the Mafia that, according to Jameson, serves the ideological function of substituting ethical questions of individual criminal aberration for genuinely political (and economic) ones of capitalist depredation, while also, at the same time, expressing a utopian longing for the collectivity imagined in the fantasy of the powerful and close-knit Mafia family. In *The Godfather II*, however, this mythic structure, says Jameson, "falls as it were into history itself, which submits it to a patient deconstruction that will in the end leave its ideological content undisguised and its displacements visible to the naked eye" (p. 147). Only in the second film, according to this reading, do the contradictions of capitalism explode the mythic generic structure of the Mafia film that is designed to repress them.

Jameson provides valuable insights into *The Godfather II*, on which I will be drawing presently; and it is clear that, as a Marxist, he welcomes the "fall" that the historicizing tendency of the second film represents. Nonetheless, his opposition of history to myth oversimplifies the first film in a way somewhat similar to (though it is more intellectually complex than) the merely moral or aesthetic nostalgia for Brando-as-Vito that the viewer may feel after Pacino-as-Michael has taken over the role of protagonist and Godfather. As we have seen, the superficially attractive persona of Don Vito is demystified almost from the start, and certainly from the scene of the bloody horse's head in Woltz's bed (which comes only slightly more than half an hour into the film). In a parallel way, the pressure of history and the corresponding impossibility of distinguishing clearly between the Mafia and "legitimate" capitalism do not, in fact, wait for *The Godfather II* to be registered, but are powerfully represented in the initial installment of the trilogy: so that the historicizing deconstruction that Jameson accurately identifies is at work much earlier than he allows. Primitive accumulation—the moment of violence and crime that is foundational to capitalism and untranscendable by it—is, as we have already seen, inscribed in the film's opening scenes in the Don's study, though through the most profoundly allegorical kind of representation. After this point, the inscription of primitive accumulation becomes increasingly *less* allegorical, not only as the whole trilogy unfolds but even within the first film.

Of considerable importance here is the theme of Don Vito's political connections, first sounded with regard to the case of Nazorine and Enzo and central to the near-fatal miscalculations that Vito makes in his dealings with Sollozzo. The elaborate network of influence that Vito has established with a variety of judges and politicians makes it impossible to sustain Jameson's notion that the film sees the Mafia as aberrational or essentially heterogeneous to the normal and "legitimate" structures of American society. The view Jameson describes is, indeed, the (strictly ideological) view taken by the much earlier films—*Little Caesar* (Mervyn LeRoy, 1931), *The Public Enemy* (William Wellman, 1931), and *Scarface* (Howard Hawks, 1932)—that established the generic conventions of the Hollywood mob movie and that might reasonably be taken as the chief precursor-films to Coppola's work. But the central originality of *The Godfather* is Coppola's deconstruction of the binary opposition, upheld by LeRoy, Wellman, and Hawks, between legitimate and illegitimate centers of American power: and not only through Don Corleone's own political connections but also through those of some of his adversaries as well. For instance, the Corleone family is temporarily baffled, in its quest for revenge against Sollozzo after the shooting of Vito, by the fact that the heroin dealer has hired as his personal bodyguard a high-ranking police officer, Capt. McCluskey (Sterling Hayden). Tom Hagen makes clear, in discussions with Michael and Sonny, that a New York police captain does not necessarily lose any of his respectability, power, or prestige merely by becoming an enforcer for the drug rackets.

Interestingly enough, though, Vito himself does feel a sentimental yearning for respectability that logically seems to imply the kind of sharp distinction between legitimate and illegitimate power that his own career exposes as untenable. In a memorably poignant scene after Vito has been permanently weakened by Sollozzo's bullets and Michael has become his successor, he gives explicit voice to what has long been implied: that he did not wish Michael, always his favorite child, to follow in his own footsteps. "I never wanted this for you," he tells Michael. Instead, he envisioned his son as "Senator Corleone. Governor Corleone. Something". But the poignancy of such longing for legitimacy—which becomes one of the overarching motifs of the trilogy until it is pretty much abandoned altogether toward the end of *The Godfather III*—derives, of course, from its plain impossibility. Michael, though himself capable, like his father, of feeling such longing, also sees the true situation quite clearly almost from the beginning. Not long after his own path as a crime boss has become irrevocable, he responds to Kay's disappointment that he has, after all, and against his own earlier intentions, become a man like his father, by insisting, "My father's no different than any other powerful man. Any man who's responsible for other people. Like a senator or a president". This is offensive to Kay's New England WASP sensibilities, and she replies, "Do you know how naïve you sound? … Senators and presidents don't have men killed". Michael's response is definitive: "Who's being naïve, Kay?" It is worth recalling that, as the film was being made, the president of the United States, with the support of most US senators, was having hundreds of thousands of people killed in a criminal war that would provide the raw material for Coppola's most considerable cinematic achievement outside the *Godfather* trilogy.[14]

Moreover, the first film's dismantling of the dichotomy between legitimacy and illegitimacy obtains on the level of the American economy as well as on that of the American polity. Though the point is considerably elaborated in its sequels, *The Godfather* itself makes sufficiently clear that what is essentially at stake in the workings of organized crime is nothing more or less than capitalism itself. Indeed, Mafia capitalism, precisely because of its illegality and its corresponding relative autonomy from the ordinary systems of government regulation, might be considered to be capitalism at its freest and thus capitalism as most strongly and thoroughly—and violently—itself. This is one reason that organized crime can so conveniently figure the persistence of primitive accumulation, that "dangerous supplement" integral and even fundamental to "normal" capitalism that the latter vainly strives to disavow. The matter is neatly encapsulated in a remark that Sollozzo makes to Tom Hagen shortly after the shooting of Vito. Sollozzo, attempting to make a peace with the Corleone family and thus head off full-scale retaliation, comments: "I don't *like* violence, Tom. I'm a businessman. Blood is a big expense".

Sollozzo (whose relative frankness is in general one of his most distinctive characteristics) is telling the truth. He is a businessman, a capitalist, and neither better nor worse than that description should imply. His interest is in generating fabulous superprofits from the sale of heroin (the superprofits that led Tom and Sonny to urge their father to accept Sollozzo's deal in the first place), and he has no special fondness for gun play: just as capitalism can sometimes operate happily enough through the "normal" production and extraction of surplus-value. But the overt violence of primitive accumulation is sometimes called for in any capitalist system, just as Sollozzo does not hesitate to have Don Vito shot down when the Don's stubborn refusal to accept his offer threatens the serious business of profit-making. Gun violence amounts to a dangerous supplement indeed to Sollozzo's business: more dangerous, even, than Sollozzo himself appreciates.

A more elaborate and even less allegorical representation of the fundamental congruence between organized crime and capitalism in general is provided later, in the extraordinary scene of the conference between Don Vito and the heads of the other Mafia families. The intra-Mafia war, touched off by the near-fatal shooting of Vito, has been intensified by Michael's execution-style murder of Sollozzo and Capt. McCluskey in a sleepy Bronx restaurant, and has most recently reached a climax with the machine-gunning of Santino at the toll plaza. Vito determines to forego vengeance for his oldest son and to bring hostilities to an end (in large part so that his especially beloved Michael can safely return home from the Sicilian exile in which he has been hiding). As Don Corleone opens the meeting by naming some of the fellow crime bosses with whom he sits—some of whom are, like him, based in New York, but others of whom have come from as far away as Missouri and California—we realize that we are witnessing sober corporate negotiations. Like a board of company directors, a group of somber middle-aged white men wearing expensive suits sit around a luxurious conference table and discuss business. The pros and cons of the trade in heroin are examined, and it soon becomes evident—even to those, like Vito, who had resisted the move into narcotics—that the pure capitalist logic of profit-making is in this case simply too great to be withstood, whatever the risks ("There's a lot of money in that white powder," as the late Santino had said to his father). Ways are therefore agreed upon to organize the sale of heroin as prudently as possible. The political connections that are Vito's special resource will be crucial in the effort; and Don Barzini (Richard Conte)—who appears to function as the chairman of the board, so to speak—states flatly that Vito *must* share this resource with his colleagues. Don Barzini adds: "Certainly, he can present a bill for such services. After all, we are not communists".

Indeed they are not. The remark, which receives an appreciative chuckle of agreement around the table, may at first seem a bit surprising, since communism was not, of course, a live political option in the America of the 1950s, in which the action is taking place. But it is fair to assume that all the men around the table remain close to their Italian roots. They would all know not only that Italy, at this time, boasted a Communist Party of major electoral strength, but also that, only a few years previous, in the late 1940s, the Italian CP came reasonably close to winning state power, and was thwarted only by a massive right-wing coalition that included (in addition to the US government, the Italian Christian Democratic Party, and the Roman Catholic Church) the Italian branch of their own organization.[15]

They would thus have a good appreciation that, as Don Barzini implies, capitalism and communism remain the two real, and mutually exclusive, alternatives in any developed society. And they have no doubt whatsoever as to which side they are on. At the conference over which Don Barzini presides, perhaps more profoundly than at any other point in the film, we see the "new tragic realism" that Pauline Kael famously—and shrewdly—detected in *The Godfather*.[16]

From Sicily to America

The Godfather is, then, itself a film of such keen historical awareness that its sequel presents us with no definable "fall" into history. But *The Godfather II* certainly does extend and deepen the historicizing project of its predecessor in ways that may seem almost inevitable when we consider the two films together but that could not have been predicted in advance. As we begin to examine in detail the second film of the trilogy—sometimes claimed as the only sequel in movie history to be as good as, or maybe even better than, its original—it may be useful to consider briefly the category of the cinematic sequel.

There had, of course, been sequels of a sort for almost the entirety of the history of film; James Whale's *Frankenstein* (1931) and *Bride of Frankenstein* (1935) provide a noteworthy and relatively early example. But perhaps no Hollywood director before Coppola had ever explicitly and formally designated a film as being the second part of an earlier film. Whether or not such a designation was completely unprecedented, there is no question that the title of *The Godfather, Part II*, when it first appeared on theater marquees in 1974, had considerable force of novelty: not only because of the unfamiliarity, at that time, of the general formulation but also because of the particular terms involved. If we consider it simply in and of itself (something that is a bit difficult to do at this point in time), *The Godfather* is as skillfully and satisfyingly *finished* a work of art as Hollywood has produced. The famed cross-cutting toward the end—in which scenes of Michael in church, standing as godfather to Connie's infant son, are interspersed with scenes of his hired killers, murdering his important rivals within the Mafia—brilliantly dramatizes the path he has taken, irretrievably, as a crime boss. And much the same point is reinforced, in a minor key as it were, in the film's final scene, where a forlorn-looking Kay Adams (now Kay Corleone) is literally shut out of the study where Michael's subordinates are abasing themselves around him and addressing him by the title, "Don Corleone," that had been reserved for his late father. Today we are accustomed to movies that end in ways that seem designed to stimulate curiosity about a possible sequel. But it would be hard to name a movie of which this is *less* true than *The Godfather*.

Yet the very title of the second film clearly proclaims that the first film was not finished after all. *The Godfather II* does not, however, aim primarily to satisfy simple curiosity about "what happened next" in the story: though it does indeed serve this now conventional function of the sequel. Instead, the second film retroactively reconfigures the structure of its predecessor, so that what had been a complete and self-contained narrative becomes, through a kind of cinematic *Nachträglichkeit* or back-illumination, the middle term of a three-part account of capitalist development. As if to emphasize that its ambitions are considerably larger and more complex than what might normally be expected of a sequel today, *The Godfather II* begins with several scenes that tell us nothing about what happened next, vis-à-vis the first film, but a great deal about what happened *before*—that is, about the origins of the situation on which all the post-Second-World-War action of *The Godfather* depends.

After a brief shot (just before the main title) of Michael's hand being kissed by a subordinate—a direct reference back to Michael's consolidation of his position as Godfather at the end of the earlier film—the movie proper opens in Sicily: and a Sicily rather different, in function as well as in time period, from the Sicily that appears in the earlier film. In *The Godfather*, Sicily is the location of Michael's exile from America after his assassination of Sollozzo and McCluskey. Though this segment of the first film is fairly eventful (Michael marries a beautiful local woman, who, thanks to the treachery of one of his bodyguards, is blown up by a bomb intended for him), it is nonetheless an *interlude* in the structure of the film as a whole. The action that takes place in Sicily is distinct from and relatively heterogeneous to the film's main action. In *The Godfather II*, by contrast, Sicily is primary and foundational. The year is 1901: a nice touch indicating the dawn of the twentieth century (and, perhaps, an inspiration for Bernardo Bertolucci's somewhat parallel cinematic narrative of capitalist history, *Novocento* [1976], which also begins in 1901 and also stars Robert De Niro).[17] Vito (the child actor Oreste Baldini) is nine years old. As the film begins, the local Mafia head has murdered Vito's father and, fearing familial retaliation, proceeds to murder his older brother and his mother as well. He tries to murder Vito too, who, by an extraordinary stroke of luck, escapes to an emigrant ship bound for America. Once in New York, he is diagnosed with smallpox and sentenced to a quarantine of three months.

This ill, friendless, penniless, utterly isolated orphan, who cannot speak a word of English, will grow up to be the fabulously wealthy Godfather who keeps judges and politicians in his pocket like (as Sollozzo will put it) so many nickels and dimes. The final shot of the opening sequence offers an image of what might appear to be all but hopeless misery. We see the young Vito alone in his tiny, bleak, prison-like cell on Ellis Island. Yet the boy does not seem particularly downcast. As if confident that, despite all apparent probability, life has much better things in store for him, he sings a little song to himself; and that classic American symbol of immigrant hope, the Statue of Liberty, is clearly visible through his cell's small window.

What needs to be stressed, though, is that the remarkable story of Vito's rise is not merely the story of an individual. Though it does, indeed, amount to a (highly revisionist) version of the familiar rags-to-riches tale of immigrant success in the land of opportunity, it is also the story of the movement from one social system to another. The Sicily from which Vito springs is shown as a terribly impoverished and overwhelmingly rural land. Though it cannot quite be considered pre-capitalist in the strictest sense—since by 1901 Italy as a whole (and not only the cities of its industrial north) was integrated into the world capitalist system—it is pre-capitalist in the sense of still displaying many late-feudal survivals. Not only is there no developed industry in sight, but neither, also, is there any properly bourgeois structure of legality. Whereas, in the America of Vito-as-Godfather, organized crime is complexly interlinked with the regular administrative system of law and justice, in the Sicily of Vito's birth any such "legitimate" system appears to be absent altogether. The Mafia chieftain Don Ciccio (Giuseppe Sillato) rules almost like a feudal baron, with personal authority backed by naked armed force. When he has it announced to all and sundry that rewards await anyone who turns in the young Vito—and that terrible retribution awaits anyone who assists or hides him—it seems clear that his control of his domain is unshared. Unlike the later Vito, he has no need for judges or politicians.

There is, of course, considerable irony in the fact that Vito (played by De Niro throughout all of *The Godfather II* after the opening sequence that ends in Ellis Island) should ultimately go into the same line of work as the man who slaughtered his family. Indeed, it is his success as a New York Mafia boss that enables him later to return to Sicily from a position of strength and then to murder Don Ciccio in precisely the kind of vengeance that Don Ciccio had feared. But the deeper irony—the deeper significance—is, again, less individual than social. The almost pre-capitalist Sicilian Mafia may enjoy more *unshared* power, within a fairly narrow geographical compass, than its American counterpart. But the resources of America's commercial capitalist society, which are incomparably vaster than anything to be found in Sicily, enable the American Mafia—led in part by Don Vito Corleone and later by Don Michael Corleone—to acquire far greater wealth and wider influence than anything that Don Ciccio could even imagine.

It is important to notice the exact path that leads Vito to fortune and power. What Coppola shows is sharply distinct from, and even opposed to, the usual sentimental tale of immigrant success, in which honesty and patient hard work lead to a gradual rise from working-class poverty to middle-class comfort. Such, conceivably, has been the case with the undertaker Bonasera or the baker Nazorine, but Vito's story is very different. When we first see him as a young adult, he is indeed honest and hard-working; but such virtues are conspicuously failing to yield any great rewards. He works as an assistant in a small grocery store, and lives with his family in a miserable slum apartment. When he first (and accidentally) encounters a representative of organized crime—the Black Hand boss Don Fanucci (Gaston Moschin)—he is shocked by the man's cruelty (Don Fanucci threatens to cut up a young girl's face if her father gets behind in his payments of protection money) and wonders, with naïve feelings of ethnic solidarity, "If he's Italian, why does he bother other Italians?" (the line itself is spoken in Italian). Soon thereafter, Vito himself is "bothered" by Don Fanucci, who demands that the grocer employing Vito give his job to Fanucci's own nephew. Despite his genuine fondness for Vito, the grocer feels he has no choice but to comply: so that Vito, through no fault of his own, and despite all his honesty, good will, and industriousness, is now out of work. It is unclear how he will be able to provide even minimal sustenance for his family or the rent on the wretched flat where they live. America's claim to be the land of opportunity for those willing to work hard and play by the rules has proved false in Vito's case. We understand more fully now why the middle-aged Vito in the earlier film should be so scornful of Bonasera's uncritical trust in their common adoptive homeland.

After losing his job, Vito drifts into petty crime—at first, almost without really meaning to—and becomes a partner in a small stolen-goods operation that keeps him afloat economically but that is not visibly generating a great deal more income than his old position as a grocery clerk did. The real turning point in his fortunes occurs after his business comes to Fanucci's attention: Fanucci demands to "wet his beak," that is, to collect a share of the take. On his own initiative, and without fully consulting his partners, Vito decides to refuse Fanucci's demand. He determines instead to murder Fanucci and to take over Fanucci's position as the neighborhood crime boss. The killing takes place during the festival of San Gennaro (Saint Januarius, the patron saint of Naples) in Little Italy; and the cameras alternate between shots of the street festival itself (including a priest's recital of Latin prayers) and shots of Vito as he stalks and then guns down Fanucci. The viewer is irresistibly reminded of the cross-cutting near the end of the earlier film between Michael in church and Michael's professional killers as they blast away at his enemies. The comparison is important, for the murder of Fanucci establishes the Corleone criminal empire that Michael, years later, will inherit, consolidate, and expand.

It is important to notice that Vito's decision to take the plunge into major, violent crime seems at least partly motivated by the bout of pneumonia from which his son Fredo is suffering. That his family is still forced to live in a cold, drafty tenement painfully illustrates for Vito the continuing vulnerability of the Corleones. After establishing himself as a crime boss, Vito, ever the family man, will be able to give his family the best of everything. But, years after Fredo survives his childhood illness, the criminal empire Vito founds will also result, at the end of this film, in Fredo's being murdered by Vito's youngest and dearest son, Michael. After shooting Fanucci, Vito returns home to hold the infant in his arms and to murmur (in Italian), "Michael, your father loves you very much".

When we next see Vito, he is a man of wealth and influence, though not yet on the scale that he will one day command. But we see him already dispensing favors to humble dependents, just as he does in the opening scenes of *The Godfather*. The path by which De Niro's character will become Brando's is clearly implicit, and the film has no need to detail it further. We can sum up the story of Vito in *The Godfather II* by saying that it shows explicitly and in detail what is only suggested in the earlier film: that "behind every great fortune there is a crime," to quote the aphorism that Mario Puzo attributes to Balzac and uses as the epigraph of his novel. The term "great fortune" should, of course, be understood to mean not only this or that particular private holding but all the immense riches of capitalism itself. Vito's passage from Sicily to America cannot be understood simply as a journey from less to more opportunity. In fact, though his ocean-crossing does put Vito beyond Don Ciccio's murderous reach (in a nice illustration of Ciccio's provincial limitations), Vito in New York, as long as he confines himself to lawful activity, can attain a standard of material consumption only marginally, if at all, superior to that of a Sicilian peasant. What the shift from Sicily to America really signifies is the passage from a remote backward region of Europe—where the crimes of primitive accumulation, however vicious, have been unable to command sufficiently massive resources to allow for full-scale and thoroughgoing capitalist take-off—to the increasingly powerful economy of North America, where primitive accumulation, both foundational and ongoing, has produced very great capitalist fortunes indeed. Vito's murder of Fannuci is more an instance than an allegory of primitive accumulation, and founds his own particular great fortune, which is completely at one with the stupendous dynamism of US capitalism as a whole.

It is worth noting that Puzo's epigraph represents a slight misquotation or paraphrase (though a common one). What Balzac (who was Marx's favorite novelist) actually wrote in *La Père Goriot* (1835) is, "The secret of a great success [*Le secret des grandes fortunes*] for which you are at a loss to account is a crime that has never been found out [*un crime oublié*], because it was properly executed".[18] This version is perhaps even more pertinent to the discussion at hand. The murder of Fannuci is never found out, and Vito goes on to enjoy great success; and the *Godfather* trilogy as a whole displays the largely forgotten (or repressed) crimes of American capitalism that have been very properly executed (*proprement fait*, in Balzac's French) indeed.

From America to Cuba and back again

The scenes of *The Godfather II* devoted to Vito—despite their vital importance in supplying the pre-history of *The Godfather*—comprise only a minority of the film: roughly an hour out of the entire running time of three hours and twenty minutes (or nine out of thirty "chapters" in the DVD format). They are interspersed with scenes that focus on Don Michael and that, in the usual manner of a sequel, continue the action beyond the point where it ended in the first film. The transitions between the early-twentieth-century scenes and the later ones are managed by an especially artful series of fades and dissolves, and it is worth attending to Coppola's technique here; for it amounts to a good deal more than a mere film-school *tour de force*. The point is that the past always lives within the present, indeed that (as William Faulkner famously insisted) the past, far from being dead, is not even really past: as when, for example, the shot of the child Vito in his Ellis Island cell dissolves into one of his grandson, Michael's son, Anthony Vito Corleone (James Gounaris), as he prepares to make his first communion. The scenes are separated by 58 years, and the material circumstances are about as different as could easily be imagined. In contrast to the extreme bleakness and poverty of Vito's situation, Anthony's big day is celebrated with an expensive open-air party, complete with a live band and a guest list that includes a US senator. The scene recalls that of Connie's wedding in the first film, but this occasion is even grander. Michael has become a public philanthropist, donating a large sum to the local university; and, whereas elected officials had avoided being seen with the Corleones at Connie's wedding (though all of Vito's political friends discreetly sent gifts), Senator Geary (G. D. Spradlin) eagerly speaks at the party thrown for Connie's nephew. FBI agents had brazenly walked among the guests' cars at the wedding, snooping around and casting a pall over the festivities. But here uniformed police officers work as Corleone servants. Despite the huge difference in situation, however, the boy Vito and the boy Anthony physically resemble each other; and Vito's past lives in Anthony's present and future. The criminal career that lifts Vito out of poverty has a major impact on Anthony's life, in this film, and, even more, in *The Godfather III*.

Indeed, so brilliantly wrought is *The Godfather II* that one can almost imagine it as a stand-alone film, with all the action of *The Godfather* merely implied. In actuality, though, the scenes that focus on Michael amount to the third part of a narrative that chronologically begins with Vito's rise from impoverished orphan to wealthy crime boss and continues with his retirement and his succession by Michael.

In *The Godfather*, Michael saves the family business from attack by Sollozzo and his associates when he kills Sollozzo and McCluskey; and then, toward the end of the film, as we have seen, he eliminates most of the family's remaining rivals in a quick series of spectacular murders. At the beginning of the Michael-centered portion of *The Godfather II*, the Corleone empire is thus stronger than ever. Michael has moved the family from New York to Nevada, where it is becoming heavily involved in the Las Vegas casino and hotel business. Michael appears to be perhaps the most important crime boss in America, with the financier Hyman Roth his only real equal. Roth—who is developed as a character to a far greater extent than is any of Vito's peers in the earlier film—is, in fact, crucial to the story. For one thing, organized crime, considered as a kind of parallel capitalist system to normal or "legitimate"—and WASP-dominated—free enterprise, is, as we have seen, defined partly by its ethnic character; and Roth's Jewishness, as noted earlier, makes clear that it is marginality vis-à-vis the "truly" American WASPs, rather than Italian heritage as such, that is most fundamentally at issue here. Roth is known within the Mafia as "the Jew in Miami," a remarkable appellation when one considers the size of Miami's Jewish population; and Roth, like Michael, appears to have a healthy share of ethnic pride without, however, being excessively preoccupied with it. Roth's real-life model Meyer Lansky (who was still alive when the film was released, and is said to have admired Strasberg's performance) was often called "the banker to the mob," a phrase not actually used in the film but one that describes Roth's apparent function pretty well. There is, of course, a stereotypically Jewish note here, in view of the historic prominence of Jews in the banking and money-lending business.

Despite their shared ethnic marginality, however, neither Roth nor Michael is content to be a boss in a merely *alternative* capitalist system parallel to the "legitimate" one run mainly by WASPs. This is the great leap forward that Michael makes from the position he inherited from his father. Vito becomes a rich, powerful capitalist who at many points *resembles* the bosses of "normal" capitalism. But with the expanded and "improved" version of organized crime run by Michael Corleone and by Hyman Roth (the latter of whom, we learn, had worked closely with Vito for decades), there is no longer a question of mere resemblance. Instead, the distinctions between "legitimate" and "illegitimate" capitalism dwindle almost to the vanishing point.

Perhaps the most illuminating scene in this regard is the business conference in the presidential offices of the Cuban dictator Batista (Tito Alba). The president welcomes and thanks "this distinguished group of American industrialists" that includes Michael ("representing our associates in tourism and leisure activities") and Roth ("my old friend and associate from Florida") alongside representatives of companies with names that not only sound perfectly respectable but that are designed to suggest real-life American corporations once powerful (and nefarious) in Batista's Cuba: for instance, "the General Food Company" (probably United Fruit, with its massive and notorious human-rights violations) and "the United Telegraph & Telephone Company" (an obvious stand-in for what an investigative journalist once called the sovereign state of International Telephone & Telegraph). The president is deeply proud of a solid-gold telephone presented to him as a personal gift by the telephone company, and he passes it around for all his guests to admire. This gaudy and virtually obscene signifier of wealth is reminiscent of one of the earliest forms of primitive accumulation, the large-scale theft of New World gold in the early modern period by Spain and other European powers. The phone itself is of course thoroughly *post*modern in style; and it is a reminder of the ongoing (and, if you like, "postmodern") crimes of capitalism such as those perpetrated by the men around the conference table.

The conference cinematically "rhymes" with the one presided over by Don Barzini in the earlier film. But, again, whereas Vito takes part in a conference that is a good deal *like* an ordinary business meeting, the conference in the second film *is* an ordinary business meeting. Michael sits as equal to, and a full partner with—and, indeed, is finally almost indistinguishable from—the "normal" capitalists in Batista's conference room. Under Michael's leadership, the Corleone family's empire has not only expanded in wealth and scope but has effectively merged with the respectable capitalism that in Vito's heyday it had only resembled. As Roth explicitly stresses, an important part of this development is the increasingly close co-operation between the mob and the apparatuses of the bourgeois state itself. Vito's political connections are extensive and indispensable to his great success; but it is a safe bet that Vito never sat with any nation's president to plan joint business operations, as Michael does. It is altogether appropriate that, in one of his most memorable lines, Roth should reach for the name of one of the (then) most iconic institutions of American industrial capitalism to celebrate the unprecedented success that he and Michael are enjoying: "Michael, we're bigger than US Steel!"

Such grandeur cannot, however, conjure away the always underlying violence and instability of capitalism: a point the film illustrates in many ways. Some of the violence in *The Godfather II* takes specifically Mafia forms and is closely allied to the violence in *The Godfather*. One especially disturbing scene, for instance, directly corresponds and alludes to the scene of the horse's head in the first film. When Sen. Geary gives Michael some trouble about his business holdings in Las Vegas—and, to make matters worse, gratuitously insults him, his family, and Italian-Americans in general—he creates a problem parallel to that which the studio head Woltz creates for Johnny Fontane. Once again, Tom Hagen is the unfailingly polite and soft-voiced fixer on the scene. He arranges for Geary (after apparently being drugged) to wake up with a prostitute whom the senator knows well, but whom he now finds tied to the bed-frame and gruesomely cut to death. Understandably frantic and unable to remember exactly what happened, the senator realizes that he has no choice but to align himself with the Corleones and to accept their offer of help in covering up the crime that would otherwise ruin his career and his life. Perhaps more chilling, even, than the image of the beautiful young woman lying naked and lifeless on the bed, partially covered with a blood-soaked sheet, is Tom's impeccably calm manner as he explains how he can make Geary's problems go away: "This girl has no family. Nobody knows that she worked here [i.e., in what appears to be an expensive brothel operated by Fredo Corleone]. It'll be as though she never existed. All that's left is our friendship". The woman is a mere pawn in the Corleones' intricate chess game, killed without even the courtesy of being named or blamed. As with all the most typical crimes of capitalism, murder is purely instrumental—as instrumental as the "friendship" with Geary—and with no harsh feelings whatsoever. ("Never hate your enemies," as the older Michael says in *The Godfather III*. "It affects your judgment".)

Violence also underlies the most important personal relationship of the film, that between Michael and Hyman Roth. The two are technically partners, and each makes a considerable pretense of regarding the other as a good deal more than a mere partner too. Roth, Vito's old friend and colleague, appears to regard Michael as a son-figure, a bright and respectful young man whom he can nurture and teach. Michael, in turn, professes to revere Roth as a wise and brilliantly accomplished mentor from whom he has much to learn. Nonetheless—and despite the fact that the apparent feelings of personal fondness that the two have for one another may well be at least partially genuine—the logic of free, unregulated profit-making dictates that the two are fundamentally rivals, each aspiring to unshared dominance of their joint enterprise. Roth, accordingly, has the master bedroom of the Corleone lakefront mansion in Tahoe machine-gunned as Michael and Kay are retiring for the night. The two barely escape with their lives. The scene comes fairly early in the film, just a little more than half an hour in; but it is only later that the viewer realizes the shooting to be Roth's work. Michael, however—who in the course of the film is revealed to be the sharpest of all the Mafiosi, more clever even than Roth or Vito—grasps the truth all along, and, near the end of the film, manages to have Roth shot to death at the Miami airport, even though the aged financier is surrounded by federal agents in the process of taking him into custody.

Where *The Godfather II* makes a major conceptual advance over its predecessor—particularly in the representation of violence—is in its treatment of a conflict very different from Michael's lethal rivalry with Roth or the Corleones' murderous blackmail of Sen. Geary. The deeply political nature of Coppola's filmmaking makes itself most explicit in his decision—virtually unprecedented in the history of the mob movie—to incorporate into his saga no less a political event than the Cuban Revolution. Though the fact is not at first obvious during the film's Cuban scenes, it turns out that we are seeing the country during the very last days of the Batista dictatorship. Indeed, the climax of the Cuban portion of *The Godfather II* comes with a lavish New Year's Eve party in the presidential palace on 31 December 1959—that is, just as Fidel Castro and his rebel soldiers of the 26th of July Movement are marching victoriously into Havana to proclaim the triumph of the revolution the following day. The party is interrupted by the humiliated dictator's announcement of his resignation and flight. Up until this point, though, the veteran Cuba hands—most prominently Roth and Batista himself—are unconcerned about the rebels, who they expect to be as ineffective as their predecessors have been for decades. But Michael, always more penetrating than those around him, suspects otherwise. As he is being driven through the Havana streets, he sees a rebel being arrested by Batista's military; rather than be taken alive, the man shouts "Viva Fidel!" and explodes a grenade, killing himself but taking a high-ranking officer with him. Michael is struck by the fact that, as he points out, the soldiers are paid to fight, whereas the rebels are not. "What does that tell you?" asks Roth. Michael replies: "They could win".

And so they do. Michael, of course, has no sympathy for the revolutionaries; like Don Barzini and the rest of the Mafiosi, he is not a communist. His prescience about the potential imminence of revolution merely leads him to decline to invest the large sum of money in Cuban gambling operations that Roth, Batista, and their associates had hoped for and expected. But, for the film itself, the point is more properly political. In films as violent as the *Godfather* trilogy, the act of exploding a grenade is, in and of itself, a fairly routine kind of occurrence. Yet the difference between this and the other acts of violence we have witnessed is fundamental. The rebel soldier willing to kill and to die for the revolutionary cause does not act for the instrumentality of profit-making (nor for a merely personal grudge, as Vito does when he murders Don Ciccio). For him, violence is, on the contrary, a means to bring about a new society, one dedicated to the abolition of the profit motive and thus of capitalist violence itself.

The whole incident shows that capitalism is unstable not only in the sense of proceeding by fits and starts of violence, by the persistence of primitive accumulation. It is unstable also, at least potentially, in the sense of being capable of being overthrown. The scene of the rebel soldier therefore amounts to a *novum* (in Ernst Bloch's term), a genuine revolutionary novelty. Of course, to portray the actual building of a revolutionary socialist society in Cuba lies far beyond the film's ambitions (huge though the latter are). Yet, just as Don Ciccio's regime in Sicily shows an *almost* pre-capitalist alternative to America's bourgeois status quo, so the heroic joy of Fidel's soldiers as they march through the Havana streets on New Year's Eve shows an *almost* post-capitalist one. Michael, naturally, returns to the United States and to business as usual, and takes the action of the film with him. But, as *The Godfather II* traces a progress from the agrarian Sicilian backwardness in which Vito is born to the advanced monopoly capitalism in which his son Michael is a major player, the Cuban interlude suggests that history need not halt its march with capitalism. Primitive accumulation, perhaps, will not have the final word after all.

The global horizons of Michael Corleone

Or will it? This is, in a sense, the question that haunts the entirety of *The Godfather III*. Not the least important thing to happen in the sixteen years that separate the second and third films of the trilogy is the change in the significance of the Cuban Revolution. To be sure, the widespread hopes (and fears) during the 1960s that the Fidelista victory might herald a global wave of revolutionary liberation had already begun to fade considerably by 1974, when *The Godfather II* came out. But such hopes were by no means dead, and the heroic period of the 26th of July Movement's triumph was still a vivid memory. The doomed rebel's cry of "Viva Fidel!" still had the capacity to thrill. The political climate was very different by 1990, when the third film was released. Bureaucratic ossification in Cuba had become increasingly rigid and evident, and the European Stalinist states with which Castro was allied were in (or beyond) an advanced state of collapse. US-dominated capitalism seemed decisively victorious. *The Godfather III* is very much a product of this moment—a moment of global capitalist triumphalism—even though the film's actual setting is more than a decade earlier, in the 1970s.

Before examining the film in detail, it is, however, necessary to address the widespread complaints that *The Godfather III* is inferior to its predecessors, so much inferior, as some have maintained, as even to render problematic the whole notion of a trilogy. It is true that, if one insists on treating the three films as separate works, the third one does fail, in some ways, to meet the (almost impossibly high) standards of the first two. The story-line of *The Godfather III* is somewhat episodic, not quite matching either the finished narrative perfection of *The Godfather* or the extraordinary historical agility and incisiveness of *The Godfather II*. There is also a decline in the quality of the acting, though here again the standards of comparison are stratospheric. The main burden of acting in the first film is carried by Brando and Pacino together, and in the second film by Pacino and De Niro—that is, at least arguably, the finest Hollywood actor of one generation and the two finest of the succeeding generation, all at their very best. In the third film, Pacino carries the main burden alone (a metaphor, perhaps, for the way that increasing success brings increasing isolation for Michael), and, though his performance is never less than thoroughly competent, it lacks (as does most of Pacino's later work) the special intensity and power he brought to playing the younger Michael. Furthermore, whereas in the earlier films all the supporting performances are strong (with Robert Duvall, James Caan, Lee Strasberg, and Diane Keaton turning in especially fine work), the abysmal job that Sofia Coppola (the director's daughter) does as Michael's daughter Mary is a serious flaw in the third film. Even Coppola himself has seemed to regard *The Godfather III* as of less than equal stature to its predecessors. His preferred title for the film was "The Death of Michael Corleone"—which was rejected by Paramount for box-office reasons—and the implication is presumably that the third film is to be seen more as a coda to the first two than as the final third of a genuinely three-part structure.[19]

Nonetheless, I will argue that *The Godfather III* is indeed a worthy conclusion to a great trilogy. In strictly formal terms, the elaborate parallelism of images and motifs established between the first two films continues here, and makes it hard to consider the third film as a mere coda. Even more important, the fundamental thematic concerns of the earlier films reach a culmination in the third film so logical as to seem, in retrospect, inevitable. The third film, in this way, recapitulates the success of the second in making the earlier material, so wonderfully finished in itself, turn out to be not yet complete after all. Jonathan Rosenbaum, one of the more quirky *Godfather* critics but not one of the least perceptive, has actually argued that the final film is "conceptually and morally" superior to the other two.[20] Though my reading of *The Godfather III* will be very different from his, I maintain that this judgment is less hyperbolic than it may seem.

We can begin to explore how the film continues the saga of primitive accumulation initiated and continued in its predecessors by considering the role of the Roman Catholic Church. In the first two films, it is noteworthy not only that the Church plays a fairly prominent role—unsurprisingly for a story about a family of Italian Catholic background—but that specifically religious ceremonies appear at key narrative points. *The Godfather* begins by highlighting the sacrament of Holy Matrimony, as Connie's wedding celebration and Vito's concomitant granting of favors dominate the opening action. The movie's conclusion gets underway with the sacrament of Baptism, when Michael serves as godfather to his infant nephew. The first scene of the Michael-centered plot of *The Godfather II* features the sacrament of the Eucharist, as young Anthony Corleone makes his first communion. The other, Vito-centered narrative line of the film reaches its climax with the murder of Fanucci, which, as we have seen, takes place during the festival of San Gennaro: not one of the seven actual sacraments of the Church but still (as the scene makes clear) an event of deeply Catholic religious significance. The third film continues this pattern. After an initial panning shot of the Corleones' abandoned Tahoe estate (which shows, among other things, a statue of the Madonna), the action proper begins with a ceremony in which Michael is being awarded a solemn Papal honor, induction as a Commander of the Order of Saint Sebastian: "one of the highest honors the Catholic Church can bestow upon a layman," as we are informed by one of Michael's publicists. Not counting some voice-over by Michael, the first words in the film are spoken in Church Latin, by an archbishop.

Yet the Church not only has a presence in this film far more prominent than in *The Godfather* or *The Godfather II*; its presence is also very different in kind from anything in the earlier installments of the trilogy. In the first two films we see the *American* Catholic Church, a church of immigrants and their descendants; and Catholicism (like Hyman Roth's Judaism) is significant not so much for properly theological reasons as because of its inseparability from the ethnic marginality of non-WASPs. Even at Connie's grand wedding party, Vito, as we have seen, must endure the impertinence of the FBI. Even at Anthony's still grander first-communion celebration, Michael must endure the obnoxious anti-Italian bigotry of Sen. Geary. Though Michael's party celebrating his Papal honor takes place in New York (where he has returned to live after leaving Nevada), we quickly see that the ecclesiastical—and other—horizons of the Corelones now extend far beyond the American shores to which Vito came as an impoverished refugee. At Michael's party, private talk between his attorney B. J. Harrison (George Hamilton) and Archbishop Gilday (Donal Donnelly), who presided over the induction ceremony, soon turns to the Vatican and its vast network of financial holdings. It is clear that we are dealing here not with an immigrant church marginalized within a predominantly Anglo-Protestant nation, but with the Holy See itself: one of the historic centers of European political and economic power.

Michael's involvement with his church is revealed to be a matter of higher and higher—and more and more corrupt—finance as the film progresses. At his party, he has his daughter Mary, acting as titular head of a philanthropic foundation named after his father, present Archbishop Gilday with a check in the amount of $100 million for Catholic charitable efforts to aid the poor of Sicily, the Corleones' ancestral homeland; and it is natural to assume, at this point, that this generosity has a great deal to do with the Papal honor he has just received. Before long, however, we learn that the story is much more complex, and much more sinister, than any apparently simple *quid pro quo* between a huge charitable donation and being made a Commander of the Order of Saint Sebastian. In an important scene a bit later, in which Michael and Gilday speak privately, it transpires that the archbishop has been running the Vatican Bank, and that, owing to unspecified shenanigans involving him and certain unnamed "friends," he has managed to lose $769 million of the bank's money. Gilday asks Michael to make good most of the deficit, and Michael is willing to do so: but not simply for the sake of charity. He is interested in taking over a multinational holding company called Immobiliare—the "largest landlord on earth, real estate all over the world worth $6 billion," as B. J. Harrison helpfully explains—in which the Vatican holds a crucial 25% of the voting stock. If the Vatican votes to support the Corleone bid, giving Michael control of Immobiliare, then, he says, he will save the archbishop from the embarrassment (or worse) that otherwise awaits him. The deal is struck. Michael intends to turn the company into a new kind of European and international conglomerate, a move that, as the archbishop points out, should make Michael (who must already be a billionaire) one of the very richest men in the world. As the two men talk, huge maps of the world on the walls behind them signify the global scope of their dealings.

As the film unfolds, the plot thickens yet further. While pretending to be allied with Michael, Gilday turns out to be secretly working with a rival faction within (and beyond) the Vatican, one that is determined to block the Corleone takeover of Immobiliare. "We're back with the Borgias!" complains Michael after a meeting in Rome in which it becomes apparent that his bid for the company is not proceeding as smoothly as he had thought it would. His reference to the famously corrupt and murderous Spanish-Italian noble family, which at one point controlled the Papacy, is even more appropriate than Michael himself, for all his acuteness, may yet grasp.[21] For, by film's end, it is clear that Gilday's co-conspirators include important sections of the Italian Mafia, who, of course, do not shy away from homicide in pursuit of their aims. Their targets include not only Michael himself but even the new Pope, John Paul I (Raf Vallone), who is determined to clean up the financial corruption in the Holy See that he inherited from his predecessor.

Except for the sincerely pious John Paul I—who, while still Cardinal Lamberto, hears Michael's confession in the only scene in the entire trilogy in which actual religious faith is registered—the Church in *The Godfather III* appears, indeed, as a political and financial rather than a spiritual and theological institution. Its high officials participate in the global financial and political elite that includes ruling-class types from Swiss bankers to Italian Mafia dons. The ultimate ringleader of the anti-Corleone conspiracy with which Archbishop

Gilday works is one Don Licio Lucchesi (Enzo Robutti), an Italian politician based on Giulio Andreotti—who was not only a power within the Italian Mafia (and who at one point was actually convicted of murder in the death of an anti-Mafia journalist) but who was also one of the most important figures in the history of the Italian Christian Democratic Party, serving in many high governmental posts, including three terms as Italy's prime minister.[22] "Finance is a gun. Politics is knowing when to pull the trigger," says Don Lucchesi. This aphorism sums up much of what the film demonstrates about the unity of power elites "legitimate" and "illegitimate". Bankers, politicians, archbishops, and crime bosses are all, finally, in pretty much the same business.

In *The Godfather III*, then, the Corleone family business is more advanced than its earlier incarnations in two major ways. The most obvious advance is in sheer scale. The rise is not just from Vito's relatively humble position as a neighborhood boss in the Little Italy section of New York City, but even from the position that Michael himself occupies by the end of *The Godfather II*. After the death of Roth, Michael is the wealthiest crime boss in the country, and he controls economic interests that extend far beyond such traditional Mafia activities as bootlegging and illegal gambling, in which his father made his fortune. At a hearing of a US Senate committee investigating organized crime, Michael points out that he owns stock in utterly respectable corporations. Still, Michael in the second film is only a *national* power, with influence that does not appear to extend beyond the United States and its semi-colonial dependencies. In the final installment of the series, however, the increasing globalization of capital is a mighty tide that has lifted the Corleone boat to a multinational level. Michael's allies and adversaries are now among the most influential political and economic powers on the planet. The *Godfather* saga is, as we have seen, always a deeply American narrative; and the rise of the Corleones recapitulates the larger intercontinental processes by which the New World, once a mere dependent outgrowth of the Old, returns to confront its former masters on (at least) equal terms. Vito flees Europe as a young boy, because, even within one of Europe's most impoverished regions, he is so powerless that he must run for his life. Vito's son returns to Europe to deal, as a peer, with men who are orders of magnitude more powerful than Don Ciccio could ever hope to be.

Concomitant with the expansion of the Corleone empire is its increasing respectability. Though Michael sees from the beginning that the distinction between "legitimate" and "illegitimate" capitalism is largely a matter of hypocrisy, he nonetheless yearns to transcend the Mafia environment in which he has been raised. In the first film, he vows to Kay that within a few years the Corleones will be involved only with legal businesses; and their marriage breaks up in the second film in large part because of his inability (or unwillingness) to keep this promise. True, he may sit (as his father never did) in a presidential conference room alongside executives of food, communications, and other "normal" companies. But, after all, the president in question (who is about to be overthrown anyway) rules only a small tropical island; and Michael's core business interests are still criminal in the technical and legal as well as in the moral sense. In the third film, however—with Kay now happily remarried but still ardently desired by him—Michael has finally succeeded in keeping his old pledge. As he carefully explains to Archbishop Gilday, the Corleone businesses are now strictly legal; and Michael operates as a billionaire international businessman among other international businessmen. When his ambitious nephew Vincent (Andy Garcia)—a young Mafia operative and Santino's out-of-wedlock son by his mistress Lucy Mancini, with whom we see Santino having sex during Connie's wedding celebration near the beginning of the first film—asks Michael for a job, Michael replies, "As what? Tough guy? I don't need tough guys. I need more lawyers". In *The Godfather*, Vito appears in the newspapers only in sensational tabloid stories about organized crime. In *The Godfather III*, we see stories about Michael in the business pages of *The New York Times*, *The Financial Times*, and *The Wall Street Journal*: the most sober and respected of papers among the global elite.

The problem, of course, is that, as Don Lucchesi illustrates more precisely than any other single character in the film (or the entire trilogy), the distinctions between the global elite and the Mafia are mainly illusory. As the film progresses, it seems that the extent to which this is true comes as a bit of a surprise even to Michael, for all his insight and experience. "All my life," as he says to his sister Connie, "I kept trying to go up in society, where everything higher up was legal, straight. But the higher I go, the crookeder it becomes. Where the hell does it end?" The remark may express a moment of sentimental self-indulgence on Michael's part, for, taken literally, it could hardly represent the considered opinion of the man who, decades earlier, could already see through Kay Adams's naïve assumption that senators and presidents don't have men killed. His concluding question is surely rhetorical, for Michael knows that "it" (the pronoun here recalls the Freudian *Es*, or, in Latin, "id," or, in English, "it," the dark, surging, transpersonal force that cannot be completely transcended or repressed) *never* ends. Moreover, "it" is represented, for Michael, not only by the fact that, after arriving in Europe, he finds himself the target of Lucchesi's conspiracy, which includes elements of the same organization—the Italian Mafia—that forced Vito to *flee* Europe, and that manages to recruit even the old Corleone family friend Don Altobello (Eli Wallach) to its cause. In neatly quasi-Freudian fashion, "it" is to be found also in those parts of Michael's own past that he has tried so hard to repress: which, however, themselves turn out to be inseparable from the future to which he aspires.

The return of the Corleone repressed is seen most spectacularly in the most graphically violent scene of the film, the scene of the Atlantic City massacre. Michael has long been regarded as the ultimate authority within the American Mafia, especially in the New York area. Vincent compares him, in this regard, to the Supreme Court. Though Michael, throughout the film, tries to cut his ties to his old associates, they are not happy about foregoing the leadership and economic opportunities that he had always provided. In particular, they are eager (as Don Altobello tells Michael) to take part in the Immobiliare deal, with its promise of vast profits. But Michael cannot allow that, since he intends the Immobiliare takeover to complete his separation from the Mafia and his integration into the world of "legitimate" capitalism once and for all. Especially disappointed by Michael's refusal—because he had also been shut out of earlier deals that Michael had intended to be his final connections with organized crime—is Joey Zasa (Joe Mantegna), a cocky up-and-coming don who controls what was once Vito's neighborhood crime ring. At a conference of crime bosses on the top floor of a luxurious Atlantic City hotel, Joey denounces Michael and the others, leaves, and then, having chained shut the doors of the large banquet room, executes an extraordinary attack: machine-gunners in a helicopter outside fire hundreds (or perhaps thousands) of rounds of ammunition through the room's big windows. Michael survives (with Vincent's help), to deliver perhaps his single most memorable line in the film (one repeatedly recalled and parodied in *The Sopranos* [1999–2007], David Chase's great television drama about the mob): "Just when I thought I was out, they pull me back in".

Of course, the fundamental reason that Michael can never get out is that there *is* no "out". Michael sees at once that Joey Zasa is basically just a small-time enforcer, lacking both the intelligence and the ambition required to initiate or plan anything as grand as the Atlantic City massacre; and that someone else must therefore be the real brains behind the operation. What he does not learn until later is that the massacre was the brainchild of Lucchesi himself, one of the masters of that world of global finance and politics that Michael is in process of joining. Michael cannot use the Immobiliare takeover to escape his violent past: not only because his past always catches up with him but also because equal or greater violence will always be ahead of him, so to speak, waiting for him. In a way, the shrewdest commentator within the film on these realities is Kay, no longer the naïve New England maiden. Well before the violence in Atlantic City, and without any specific knowledge of the Immobiliare deal or the machinations of Lucchesi, Kay says to her ex-husband at the party celebrating his honor from the Pope, "You know, Michael, now that you're so respectable I think you're more dangerous than you ever were. In fact, I preferred you when you were just a common Mafia hood".

The personal relationship in the film that most vividly shows Michael's inability to separate himself from criminal violence is that between him and Vincent Mancini. When he tells Vincent that he needs lawyers, not tough guys, Michael is expressing the perennial, and perennially vain, dream of capitalism: the dream that the system might someday work by entirely peaceful, lawful methods, without the continuing need for the murder and thievery of primitive accumulation. But capitalism cannot, in fact, do without these things, and Michael cannot do without Vincent. Just as he cannot deny the ("illegitimate") blood tie that connects him to his older brother's son, so he cannot deny his need for Vincent's consummate mastery of the violent arts. Michael would probably never have left the Atlantic City hotel alive had it not been for the bodyguarding skills of Vincent, the tough guy. Not only does Michael give Vincent the job he at first refuses, but he then proceeds to instruct him on how to be a crime boss. Vincent shares many of his father's qualities (even though Sonny was shot to death before Vincent was born): physical prowess, a brash and outgoing manner, a hot temper, sexual charisma, and a taste for violence. Michael teaches Vincent to combine such characteristics with cool thinking and careful planning, and to avoid being undone by his own impulsiveness. Vincent's rise is strongly supported by Connie, who in this film has matured from a giddy playgirl to Michael's effective second-in-command and informal *consigliere*. As Michael is bedridden with diabetes, Connie tells her nephew, "You're the only one left in this family with my father's strength". Michael agrees. He legitimizes

Vincent—"Nephew, from this moment on call yourself Vincent Corleone"—and anoints him as his successor as Godfather. In a late scene, several Corleone subordinates gather around Vincent to kiss his hand and address him by Vito's old title, Don Corleone.

Vincent does a good job, justifying Michael's and Connie's confidence. He infiltrates the conspiracy against Michael, even outwitting the mighty Lucchesi himself in a face-to-face meeting, and gathers vital intelligence. He recruits the best hired guns available, and carefully plans the defense of his uncle against the attack they both know is coming; he also instigates a series of preemptive strikes against the attackers. Thanks mainly to Vincent, the film, like its predecessors, ends with the destruction of Michael's enemies. In *The Godfather*, Moe Green and the heads of the Five Families of New York are gunned down while Michael attends the baptism of Connie's baby boy. *The Godfather II* concludes with the deaths of Hyman Roth, of the disloyal Corleone brother Fredo, and of the informer Frankie Pentangeli (Michael Gazzo). As *The Godfather III* ends, Archbishop Gilday is shot down, Don Altobello is poisoned, and Don Lucchesi is stabbed to death in an especially grisly fashion. Though Michael is wounded in the attack on him, he survives, and dies years later, of natural causes like his father before him. It may seem that he has won.

But he has not. Violence can never be perfectly or precisely scripted, not even by one as talented in such things as Don Vincent. The main setting of the film's conclusion is the Sicilian opera house where Michael's son Anthony (Franc D'Ambrosio), now a professional singer, is making his triumphant operatic debut in a starring role. After the show ends, and the audience is descending the stone steps of the theater, a bullet intended for Michael hits his daughter Mary, horribly bathing the front of her evening gown with blood. Looking at her father, she falls to her knees, manages to squeeze out the single word, "Dad," and then drops down dead.

So for Michael it has all, ultimately, come to nothing. In the voice-over at the beginning of the film, Michael addresses Anthony and Mary in a letter he is writing to them: "The only wealth in this world is children. More than all the money, power on earth, you are my treasure". This note is consistent with Michael's character as it has been developed throughout the trilogy. He has always been a family man, if less successfully so than his father before him. (It is noteworthy that, like Vito, and unlike Santino, Fredo, and even, in his discreet way, Tom Hagen, Michael consistently foregoes extramarital dalliances; after Kay, the mother of his children, leaves him, he does not even remarry, but instead installs Connie as the lady of his household. It is also noteworthy that, of all murders for which he is responsible, Fredo's is the only one that seems to cause him anything like genuine remorse.) "I would burn in Hell to keep you safe," he says at one point as he hugs and kisses Mary, his favorite of his two children, as he was his own father's favorite; and the sentiment is, in merely psychological terms, perfectly sincere. But the notion that he could actually keep Mary, his most cherished treasure, safe from the fall-out of his business operations is as vain as the notion that the business itself could be conducted without benefit of tough guys, without violence.

The death of Mary Corleone is one of the great cinematic representations of hot, raw, unmitigated grief. Kay, Connie, Anthony, and Vincent (who had loved his cousin) are all devastated, but the main emphasis is on Michael, who ignores his own gunshot wounds and desperately holds and hugs Mary's still warm corpse, as if his touch could somehow bring her back to life. A few moments later he throws back his head and screams in agony, though for the viewer the scream is silent until its last few seconds. In what is perhaps Pacino's finest bit of acting in the film, Michael's face is a mask of unspeakably terrible, unalloyed pain.[23] Mary's death is a loss compared to which the hundreds of millions, or billions, of dollars that deals like the takeover of Immobiliare might bring him are trivial.

There immediately follows a series of brief flashbacks: Michael dancing with Mary at the party celebrating his Papal honor, Michael dancing with his Sicilian wife Apollonia (Simonetta Stefanelli) at their wedding, Michael dancing with Kay at Anthony's first-communion party. These are the three women whom Michael has loved unconditionally, and in each part of the trilogy he loses one of them because of his business: Apollonia when she is killed by a car bomb meant for him in *The Godfather*, Kay when she divorces him in *The Godfather II*, and now Mary in *The Godfather III*. The scene then dissolves to one of Michael as an old man, sitting on a chair and then falling over, evidently dead from a heart attack. Though Michael's death somewhat "rhymes" with Vito's own death by apparent heart attack, the differences are more noteworthy than the similarities. Vito dies at the home where his family lives, in the lush green garden where he spends much of his retirement time, surrounded by good food and drink; and, despite the losses that he himself has suffered (most notably the loss of his oldest son), he dies while playing happily with a grandchild, the young Anthony. Michael, by contrast, dies in an unidentified (though probably Sicilian) place of sun and rock; and, except for two small dogs who (in contrast to Vito's cat at the beginning of the first film) are pretty much ignoring him, he dies alone. Before he collapses, his face wears the gaunt, empty expression of a broken man who has long ago lost anything to live for. After his collapse, the screen cuts to black, and the credits come up; the trilogy is done.

But there is, of course, no reason to suppose that the violence integral to the Corleone empire established by Vito's murder of Don Fanucci has—or can, or ever will—come to an end. Mary is only the most recent victim that the viewer of the trilogy happens to see. The crime and violence of primitive accumulation are inseparable from capitalism itself: and, as the capitalism of the Corelones becomes richer and grander and more respectable—as it becomes more and more like "normal" capitalism until it is completely indistinguishable from it—the violence only gets worse, finally resulting in what is, from Michael's viewpoint, the worst imaginable outcome in the world, the violent death of his beloved daughter. Not for nothing is she named after the most precious of all women—of all mortal creatures—in the Roman Catholic faith that Michael, as the confession scene with Cardinal Lamberto suggests, has never quite given up. When Michael tells Connie that the higher up in society he goes, the more crooked everything gets, he still has no inkling of just how cruelly crooked his own existence is yet to become. All his life, Michael has, in effect, hoped that primitive accumulation might be a supplement to capitalism in the colloquial rather than the dangerous, Derridean sense: that is, something essentially incidental and dispensable, something that can ultimately be left behind. As a withered old man who falls over in his chair to die alone, Michael has finally, at terrible cost, learned better.

Hobbes after Marx, Scorsese after Coppola: On *GoodFellas*

From Coppola to Scorsese

*G*oodFellas—which I take to be the absolute summit of Martin Scorsese's filmmaking career, surpassing even *Mean Streets* (1973), *Taxi Driver* (1976), *Raging Bull* (1980), *The King of Comedy* (1983), *The Last Temptation of Christ* (1988), *The Age of Innocence* (1993), *Casino* (1995), and *Bringing Out the Dead* (1999), among his other strongest works—came out in 1990, the same year as the final third of Francis Coppola's *Godfather* trilogy. Though the timing is almost certainly a co-incidence, it is a highly appropriate one. For Scorsese's film of 1990 is, like Coppola's, defined—though of course it is much less obviously or directly defined—by the first two installments of the *Godfather* series. This is not to deny that some of the seeds of *GoodFellas* can be found in Scorsese's earlier work and also, for that matter, in films by other directors as well. Raoul Walsh's *White Heat* (1949), in which James Cagney's character is clearly the direct model for Joe Pesci's in *GoodFellas* (and also for Pesci's character in *Casino*), is one pertinent example. But *GoodFellas* is a mob movie in a way and to a degree that *White Heat* and even *Mean Streets* are not, and, indeed, that hardly any really first-rate Hollywood film before *The Godfather* (1972) is. In *White Heat*, for example, there is no real "mob," no large-scale criminal organization, just a small, mobile band of robbers. As for *Mean Streets*, most of its action (like some of the action of *Raging Bull*) takes place on the fringes of the Mafia. But the inner workings of organized crime are incidental—not, as in the genuine mob movie, central—to the film's narrative and to its character development. Indeed, Coppola's overwhelming success has made it easy to forget that, prior to 1972, the mob movie was a relatively minor genre. It had a certain presence in the Hollywood repertoire, but had never attained the kind of major success enjoyed by the Western or by film noir. As a matter of fact, the genre's relatively undistinguished history helped to make for considerable studio resistance, at first, to turning Mario Puzo's novel into a big-budget film.

The Godfather and its immediate sequel, *The Godfather, Part Two* (1974), changed all that, of course. By 1990, the pre-eminence of Coppola's masterpieces within the genre of the mob film was incontestable (though Brian De Palma had made an important contribution to the form with *Scarface* [1983]—a remake vastly superior to Howard Hawks's 1932 film of the same name—as had Sergio Leone with *Once Upon a Time in America* [1984]). The best way, I think, to understand *GoodFellas* is to see it as the only successful attempt to make a mob movie of a stature truly comparable to that of the *Godfather* films: and, moreover, one that understands that it would have been quite impossible to rival Coppola's work by attempting anything profoundly similar to it. Samuel Beckett famously maintained that James Joyce had written literature that expanded the resources of language to the utmost, beyond what any other author could hope to do; and that, therefore, the only way to follow Joyce's incomparable achievement was to go in the exactly opposite direction and to contract language to the maximum extent feasible. In somewhat the same way, Scorsese (whether with full self-consciousness or not) implicitly offers to rival Coppola by making a mob movie that is as much opposed as possible to the *Godfather* films.[24] Scorsese himself has, in fact, more than once seemed to imply as much.[25]

In this chapter, I will keep the antithetical precedent of the *Godfather* trilogy steadily in view as I analyze what seem to me the three most important aspects of the mob lifeworld as represented by *GoodFellas*: the essentially proletarian nature of the stratum of the Mafia inhabited by the film's characters, where the rewards of crime generally turn out to be considerably more meager than they may at first seem; the Hobbesian near-anarchy of violence, fear, and insecurity that characterizes everyday life in this proletarian stratum of the mob; and the attendant solitariness in which the characters of *GoodFellas* necessarily live.

The view from the Mafia's factory floor

Perhaps the most obvious way that *GoodFellas* adopts a strategy opposite to that of the *Godfather* films concerns the radically different coigns of vantage from which the two filmmakers examine the workings of the Mafia. Coppola's interest is almost entirely in top management. The Corleones themselves are the main examples, of course, but other examples include such secondary characters as the Tattaglias (the Corleones' arch-rivals in New York in the first film), Virgil "the Turk" Sollozzo, Moe Greene, Don Barzini, Don Tommasino (Michael's protector in Sicilian exile in the first film, who returns in the third), Hyman Roth, Frankie Pentangeli, and, in the third film, Don Altobello and Don Lucchesi. Such ruling-class types prefer to conduct business in private, and the spaces most prominently featured in the *Godfather* films are indeed private ones: especially the fortress-like mansions, but also the offices, suites, and conference rooms of the mighty. In few respects is Coppola's trilogy more profoundly a saga of American big business from the perspective of the boardroom than in the rigorous separation it observes between the machinations of the top bosses and the actual work on which all the wealth of the enterprise ultimately depends. Don Vito Corleone's fortune is based primarily on businesses like bootlegging and illegal gambling; but never do we see a bet taken or a drink served. Coppola's interest in the Mafia is macroeconomic (and macropolitical).

GoodFellas, by contrast, is very much a street-level film, with a keen interest in the microeconomics of organized crime.[26] Much of the action takes place literally on the streets of New York City (mainly the unfashionable borough of Queens), and most of the rest is set in places like bars, inexpensive restaurants, airports, and prisons: all public spaces in which privacy is at a minimum. The highest-ranking Mafia official in the movie is Paulie Cicero

(Paul Sorvino), a mere neighborhood boss who, on a hypothetical organization chart of the mob, would surely be placed at least two or three levels below Michael Corleone; and even Paulie is a secondary character. The protagonist is one Henry Hill (based on an actual person of the same name and played by Ray Liotta as an adult, and by Christopher Serrone as a youngster), a proletarian type who, far from being born into Mafia aristocracy, is not even born into the Mafia at all. Coming from working-class poverty in a mixed Irish-Italian family, Henry as a child just happens to live across the street from a cabstand and a pizzeria that function as mob fronts and hang-outs for lower-level Mafiosi. Observing the goings-on there from his parents' front window, Henry aspires to what he imagines to be the free, easy, and glamorous life of the mobsters: "I mean, they did whatever they wanted. They double-parked in front of a hydrant, and nobody ever gave them a ticket. In the summer, when they played cards all night, nobody ever called the cops". It is striking how pathetically modest are these examples of privilege, cited by Henry in voice-over, that convince him that being a gangster is somehow "better than being president of the United States". As a schoolboy, he crosses the street to join the mob at the lowest level—doing such odd jobs as parking cars, serving food, and delivering messages—and gradually works his way up to modest success as the owner of a mob-connected restaurant and, later, as a dealer in cocaine.

The film gives considerable emphasis to the hard work required for such a rise. A pertinent example, relatively early in *GoodFellas*, is the sequence that shows Henry learning the hijacking business as an assistant to Jimmy "the Gent" Conway (Robert De Niro), his closest friend and chief mentor in the mob. Armed, they stop 18-wheel delivery trucks on lonely night roads, and Jimmy demonstrates how to acquire the goods with minimal bother. He demands to see each driver's identification card, and then, after reminding the driver that he now knows the driver's name and address, returns the card without further ado and with a $50 bill (a very considerable sum for a truck-driver in the 1950s, when this action is taking place). The effect is not just to make potential adversaries co-operative but even to make them accomplices in the hijacking enterprise. Soon drivers in the area are not only handing over their wares without even token resistance but also alerting Jimmy in advance to the more valuable loads.

It is all a fairly plebeian operation. The trucks in question are not carrying valuable works of art, precious gems, gold ingots, or sacks of cash, but quite ordinary items—liquor, cigarettes, razor blades, shrimp, lobsters—of the sort that can be sold quickly and almost anywhere. "Shrimp and lobsters were best," Henry informs us. "They went really fast". This activity naturally comes to the attention of the authorities, who dispatch what Henry, in voice-over, describes as "a whole army" of police to stop it. Jimmy handles the challenge with typical smoothness and efficiency; he simply co-opts the police assigned to arrest him, making them partners and sharing his take with them. In a sense, this is official corruption of the same general sort that plays such a large role in the *Godfather* movies. But there is an immense gulf in scale between Vito Corleone issuing instructions to congressmen and judges, on the one hand, and Jimmy Conway handing over a few cartons of Pall Malls to uniformed beat cops, on the other.

A later, more intricate example of the money-making enterprises in which Henry is involved, and one in which he is the prime mover, concerns a restaurant-owner named Sonny Bunz (Tony Darrow). Sonny is having some trouble with Tommy De Vito (Pesci), Henry's other best friend and a man whose unpredictably violent temper makes him one of the most feared local Mafiosi. Posing as Sonny's friend—and the two do, apparently, have a real personal acquaintance—Henry arranges for Paulie to become a "partner" in the restaurant. This instantly guarantees the restaurant-owner protection, not only from Tommy but also from the police and from anyone else who might be in a position to cause Sonny difficulty. But it also means that Sonny is obliged to pay Paulie a fixed, substantial weekly sum in protection money, regardless of his restaurant's economic performance. Even worse for Sonny, Paulie is now able to buy a wide variety of mundane consumer goods on the restaurant's line of credit—everything from cases of Scotch to washing machines and television sets—which his organization immediately resells in the neighborhood at a steep discount. Since the bills from the suppliers will never be paid, the resales generate pure profit. Eventually, of course, the Bamboo Lounge (the almost painfully pedestrian name of the restaurant, which features an ersatz Hawaiian theme) is driven so far into debt that it is unable to borrow a dime from the bank or to purchase anything on credit. Bankruptcy is the only option: whereupon the gangsters simply burn the place to the ground. (In a finely ironic touch, they use the restaurant's own matchbooks—which have "Bamboo Lounge" printed on the covers—to do the deed). Henry and his associates in Paulie's neighborhood crime ring have enriched themselves nicely, while Sonny—who originally entered into the arrangement with Paulie in order to protect himself and his business—is left with nothing. "Fucking shame," as Sonny understandably comments.

The episode is a good example of the street-level work of organized crime. Multiplied hundreds or thousands of times, it represents the basis of the vast fortunes possessed by the top Mafia bosses (like the Corleones) whom the movie never shows or even mentions. In and of itself, however, Henry's scheme, like Jimmy's hijacking business, is relatively small-time. As its name implies, the Bamboo Lounge is far from being the classiest joint in town. At one point, when (unaware of Henry's long-term scheme) Sonny thinks he is trying to convince Paulie to become his business associate, Sonny rather pathetically brags that one of the restaurant's strong points is that it is frequented by prostitutes. At the end, Henry's continuing proletarian status is emphasized by the fact that he and Tommy must personally perform the tricky, dangerous labor of arson.

The principal psychological irony on which *GoodFellas* is structured is, then, the constant gap between Henry's deeply enchanted view of the gangster lifeworld, on the one hand, and the modest scale of anything that he actually manages to achieve by being a part of it, on the other. At bottom, he never grows beyond the awestruck kid who thinks that being able to double-park a car beside a fire hydrant is better than being president of the United States. This attitude persists to the end of the film, when Henry, in order to save his life, has turned state's evidence against his friends and associates, entered the federal government's Witness Protection program, and left the mob life behind. At this point, with all the people who have meant the most to him ardently desiring to have him murdered, one might think that Henry would finally have gotten over his love affair with the Mafia. But no. He misses his old life dreadfully, and, in a phrase that the film has made a part of the American language, remembers longingly that he and his fellow gangsters "were treated like movie stars with muscle": not reflecting that his life was never at all like that of a movie star, and that he never had any real "muscle"—he never exercised any real power--except on a quite small scale.

This is not to say that Henry manages to gain *no* impressive rewards. The best and probably the most widely discussed example is the great sequence at the Copacabana. Wishing to impress his new girlfriend Karen (Lorraine Bracco), whom he later marries, he takes her on a date to the famed nightclub, where Henny Youngman (playing and, rather gamely, parodying himself) is doing his stand-up comedy act. The scene of the young couple's entrance is one of Scorsese's most renowned. It is all shot with a Steadicam in a single take: and the smooth, unbroken movement of the camera suggests the ease and gracefulness with which Henry is escorting Karen into an exciting world of privilege and show-business glamor. Finding a line of people waiting on the sidewalk to get into the Copa, the two duck into a side entrance, go down a flight of stairs, and then make their way along a series of hallways and through what seems to be the main kitchen before emerging onto the nightclub's floor. Henry distributes $20 bills to Copa employees along the way, and, once on the floor, finds himself greeted by name by the host—who, despite the fact that many other customers have been waiting for tables, immediately orders one for Henry and Karen. It appears almost as if by magic, literally whisked above the heads of a number of seated patrons and then set down right in front of the stage: so that Henry and Karen have been given, with no wait whatsoever, two of the best seats in the house. A man at a neighboring table (apparently one of Henry's fellow mobsters) sends the couple a bottle of champagne, and Henny Youngman, trademark violin in hand, begins his act. What young couple (Henry is 21 at this point, and Karen appears to be about the same age) from modest backgrounds would not find the experience delightfully heady? Karen is just as impressed as she is meant to be, and the wedding follows before long.

In no other scene in *GoodFellas* does Henry come closer to enjoying the ease, excitement, and glamor that from childhood he has associated with the lifeworld of organized crime. Even here, however, we should consider what is actually shown rather than merely accept everything as it appears from Henry's always enchanted viewpoint (and now from Karen's newly enchanted viewpoint as well). *GoodFellas* does, indeed, subtly discourage such deflationary realism, for it is, in a loose sense, a first-person film; in fact, a rare first-person *plural* film, with the voice-over by Henry and Karen guiding us through the action, and many camera angles suggesting the view from their eyes.[27] Yet, as ever with Scorsese, psychological subjectivity is sufficiently balanced by naturalistic objectivity that it is possible to see not only from the protagonists' perspective but beyond that perspective as well.

What, objectively, do we see in this scene? The Copa was at the time probably the most famous nightclub in the world. Scorsese himself, in a discussion of *GoodFellas*, has remembered that, "when I was growing up, the Copacabana was like a palace; you couldn't get any higher in style and class".[28] Still, it is worth considering that the Copa was, after all, a popular tourist spot that catered to a wide clientele—not any sort of genuinely exclusive private club. Though Henry is treated better than the ordinary members of the general public—the people waiting patiently outside on the sidewalk—he is not treated quite like an authentic big shot either. In that case, he would, surely, have been immediately ushered in through the front door (or maybe through a special private entrance) rather than left to find his own circuitous way through the kitchen. On the floor, the quality of the entertainment is indicated by the desperate staleness of Henny Youngman's jokes (e.g., "Dr. Wellsler is here. Wonderful doctor. Gave a guy six months to live. Couldn't pay his bill. Gave him another six months"). Since Youngman was in reality (as most viewers of the film in 1990 would have been old enough to remember) a much better stand-up comic than the brief footage of him here suggests, it is fair to assume that the effect of cheesy mediocrity is deliberate. Finally, even if we allow for the fact that Henry and Karen are young and inexperienced enough to find traipsing through the kitchen to be rather exciting, and rusty jokes delivered by a big-name performer to be genuinely enjoyable, it still remains to ask exactly what, in this scene, has been gained. The answer is just a pleasant evening on the town for the young couple and, from Henry's viewpoint, the chance to impress a good-looking woman whom he ardently desires: not bad, but hardly the sort of thing that would generally be considered better than being president of the United States.

A somewhat similar though less elaborate moment occurs later in the film, after Henry and Karen have become an established married couple, and soon after Henry has become newly affluent, thanks to a cocaine operation he is running out of Pittsburgh. They have spent some of their recent wealth on redecorating their house, and Karen is fantastically proud of her home's new look. As they entertain a pair of friends—Morrie Kessler (Chuck Low), a wig dealer with mob connections, and his wife Belle (Margo Winkler)—Karen can hardly contain her excitement and enthusiasm as she urges Belle to admire the Hill residence. What we see is perhaps somewhat expensive—though it does not look *very* expensive—but it is, without question, stupendously gaudy and over-the-top: for instance, garish and excessively "busy" wallpaper, an overstuffed sofa with a zebra-striped throw ("And this we just had to have made special," explains Karen), and a few outsized orange-red plastic flowers. Karen's enthusiasm only becomes more ardent as the décor becomes more ridiculous. "Watch the wall with rock," she instructs Belle, as she flips a switch; and a wall decorated with a tawdry artificial-rock pattern recedes to reveal shelves on which are placed bottles of liquor and several electronic appliances. "The electricians did it special," Karen brags. She then turns her (and Belle's, and our) attention to a modern dining-room table of which she is particularly proud because it was "imported" and "came in two pieces". We are bound to be struck by the meretriciousness of the rewards for which Henry is daily risking prison and death: especially if we happen to recall, in contrast, the genuinely luxurious and tasteful décor of the Corleone mansions.

We might say, then, that, if the *Godfather* films find something like high ruling-class tragedy in the Mafia, Scorsese's film finds proletarian pathos, and even bathos, instead.

"Our husbands weren't brain surgeons, they were blue-collar guys," as Karen puts it; and the ability of Henry and his peers to enjoy a standard of material consumption much higher than the blue-collar norm is both limited and occasional. From the beginning of the film to the end, the gap between risk and reward yawns wide. In exchange for taking the most terrible chances, Henry enjoys temporary spells of modest comfort but never attains real financial security. It is deeply revealing, for instance, that when, at one point, Henry urgently needs to raise some bail money, he is unable to do so except by having Karen persuade her mother to mortgage her house.

A memorable turn toward the end of *A Man for All Seasons* (1960), Robert Bolt's powerful (if historically problematic) play about Sir Thomas More, provides an illuminating metaphor here. At More's trial for treason, his old protégé Richard Rich delivers damning testimony against him, testimony that the drama assumes to be unquestionably false. Upon learning that Rich has recently been appointed Attorney-General for Wales—presumably in exchange for his perjury—More says to him: "For Wales? Why, Richard, it profits a man nothing to give his soul for the whole world. . .But for Wales!"[29] At the end of the *Godfather* trilogy, Michael Corleone may have lost his soul (in the third film he explicitly tells a priest that he is beyond redemption), and he has certainly lost his beloved daughter Mary, whom he had treasured above all else. But, insofar as any individual might rationally be said to have gained the whole world, this billionaire businessman has done exactly that. By the end of *GoodFellas*, Henry, though never portrayed as one of the more violent mobsters, has certainly committed crimes that the Catholic Church in which he was raised would consider damnable to his soul. But he has not gained the whole world in return, or even Wales. In truth, he has never really gained a great deal more than the opportunity to double-park beside a fire hydrant. And at the end, in the Witness Protection program, he has lost even that.

Marxian society, Hobbesian man

Nothing in *GoodFellas* at all *invalidates* the view of the Mafia presented in the *Godfather* films. But this is true in somewhat the same sense as that in which nothing in quantum mechanics invalidates classical Newtonian physics. The basic intellectual principle at work here is well established, though deeply counter-intuitive. Depending on the order of scale and magnitude, what is in some sense the "same" phenomenon may require radically different frames of reference in order to be understood. Perhaps the homeliest example is actuarial science. Common sense would suppose that, in order to calculate how many buildings in a certain class of buildings are likely to burn down during a given year, or how many individuals of a certain group are likely to die, one would first try to estimate the likelihood of each particular fire or each particular death, and then aggregate all these individual estimates in a merely additive process. But such is by no means the case. The actuary has only an extremely limited ability to predict individual events and no real interest in doing so. Yet, because events on a large scale may have a kind of intelligibility that individual events and events on a small scale do not, competent actuaries are capable of estimating the total number of fires or deaths with sufficient precision to guarantee, most of the time, substantial profits for the insurance companies that employ them. The paradox is that, though differences of scale are in some obvious sense quantitative ones, they may nonetheless call for qualitatively different intellectual tools.

There is, to be sure, no rigorous equivalence between filmmaking and statistically based science. But what might be called the actuarial principle can at least provide a useful analogy to one major aspect of the opposition between *GoodFellas* and the *Godfather* films. The macroeconomic concerns of the latter make for a narrative of capitalist history that begins, chronologically, with the nearly pre-capitalist agrarian society of rural Sicily and reaches one possible culmination with the Cuban Revolution, another with the financial manipulations of global capitalism portrayed in the trilogy's final installment. Though one might hesitate to describe Coppola as a Marxist in the same sense that his European peer and opposite number—Bernardo Bertolucci—can be readily so described, the *Godfather* series dramatizes processes of capital accumulation in ways that irresistibly invite the implementation of Marxist categories. *GoodFellas* not only refrains from in any way contradicting Coppola's quasi-Marxist historical narrative, but, as we have seen, devotes considerable attention to the microeconomic labor processes that collectively form the basis of the national and multinational capital flows that yield the big fortunes at the top of organized crime. Yet the vast difference in scale between the two views of the Mafia means that the predominantly macroeconomic categories of Karl Marx are of only limited direct use in understanding the street-level operations of organized crime. As we continue to analyze the details of what Scorsese's film shows, it is useful to consult a different materialist philosopher, one of opposite political allegiance to Marx and who wrote about two centuries earlier: Thomas Hobbes.

A good recent article on Hobbes is titled, "The First Counter-revolutionary;" and this phrase is useful in understanding the complex originality of Hobbes's thought.[30] Hobbes counts as a figure of the political right because, in the first place, he posits peace, or order, rather than justice as the supreme social value; and because, in the second place, he insists that a government endowed with absolute power—preferably an absolute monarchy though possibly rule by a parliament with unshared powers—is the only way that peace can be reliably maintained. Yet, however anti-revolutionary this stance may be—and Hobbes, of course, wrote in self-conscious reaction to the English Civil War of the 1640s, which he, like most modern Marxist historians, considered to be a revolution—Hobbes has little in common with the conservatism that preceded him (or the proto-conservatism, if one considers conservatism proper to originate in Edmund Burke's meditations on the French Revolution). To be a genuine counter-revolutionary means to have taken the pressure of the revolution itself. In Hobbes's situation, this required understanding that all previous justifications of monarchy—whether theological, traditionalist, or, as was most generally the case, both—had been irretrievably exploded by the social, intellectual, political, and military forces that produced Oliver Cromwell's revolutionary Commonwealth. Hobbes starts from scratch, so to speak, in producing an impeccably rational and materialist defense of absolute government, one that does not depend on mere precedent or on any imagined link between divine and earthly order (Hobbes was almost certainly an atheist, though he was prudent enough not to advertise the fact).

The main basis for his argument is outlined in the crucial thirteenth chapter of his major work *Leviathan* (1651), "Of the Natural Condition of Mankind, as Concerning Their Felicity, and Misery". By "natural condition" Hobbes means the state of humanity when unrestrained by force of law and government: and he sees it as no romantic anarchist idyll but as a horrifying condition of ruthless cut-throat competition in which justice plays no part and in which violence and fraud are the guiding principles. "Hereby it is manifest," he writes, "that during the time men live without a common Power to keep them in awe, they are in that condition which is called Warre; and such a warre, as is of every man, against every man".[31] This *bellum omnium contra omnes*, in which "every man is Enemy to every man," would render nearly all pleasant or useful human activity impossible to sustain: and the life of the individual would typically be, in Hobbes's single most renowned phrase, "solitary, poore, nasty, brutish, and short" (ibid.). Only the "common Power" of absolute government can suppress such perpetual civil war and establish peace. For Hobbes, absolutism requires no further justification.

He realizes, however, that (even to a reading public well versed in the Christian doctrine of original sin) his description of humanity's natural state may seem excessively harsh. Hobbes therefore argues, rather cogently, that the truth of his foundational assumption may be verified by the kind of empirical observation that anyone can undertake:

> It may seem strange to some man, that has not well weighed these things; that Nature should thus dissociate, and render men apt to invade, and destroy one another: and he may therefore, not trusting to this Inference, made from the Passions, desire perhaps to have the same confirmed by Experience. Let him therefore consider with himselfe, when taking a journey, he arms himselfe, and seeks to go well accompanied; when going to sleep, he locks his dores; when even in his house he locks his chests; and this when he knows there bee Lawes, and publike Officers, armed, to revenge all injuries shall bee done him; what opinion he has of his fellow subjects, when he rides armed; of his fellow Citizens, when he locks his dores; and of his children, and servants, when he locks his chests. Does he not there as much accuse mankind by his actions, as I do by my words? (Ibid.)

In the context of the current discussion, it is remarkable how directly Hobbes's examples from ordinary experience speak to the lifeworld of *GoodFellas*, to the quotidian habits and assumptions shared by Henry, Jimmy, Tommy, and their associates in the proletariat of organized crime—all of whom take great care to secure their valuables and never venture among their fellows without firearms. Though the parallel with what Hobbes describes is not completely precise, it is very nearly so. Hobbes, in the quoted passage, deliberately chooses *not* to describe the state of nature itself but leaves the reader to infer how bad the latter must be when one considers the insecurity and fear that characterize the human condition even when mitigated by the kind of laws and public officers available in seventeenth-century England. Now, the general capacity of law to suppress the war of all against all is considerably greater in twentieth-century America. But Henry and his associates have deliberately placed themselves outside the law and so arrived at a condition much closer to Hobbesian nature: roughly as close, perhaps, as the power of society's official coercive apparatuses was capable of achieving in Hobbes's England.

In *GoodFellas*, Marx's macroeconomic flows of capital operate, as it were, so far above the heads of the characters that they can barely be glimpsed. Though their determinant importance is not denied—and is, indeed, assumed—they possess no really concrete presence within the film. What *is* concretely shown on the "factory floor" of illegal capitalism that Scorsese represents—in addition, as we have seen, to the working details of street-level Mafia businesses—is the inescapable violence of a Hobbesian *bellum omnium contra omnes* that is ultimately (but *only* ultimately) determined by the exigencies of profit-making. Again, there is a radical difference between the perspectives of Scorsese and Coppola. As we have seen, the Corleones are, to be sure, by no means immune to the violence essential to their empire. Think again of Vito's near-fatal wounding at the fruit stand in the first *Godfather* film, of the machine-gunning of Michael and Kay's bedroom in the second film, of the murder of Mary Corleone on the opera-house steps at the end of the third film. But such moments are exceptional, and, significantly, all constitute major nodal points in the narrative. All represent violations of the security that more typically surrounds the Corleones in their heavily guarded private spaces, where their own hands usually remain clean. In *GoodFellas*, by contrast, nobody's hands are ever clean, nobody ever has reason to feel secure, and violence is just a normal part of everyday life. To borrow a phrase that one critic has used to describe the world of *Casino* (which, among all of Scorsese's other films, is most closely allied to *GoodFellas*), there is, for Henry and his peers, no safe haven.[32]

Henry is initiated into the omnipresence of violence on the lower reaches of the Mafia when he is still a child doing odd jobs around the cabstand and the pizzeria. About six minutes into the film, he is beaten up by his father (not himself a gangster but presented as typical of the culture from which lower-level gangsters are recruited) after the elder Hill receives a letter from Henry's school complaining of months of absence on Henry's part. The truancy is due to the fact that Henry is spending nearly all his time working for the mob; and, when he appears bruised and black-eyed before his immediate superior Tuddy (Frank DiLeo), he tells Tuddy that he may have to cut back on his job. But Tuddy will not hear of this, and immediately comes up with a solution to Henry's problem. Collecting a couple of thugs, he has the postal worker who happens to deliver mail to Henry's house kidnapped, seriously roughed up, and warned not to deliver any more letters from school to Henry's address. To punctuate the point, the hapless (and of course wholly innocent) letter-carrier's head is slammed about halfway into a pizza oven, with the promise that he will be baked to death there if he disobeys. Henry appears to take the whole incident as a welcome sign that his membership in "normal" society is fading and that his association with the Mafia is growing closer: "How could I go back to school after that and pledge allegiance to the flag and sit through good-government bullshit?"

Not long thereafter, Henry is on duty at the pizzeria when a man howling in pain from a serious gunshot wound turns up on the doorstep. Henry is slightly taken back—it is the first case of gun violence he has witnessed first-hand—but he almost immediately grasps that the most important consideration is not to tend to the man's injuries but to make sure that the gunshot victim doesn't cause any embarrassment for Paulie by dying in a building that Paulie controls. Henry, still a schoolboy at this point, responds with considerable aplomb, going astray only by using up what Tuddy (who is Paulie's brother) judges to be too many aprons to stanch the man's bleeding. Perhaps the most significant thing about this brief scene (it is only about half a minute long) is that we never hear who the man is or why he was shot. The latter question, especially, is simply not the kind that needs to be asked. In this world of perpetual civil war, a gunshot wound is as routine, and as little in need of explanation, as a paper cut in an office. Much later in the film, after the immense Lufthansa robbery that Jimmy plans has been successfully executed, it seems perfectly natural—and, of course, it *is* perfectly "natural" in precisely the Hobbesian sense—that Jimmy should try to simplify the complexities attached to having so many accomplices and helpers in the crime by just killing them all off.

To live in such a world of continual violence means that violence is always a concrete potentiality. It leaves its mark on all of everyday life even if it happens not to be taking place at a particular moment. This ever-present possibility of violence, as distinguished from its empirical actuality, is, not incidentally, precisely what Hobbes means by war: "For as the nature of Foule weather, lyeth not in a showre or two of rain; but in an inclination thereto of many dayes together: So the nature of War, consisteth not in actuall fighting; but in the known disposition thereto during all the time there is no assurance to the contrary" (ibid.).

It would be hard to name a scene in all of cinema that represents war in this exact Hobbesian sense with greater vividness and intensity than the episode in Sonny's restaurant in which Henry tells Tommy that he (Tommy) is a funny guy. Along with several other associates, the two are relaxing over what appear to be friendly drinks and conversation. Tommy, always the most outgoing of all the characters, is dominating the table with a humorous story about a run-in he had with the law following a bank job in Secaucus. At each of Tommy's punch lines the other men laugh uproariously—perhaps more so than the quality of the story really warrants, since Tommy's well-known violent temper often makes people eager to please him. Intending to take part in the general appreciation, Henry says to Tommy, "You're really funny". It seems an innocuous, even flattering, remark. But Tommy claims to take umbrage. He demands to know exactly what Henry means, and within a few seconds the atmosphere at the table has changed from convivial laughter to unbearable tension. Everyone knows that violence, even murder, between the two close friends has suddenly become an immediate possibility. The tension grows along with Tommy's apparent anger—"I'm funny, how? Funny like a clown? I amuse you? I make you laugh? I'm here to fucking amuse you?. . . .How the fuck am I funny? What the fuck is so funny about me?"—and it is impossible to tell whether he is genuinely furious or is playing a sadistic practical joke. Clearly (and rightly) terrified, Henry gambles on the latter possibility, and, after agonizingly long moments of indecision says, "Get the fuck out of here, Tommy". Tommy accepts this response—whether on the whim of the moment or because he really *was* just kidding all along—and laughter returns to the table as quickly as it had vanished. But everyone, including the viewer, clearly knows that, when life is a perpetual war, what Hobbes calls "actual fighting" may erupt at any moment without warning.

Tommy's behavior in this scene is not necessarily quite as irrational as it may superficially seem (even though his mental stability is indeed questioned at several points in the movie). In a state of (or relatively close to) Hobbesian nature, the civil authorities cannot be called upon to resolve conflicts; and so each individual's reputation for personal prowess assumes inflated importance. The actual point of the funny story Tommy tells is that he is so tough and resolute that not even a series of vicious police beatings can tempt him to turn informer: a very useful thing to have believed about oneself in the Mafia. Somewhat similarly, the notion that he might murder a close friend over an imagined (and trivial) insult can only enhance the reputation for ferocity that, on the whole, has real practical benefits for anyone in Tommy's line of work. Still, if he actually *had* attacked his partner Henry—and the clear implication of the scene is that violence has been just barely avoided—the resulting mess would not have been helpful to the serious business of profit-making. Here we see yet another dimension of the opposition between *GoodFellas* and the *Godfather* films. A now-famous maxim about violence (especially murder) that is repeated in various forms throughout Coppola's trilogy is that it's not personal, it's just business; i.e., it makes reasonable capitalist sense. From the Olympian perspective of the Corleones and their peers, this is generally true. Though accidents can of course happen—one person can be killed by a bomb or a bullet meant for another—violence in the *Godfather* series is almost always undertaken for reasons directly connected to financial gain. But on the mean streets of *GoodFellas*, where Henry, Tommy, and Jimmy live, the very omnipresence of violence means that it cannot so reliably be confined to rational business channels. When one's lifeworld is a perpetual civil war of all against all—when killing without conscience is just an ordinary part of one's job—violence that serves no truly practical purpose may explode at any time.

Such an eruption is narrowly avoided in the scene just considered, but takes place in another of the movie's key episodes: the encounter with Billy Batts (Frank Vincent). Batts is a mid-level Mafia operative whom we meet when he is celebrating his release from prison with a party in Henry's restaurant. Tommy comes in, and finds himself the target of some (not particularly good-natured) ribbing by Batts. Tommy's rage and frustration are obvious, and his friends have to restrain him from attacking Batts on the spot. For Tommy has no good recourse. Not only is Batts about a generation senior to Tommy within the mob, but, unlike Tommy or Jimmy or Henry, Batts is a "made" man, that is, one who is protected by the Mafia hierarchy and cannot be harmed without explicit authorization from the top. Tommy leaves, but returns a few hours later when the place is almost deserted, ambushes Batts, and, with Jimmy's assistance, beats and kicks the man (apparently) to death. The three friends throw Batts into the trunk of Henry's car, but, as they are driving to dispose of the body, discover their victim to be still alive. So they stop and finish with a knife and a gun what they began with fists and feet. No good can conceivably come of this murder, and none does. Later in the film, unseen (and even unmentioned) top bosses have Tommy killed in retaliation. In an exquisitely cruel irony, he is murdered at what had been falsely represented to him as the ceremony in which he himself would be promoted to the rank of made man.

The details of the Batts murder underscore how thoroughly violence—lethal violence—is interwoven with the fabric of everyday life for Henry and his pals. When Tommy returns to the restaurant, Jimmy—who never had any particular grievance against Batts—is chatting with the older mobster on terms of apparently perfect amiability. But he understands what Tommy is up to, and, when Tommy is ready for the ambush, Jimmy immediately takes part. Several shots show Jimmy kicking Batts on the floor with special determination and viciousness. No moral qualms about the murder are ever displayed (though Tommy does deliver a heartfelt apology to Henry for ruining several tablecloths in order to keep blood off the restaurant's floor). Later, on their way to bury the body, the three friends stop at the home of Tommy's mother to borrow a shovel and a kitchen cleaver. Mrs. De Vito (Catherine Scorsese, the director's mother) insists on preparing a full sit-down dinner for the boys. Though Henry seems a bit uneasy, Tommy and Jimmy not only enjoy the food and conversation with great gusto but make coded inside jokes to one another about the unfortunate Batts. Meanwhile, the camera shows the trunk of Henry's car, and a faint banging noise informs the viewer that Batts is not quite dead yet. Later, when the three friends finish him off on a lonely night road, it is with resolute efficiency.

Batts's murder so perfectly encapsulates the state of nature, of unceasing war, in which Henry and his fellows live that the episode might well be taken as the most deeply typical in the entire film, as the real moral (or rather amoral) center of *GoodFellas*. Scorsese seems to invite precisely this judgment by several strategic directorial choices. The scene on the dark road where the killing of Batts is completed forms the film's prologue. It is detached from the main body of *GoodFellas* and presented to the viewer before any characters have been introduced or any narrative situation established. In reddish tones that harmonize with the color of Batts's blood, we see Tommy repeatedly thrusting the kitchen cleaver into the still (though barely) living Batts while commanding, "Die, you motherfucker!" To make assurance doubly sure, Jimmy then fires four shots from his .38 revolver into Batts's body at point-blank range. And then, almost immediately, we hear Henry's first line of voice-over: "As far back as I can remember, I always wanted to be a gangster". Even before we really know who Henry is, his lifelong love for the mob life has thus been savagely ironized by the horrific violence just witnessed. Later, when the scene (presented from slightly different angles) is repeated in proper narrative order, Henry's voice-over supplies the most cogent expository account in the film of the Mafia's *bellum omnium contra omnes*:

> For most of the guys, killings got to be accepted. Murder was the only way that everybody stayed in line. You got out of line, you got whacked. Everybody knew the rules. But

sometimes, even if people *didn't* get out of line, they got whacked. I mean, hits just became a habit for some of the guys. Guys would get into arguments over nothing, and, before you knew it, one of them was dead. They were shooting each other all the time. Shooting people was a normal thing. It was no big deal.

Thomas Hobbes would have understood perfectly.

World without solidarity

Solitary, poor, nasty, brutish, and short: it is not by accident that, of the five adjectives in Hobbes's famous description of human life in a state of nature, *solitary* should be placed first. For solitariness is the privation that primarily determines all the others. Indeed, this point is key to understanding the specifically political opposition between Hobbes and Marx. For Marx, human beings have an intrinsic capacity for solidarity; and for Marxism the ultimate alternative to capitalist competition is a radicalized democracy in which uncoerced men and women will form egalitarian social relationships of peaceful co-operation and mutual assistance. Such is the very definition of communism. But this capacity for solidarity is exactly what Hobbes denies. For him, dog-eat-dog competition results not from social, economic, or political systems but from the fundamental and unalterable realities of human nature. Accordingly, for Hobbes it is only unlimited pressure from above, in the form of absolute government, that can establish any even relatively peaceful order among human beings: any order that offers even moderate hope of human life that will be at least somewhat rich, nice, humane, and long.

Once again, in the emphasis on solitariness, *GoodFellas* is a deeply Hobbesian film; and once again we find a basic opposition between Scorsese and Coppola. For Coppola, human solidarity is a real possibility. Though we hardly ever see solidarity take specifically communist forms in his movies (as we sometimes do in Bertolucci's), solidarity for Coppola is concretely manifest in the smallest and perhaps most ancient of social units, the family. This is quite evident, of course, in the *Godfather* trilogy, as the very title suggests. Though Corleone family solidarity is, to be sure, potentially fragile and subject to both violation from without and even betrayal from within, it is nonetheless both genuine and meaningful. Vito and Michael (and also Vincent, who in the final film becomes the third Don Corleone) are emphatically, if not always successfully, family men. Coppola's concern with the family extends, indeed, well beyond his *magnum opus*. Family ties are central to such other films of his, otherwise so different from one another and from the *Godfather* series, as *Rumble Fish* (1983), *Peggy Sue Got Married* (1986), and *Tetro* (2009); and they can be important even in films in which they are not the principal focus, like *Tucker: The Man and His Dream* (1988). The family unit maintains a kind of shadowy presence even in some of Coppola's films that do not represent it directly: as witness the allegorical father-son relationship between Kurtz and Willard in *Apocalypse Now* (1979), a shadow familial tie that is in large part responsible for giving the character of Kurtz an importance beyond his (very limited) screen time. It seems fitting that Coppola, perhaps more than any other important director, has made extensive use, both behind and in front of the cameras, of members of his own family (his father Carmine Coppola, his sister Talia Shire, his daughter Sofia Coppola, and his nephew Nicholas Cage, among others).

Though Scorsese has employed family members too (most notably his mother Catherine, who, interestingly, also acted for Coppola), neither familial nor any other sort of human solidarity is conspicuous in his films. The typical Scorsese hero is a solitary figure, and this can be fundamentally true even if, for example, he is as socially conformist in formal, external ways as Newland Archer (Daniel Day-Lewis) in *The Age of Innocence*. The most deeply prototypical of the director's protagonists might thus, in some respects, be Travis Bickle (De Niro) in *Taxi Driver*: a man who comes from nowhere and belongs to nobody; a nearly allegorical embodiment, at some points, of isolate existential *Angst*; and a character whose entire dramatic presence in the film amounts to an extended acting-out of his anguish at being unable to enjoy any meaningful connection with other human beings. His signature line, spoken to his own mirror in his drab, empty apartment—"Are you talking to me? Well, I'm the only one here"—says it all.

It could be argued, however, that *The Last Temptation of Christ* is even more radically Scorsesian than *Taxi Driver* in its fascination with human unconnectedness. Indeed, to interpret *The Last Temptation* in this way makes it easier to understand both Scorsese's interest in the material taken from Nikos Kazantzakis's novel on which the film is based—which, set in Biblical Palestine, is far removed from Scorsese's more usual setting of modern New York City—and also the director's brave determination to get the film made despite serious obstacles that included threats of physical harm. For who, after all, is Jesus (Willem Dafoe) as Scorsese (or Kazantzakis and Scorsese) present him? He is a man who, faced with the "temptation" to become a family man with a wife and children, chooses instead to be tortured to death, alone, on the cross. Solitariness does not get much more radical than that.

Henry Hill is of course very far from being such an extreme character as Travis Bickle or Jesus Christ. But Henry's very *ordinariness* in some ways makes him an especially compelling illustration of the absence—indeed the impossibility—of solidarity within the Mafia lifeworld. In this way, he contrasts not only with the likes of Travis or Jesus but also with Jimmy and Tommy, the major secondary characters within *GoodFellas*. Both are in their different ways extraordinary. Jimmy is distinguished by precocity and brilliance. A legend within the mob before the age of thirty, he had begun doing contract killings at sixteen and eventually masterminds the richest heist in American history. Tommy stands out because of his fiery temper and a propensity for violence that seems extreme even to other Mafiosi. At one point, for example, he shoots an aspiring teenage mobster in the foot when the youngster is insufficiently prompt in bringing Tommy a Scotch-and-water; and he later murders the kid for being a bit surly about the incident.

Henry, by contrast, is a classic middle-of-the-road protagonist. He is not only less violently inclined than many of his colleagues, but, in general, has a kind of vanilla or white-bread flavor—a rather *generic* quality—that Scorsese accentuates by casting. Joe Pesci and Robert De Niro are both highly distinctive performers, with signature acting styles and faces that are memorable without being classically handsome; and De Niro, before agreeing to a supporting role in *GoodFellas*, had, of course, triumphed in major starring roles like Travis Bickle and Jake La Motta in *Raging Bull* (not to mention his equally brilliant turn as the young Vito Corleone in the second *Godfather* film). Ray Liotta is more like an ordinary character actor—even though he takes the leading part in *GoodFellas*—with bland, forgettable good looks and a screen presence that is perfectly adequate without possessing anything like De Niro's or Pesci's intensity (much the same can be said of Christopher Serrone, who plays Henry as a child). Liotta is thus well qualified to play Henry Hill as a typical gangster Everyman, whose life shows the essential unconnectedness of the Mafia world more convincingly than that of a less ordinary and less middle-of-the-road character could.

The essential solitariness of mob life is well illustrated by Henry's relations with Jimmy and Tommy. Though the two men can be formally described as his best friends, it is more accurate to say that they are the closest he has to friends in an environment where authentic friendship is almost impossible. The Hobbesian (or near-Hobbesian) state of anarchic emergency in which the mob operates means that at any moment an individual's own interests, and even his own survival, may come to depend (or appear to depend) on the elimination of others, including even (in some cases especially) those to whom he has been closest. In addition, the general omnipresence of violence tends, as we have seen, to make for a certain amount of nearly random killing. Thus it is, in the scene at the Bamboo Lounge, that Henry sees with awful clarity (as Liotta's face makes painfully evident) the real possibility that Tommy, to whom he has been close since both were children, might murder him over a meaningless pleasantry.

A more complex but at least equally disturbing encounter takes place with Jimmy in another restaurant toward the end of the movie. Henry, who up to this point had managed to avoid any but relatively brief stays behind bars, has been arrested on a major narcotics charge that could send him to prison for 25 years to life. Jimmy invites Henry to meet in a diner: ostensibly to catch up and discuss Henry's legal case, but actually, as Henry sees, so that Jimmy (who had been helping Henry in the cocaine business) can try to gauge the odds that Henry will turn informer. The problem for Jimmy is not just that Henry might turn him over to the cops; even worse is the possibility that Paulie, who had strictly forbidden his subordinates to deal in narcotics, will learn of Jimmy's involvement and have him killed. Though the two old friends pretend that their conversation is friendly and casual, De Niro and Liotta create a strong undercurrent of anxiety and menace. When Jimmy asks Henry to travel to Florida to assist in a contract murder, Henry (who has never received such a request from Jimmy before) knows that, if he goes to Florida, *he* will be the victim of the hit. The man he has always liked and looked up to, the man who initiated him into serious crime, is now planning to have him killed. But this unfortunate turn of events in no way surprises Henry. It is the sort of thing he has learned to expect: "Your murderers come with smiles. They come as your friends, the people who have cared for you all of your life. And they always seem to come at a time when you're at your weakest and most in need of their help. So I met Jimmy in a crowded place we both knew". In the scene that immediately follows, Henry and Karen are talking to a federal law-enforcement official about the Witness Protection program.

Friendship is, then, in the end illusory for Henry and his fellows. There is a cruel dilemma operative here. The exigencies of this particular line of work make it impossible to socialize or form friendships with anyone outside the Mafia (as the movie explicitly emphasizes a number of times, especially through some of Karen's voice-over). But the very nature of the Mafia makes it impossible for authentic friendship to flourish within. It is a perfect catch-22.

Neither does the family in *GoodFellas* substantially mitigate the Hobbesian solitariness of the mob lifeworld. As for the family into which Henry is born, we see little of it. The most important thing about it, for the film, is just that the tiny and horribly overcrowded house where all seven Hills live happens to be across the street from a couple of Paulie's mob businesses. The only significant interaction we see between Henry and his father is the savage beating that results when Henry's truancy from school comes to light (as though a physical attack worthy of a mobster is likely to stimulate in Henry a passion for formal education). His mother's most striking appearance comes when, having made a little money from his work for Paulie's gang, Henry proudly shows her his brand-new outfit, a tailored brown suit with white shirt, tie, and shiny black shoes. "Hi Mom, what do you think?" he says with great enthusiasm. "My God, you look like a *gangster!*" she replies with horror—a true enough response that is, however, unlikely to discourage Henry, since the gangster look is exactly what he is aiming for. Henry's involvement with his family is so minimal and so uncongenial to him that we are surprised, late in the film, to discover that, as an adult, he has maintained a relationship with one of his brothers. But we never really learn anything about that relationship, and the contrast with Coppola's intent focus on fraternal relations—in the *Godfather* films and in a number of others—is striking.[33]

The viewer sees a little more of the Hill household that is established when Henry marries Karen. But it is difficult to describe what they create as a family in any but the most technical sense. Though Henry is strongly attracted to Karen as a date and a girlfriend, when she becomes his wife he quickly loses interest and begins to neglect her, preferring to spend time with his fellow mobsters or with his mistress of the moment (with each of whom his relations seem to be pretty exclusively physical). The marriage decays into a morass of shouting and arguing (save whenever Henry is handing Karen a wad of cash), and reaches a low point in a scene where Karen awakens Henry from a nap with a loaded, cocked revolver pointed directly at his face (and, in some of the shots, straight into the camera). The domestic situation is so bad that, in a somewhat humorous turn, Paulie and Jimmy feel compelled to assume the unwonted role of marriage counselors. Henry and Karen have two daughters, but neither parent seems to care much for them; and, indeed, the girls are rarely on screen except to witness their parents' fighting, or, on one occasion, to be dragged along by Karen when she goes to scream at one of Henry's girlfriends. Though the marriage endures, after its fashion, throughout *GoodFellas*, it comes as no surprise to learn, from one of the slides that follow the film proper and precede the final credits, that Henry and Karen eventually part ways.

Perhaps the scene that most brilliantly, if indirectly, illustrates Henry's lack of family connection is, on its face, a very social one: the famous scene showing what prison is like for mob wiseguys. Along with Paulie and a number of his other associates, Henry is serving a term in a federal penitentiary. Their mob connections and the ready cash they have with which to bribe guards mean that they enjoy special privileges, notably the freedom to hang out with one another apart from the general prison population, and access to good food, wine, and Scotch from outside. "In prison, dinner was always a big thing," says Henry in voice-over as the scene begins; and the camera shows a wonderful close-up of Paulie slicing garlic very finely with a razor blade, like a celebrity chef on television. Loving attention is paid to the various delicacies that comprise the mobsters' dinners—steaks, seafood, pasta with meat sauce, bread, cheese, red and white wine—and to the details of food preparation. The culinary sights and sounds are quite appetizing, and probably few viewers have watched the scene without feeling some hankering for a traditional Italian meal. We readily believe Henry when he tells us that prison, for a wiseguy, "really wasn't that bad". But the qualifying clause he immediately adds strikes a jarring note: "excepting that I missed Jimmy, who was doing his time in Atlanta". It is *Jimmy* whom he misses—not his wife and children? And then, perhaps, we realize with a start that this scene of happy dinner-time domesticity is unique in what we have seen of Henry's life. Convivial meals or other social occasions with his family have never seemed to exist for him. It may be tempting to say that Paulie's gang is his real family—except that they are all professional criminals and (probably) all murderers, so that, as we have seen, no real closeness or trust can exist there either.

Henry Hill, then, is an especially compelling type of Hobbesian solitariness precisely because—in sharp contrast to Travis Bickle or Jesus Christ, to Tommy De Vito or even Jimmy Conway—he leads a life that, in externals, is so emphatically *normal* and so full of ordinary interpersonal connections. He has steady work, a circle of professional associates, male companions with whom he socializes, a home, a wife, children, and one or another sexy girlfriend. But the point, of course, is that this network of relationships is a hollow shell, inside of which Henry is desperately alone.

Nothing in *GoodFellas* illustrates this apparent paradox better than the brilliant climactic sequence—it is almost a relatively autonomous short film unto itself—that traces the single day, Sunday, 11 May 1980, which ends with the big drug bust. Throughout the day, Henry is surrounded by other people but essentially solitary. Beginning before 7:00 a.m., he spends the day racing around, trying to attend to numerous chores, all of which involve other people and almost none of which goes well. For instance, he brings Jimmy some guns he has bought for him; but Jimmy decides he does not want them, and angrily refuses to pay. Driving to the hospital to pick up his paraplegic brother Michael (Kevin Corrigan), he nearly rear-ends another car; and, when he arrives at the hospital, Michael's doctor is so horrified by Henry's own harried, unhealthy appearance that he insists on examining him. Then Henry has to prepare a shipment of cocaine at the apartment of his girlfriend Sandy (Debi Mazar), have sex with her, and resist her furious entreaties to stay the night. He tries to arrange for his drug courier Lois (Welker White) to take the narcotics to Atlanta, but she makes mistakes and causes problems, including a surly refusal to fly without her "lucky hat". Throughout these and other hassles, a helicopter (which turns out to belong to federal drug agents) has been following Henry around.

The extreme tension and anxiety of the whole situation are accentuated, diegetically, by Henry's paranoia-inducing addiction to cocaine (like Tony Montana in *Scarface*, he samples his own wares to excess), and, extra-diegetically, by the way that Scorsese's cameras, famous for nearly always moving, are here more hurried than ever. It is almost with a sense of relief that things settle down when he is finally arrested at around 11:00 p.m. Indeed, the arresting officer provides Henry with what is, in a sense, his most reassuring human connection of the day: "Freeze!" the cop commands as he points his automatic pistol at Henry's head. "Don't you move, you motherfucker, or I'll blow your brains out!" Though it may not seem the friendliest greeting, it provides Henry with a measure of comfort. "Only cops talk that way," as Henry explains. "If they had been wiseguys, I wouldn't have heard a thing. I would have been dead".

But Henry is not dead at film's end. *GoodFellas* is not high tragedy, and has nothing of the grand "operatic" quality that so many viewers have seen in the *Godfather* films. The film ends, as it begins, on street level. While Pileggi's journalistic account ends by suggesting that, owing to the advantages he has managed to extract from the Witness Protection program, "Henry Hill has turned out to be the ultimate wiseguy" (p. 289), Scorsese's Henry Hill takes his leave of the audience on a quite different and much more plebian note: "I'm an average nobody," he tells us in his final line of voice-over. "I get to live the rest of my life like a schnook". Henry is referring to his situation in Witness Protection, and he means to contrast this life, where he "ha[s] to wait around like everyone else," with what he still feels to be the excitement and glamor of the mob. But the viewer must reflect that the central psychological irony that has determined Henry's character throughout the film—that is, the vast gulf between his incurably enchanted view of the Mafia and the cold, hard realities of what the latter actually has to offer—is still operating here: and that Henry's description of himself at the end really applies to his mob life from the beginning. From childhood to middle age, Henry has operated in something experientially very like a Hobbesian state of nature: a world where essential solitude is enforced and where lethal violence is frequently a fact and always an immediate possibility. And he has done so from a predominantly proletarian position, for rewards that, even at their best, have always been more meager than he chooses to believe, and that have never been even remotely commensurate to the terrible risks and penalties—physical, moral, legal, psychological, spiritual—that attend them. Ultimate wiseguy? From the first to the last frame of *GoodFellas*, Henry Hill is much more like the ultimate schnook.

Tony Soprano and the end(s) of the mob movie

I love movies. You know that. That smell in Blockbuster, that candy-and-carpet smell,
I get high off [it].

(Christopher Moltisanti in The Sopranos)

From film to television

"So, please let's remember that television is electronic theater and not second-rate film".[34] So maintained the great British television *auteur* Alfred Shaughnessy, advising his colleagues in the making of *Upstairs Downstairs* (1971–1975)—a series that is about as theatrical, literary, and un-cinematic as any major TV series that one could easily name. David Chase's *The Sopranos* (1999–2007)—one of the relatively few series comparable to *Upstairs Downstairs* in interest, richness, and complexity—is somewhat closer to film aesthetically: not least because the budgets available at HBO in the new millennium were considerably larger than those on offer at the BBC during the 1970s. Chase's cameras were thus allowed to range widely across a variety of indoor and outdoor places, rather than be generally confined, as in *Upstairs Downstairs*, to a few indoor sets.[35] Even so, Shaughnessy's aphorism may conveniently remind us of some of the major differences between the two forms—film and television—that are so often bracketed together.

Though cinema owes an obvious debt to theater, it is a much more emphatically multi-media form. With its confluence of words, music (even in what is misnamed "silent" film), and moving images, cinema in some ways, indeed, enjoys a deeper affinity with opera, the most multi-media of all the pre-modern art forms: as is perhaps suggested by the "operatic" quality often celebrated in many of the greatest films, including ones so different from one another as Eisenstein's *The Battleship Potemkin* (1925), Lang's *Metropolis* (1926), Kubrick's *2001* (1968), Visconti's "German" trilogy (*The Damned, Death in Venice,* and *Ludwig* [1969–1972]), and Coppola's *Godfather* trilogy (1972–1990). Film also derives from painting, drawing, and still photography—even, in some ways, from sculpture and architecture—and its debt to the plastic arts highlights, even more clearly than its debt to opera, the irreducibly visual dimension of cinema: an element whose significance can be exaggerated (as by the advocates of "pure cinema")[36] but which remains of fundamental importance.

Television, of course, has its visual component too, as the very word indicates. But, historically, the visual aspect of TV has loomed much less large than in the case of film, for various reasons. For one thing, the gargantuan size of the movie screen presents an overwhelming spectacle that cannot be matched on small screens fitted for the private residence. In addition, the visual authority of the cinematic spectacle is enhanced by the way it is "framed" in a room almost completely dark save for the light emanating from the projector itself. As with opera since Wagner, there is little to distract the viewer's eye from the show. Though it is possible somewhat to reproduce such conditions in more private spaces (especially in the "home cinemas" of the affluent), the much more typical situation for televisual viewing—in which lamps and overhead lights may be burning and in which objects of more visual interest than monotonous rows of seats are likely to be on display—further reduces the visual authority of the TV screen (especially in comparison to the movie screen) that has already been reduced by its comparatively diminutive size. Budgetary factors are generally at work here too, for the visual dimension of film or television tends to be the most expensive (leaving aside the immense salaries that a few superstar actors command). Owing to the organization and internal political economy of the television industry, creators of TV series are necessarily a good deal more prolific than filmmakers. To make a typical weekly dramatic series with hour-long installments is, after all, the equivalent of producing a full-length feature film once a fortnight. The pressure to minimize costly visual extravagances is thus intense, and is felt even in a series as well-funded and as visually sophisticated (by most televisual standards) as *The Sopranos*.

For all these reasons, then, television drama has tended to develop, as Shaughnessy's maxim suggests, in alliance with the relatively literary and distinctly un-cinematic tradition of naturalistic stage drama. Television most typically (though of course not invariably) avoids special effects, elaborate cinematographic landscape "painting," and even a large number of outdoor settings in order to focus on the mainly verbal interactions of a set of characters in enclosed spaces. A general reliance on close-ups and medium shots in preference to long shots and wide-angle panoramas further contributes to the intimate, stagy, living-room feel of the medium. Raymond Williams, in perhaps the most important sustained attempt to theorize television as an aesthetic form, has, indeed, maintained that "the television play was the ultimate realization of the original naturalist convention: the drama of the small enclosed room. . . .This was a drama of the box in the same fundamental sense as the naturalist drama had been the drama of the framed stage".[37]

Williams's words, however, most precisely describe the individual free-standing television play, of which he seems to have been mainly thinking, and which was once a considerably more prevalent form than it has since become. When we turn to the dramatic television *series*, we must consider another of television's affinities, one that distinguishes it both from film and from stage drama, and one that is more literary than either: namely, prose fiction, especially as developed in the realist novel of the nineteenth century.

The chief issues here are scale and temporality. A film (like a stage play) is a relatively brief work, nearly always meant to be consumed in a single sitting and (with some exceptions, of which the *Godfather* trilogy is perhaps the most important) independently of the consumption of other films. Film at its best thus excels in that kind of short-term intensity that Edgar Allan Poe (master of the short poem and the short story) considered essential for successful art. But it lacks the capacity for extended, complex, leisurely development that both the novel and the TV series possess. Watching an episode of a television series is in some ways more like reading a chapter of a novel by Balzac, Dickens, or Tolstoy than like watching a movie. The consumption of a film usually stands, in the immediate term, apart from the rest of one's life. But one *lives with* a long novel or a TV series, so that *Bleak House* (1853), say, or *The Sopranos* become interwoven over days, weeks, or even years with many things in one's life that have no direct connection to the New Jersey mob or to the case of Jarndyce and Jarndyce.[38]

I have, of course, sketched only the barest outline of the defining differences between film and television. But my argument will revisit and build on these distinctions in the course of maintaining the central thesis of this chapter: namely, that the relationship of *The Sopranos* to the tradition of the mob movie is paradoxical. On the one hand, the HBO series can be understood as the translation of the mob movie *into* television drama. Considered as such, *The Sopranos* ranks alongside the masterworks of Francis Ford Coppola and Martin Scorsese, and is both deeply and extensively indebted to them. On the other hand, however, the implicit claim of David Chase—the originator of the series and its principal guiding genius throughout—is not merely to rival his most formidable cinematic predecessors but to challenge them as well. *The Sopranos* is not just a TV series allied to the tradition of the mob film. It is also, in its long and leisurely development over seven seasons,[39] a deconstruction of the latter in something like the precise Derridean sense: that is, an immensely detailed and patient close reading that reveals unsuspected antinomies and aporias in the object being read. Moreover, this deconstruction (as in the strongest work of Derrida himself, though not always in the writings of his Anglo-American academic followers) is by no means purely formal but socio-economic as well.[40]

Film in television

For the moment, however, I wish only that the salient differences between movies and TV be kept in mind as necessary theoretical qualification to the establishment of one hugely important descriptive point: namely, the almost incalculable empirical debt that *The Sopranos* owes to the tradition of the mob movie in general and, above all, to Scorsese's *GoodFellas* (1990). Chase has openly spoken of the importance that this film has had for him and his colleagues,[41] but no such overt clues are required in order to see the elaborate web of intertextual relationships.

On one level, the most direct connection between the film and the series is the considerable overlap in personnel. An advanced search conducted on the Internet Movie Database yields 45 individuals credited as members of the cast or crew of both *GoodFellas* and *The Sopranos*.[42] Though James Gandolfini, who stars as the northern New Jersey crime boss Tony Soprano, does not appear to have any direct personal connection with Scorsese's film, many, perhaps even most, of his more important co-stars and supporting players do. Lorraine Bracco, who plays the female lead in *GoodFellas* as Karen Hill, the wife of Scorsese's protagonist, also plays the female lead in *The Sopranos*, as Dr. Jennifer Melfi, Tony's psychiatrist. Bracco's two parts are very different—Karen is a naïve housewife, while Dr. Melfi is a highly educated and successful professional woman—but more often the actors shared by the film and the series tend to take rather similar roles in both. Michael Imperioli, for example, who in *GoodFellas* plays the relatively small part of Spider—the aspiring teenage gangster wounded and later murdered by the sociopathic Tommy De Vito (Joe Pesci)—has a major role in *The Sopranos* as Christopher Moltisanti, Tony's protégé and cousin by marriage and also the chief exemplar in the series of the younger generation of Mafiosi. Frank Vincent, the senior mobster Billy Batts in the movie, appears in the later years of the TV show as Phil Leotardo, a senior figure in the New York mob and eventually Tony's arch-enemy. In some cases, actors with just cameo appearances in *GoodFellas* have major supporting roles in *The Sopranos*: so that the effect is of the TV series expanding on the film, of its providing, in its 86 episodes (each roughly an hour long), more detail than could possibly be included in the less than three hours of Scorsese's film. For example, Tony Sirico and Vincent Pastore, who are only briefly glimpsed in the movie, appear prominently in the television series as, respectively, Paulie "Walnuts" Gualtieri and Sal "Big Pussy" Bonpensiero, two of Tony's most important lieutenants. There is considerable overlap in crew as well as cast, most notably in the important stunt department; for instance, Michael Russo and Peter Bucossi, Chase's two principal stunt co-ordinators, have stunt credits in *GoodFellas* as well.

Chase's recruitment of so many of Scorsese's people is part and parcel of his creation of a mob ambience deeply allied to that of *GoodFellas*. Like Scorsese's film—and emphatically unlike Coppola's *Godfather* trilogy—the series operates mainly on street level, and foregrounds the nitty-gritty of Mafia life. Though Tony Soprano is considerably wealthier and more powerful within the mob than Henry Hill (who, as we have seen, never even manages to attain basic financial security), he springs from a modest background—exemplified by the lower-middle-class house that his mother Livia (Nancy Marchand) occupies until her death—and, in culture and values, remains stereotypically a "blue-collar guy," to borrow the phrase that Karen Hill uses to describe her husband and his friends. Moreover, Tony is very much a hands-on boss in both the various forms of illegal capitalism on which his income depends and the frequent spasms of violence required to keep the profit-making machine running. Like the dramatis personae of *GoodFellas*, Tony and his associates are directly involved with and fully visible in the kind of details of mob life that, in Coppola's trilogy, are typically delegated by the Corleones from the aloofness of their heavily guarded mansions.

The link between the general ethos of *The Sopranos* and that of *GoodFellas* is strengthened by countless direct allusions—mainly diegetic though sometimes extra-diegetic—that the series makes to the film. The network of allusions is made to seem particularly appropriate in that Tony and many of his fellow mobsters are film buffs and, especially, avid consumers of mob movies. Christopher is the most devoted cinephile of them all, partly for quite practical reasons. As the youngest of the major characters, he foresees that the Mafia—portrayed by the series as already on the decline—may not last his time; and so he plans for a possible second career as a writer or (especially after his literary incompetence becomes painfully clear even to him)[43] a producer of mob films. It is thus fitting that Christopher should be especially prominent in the allusions to *GoodFellas*. Perhaps the most widely remembered example occurs in "The Legend of Tennessee Moltisanti" (season 1, episode 8), when Christopher, annoyed by a surly sales clerk in a bakery, shoots the youngster in the foot, just as Tommy shoots Spider in Scorsese's film. The allusion is especially notable for the way it subtly and cleverly blurs the boundaries of diegesis. For, though Christopher, as a character, cannot know that he is being played by the same actor who plays Spider, he doubtless *does* know the relevant scene in *GoodFellas* and almost certainly admires Tommy's unsentimental toughness. "It happens," Christopher says unsympathetically when the wounded clerk expresses shock and horror that Christopher has actually shot him over his failure to wait on Christopher promptly enough.

A more unambiguously diegetic allusion occurs in "Fortunate Son" (season 3, episode 3), in which Christopher is promoted to the rank of "made man" within Tony's Mafia family. Christopher is visibly anxious prior to the ceremony, and Tony, with an easy chuckle, diagnoses the cause as "too many fucking movies—that's his problem". The allusion is, of course, to the scene in *GoodFellas* where Tommy arrives at what he thinks is to be the place of his own making, only to find that he is to be murdered instead.

Though the references to *GoodFellas* have a special importance for *The Sopranos*, the series is saturated with references to other mob films as well. Tony has a special fondness for the foundational works of the genre—*Little Caesar* (Mervyn LeRoy, 1931), *The Public Enemy* (William Wellman, 1931), and *Scarface* (Howard Hawks, 1932)—and Brian De Palma's 1983 remake of Hawks's film is also mentioned more than once. But the movies that are referred to by Tony and his associates overwhelmingly more often than any others are those of the *Godfather* trilogy. Indeed, if *The Sopranos*, as a series, is haunted to the point of obsession by *GoodFellas*, the characters who inhabit the series are haunted to a similar degree by Coppola's saga of the Corleone family. Sometimes the allusions are cleverly unobtrusive. For example, Silvio Dante (Steve Van Zandt), Tony's *consigliere* and the owner of the bar and topless-dancing club that serves as a kind of office and headquarters for the Soprano crime organization, has named his establishment the "Bada Bing!"—three apparently nonsensical syllables whose significance is that Sonny Corleone (James Caan) uses them, in a scene in the first installment of Coppola's trilogy, to humorously mimic the sound of gunfire.

More often, however, the *Godfather* films are discussed quite openly in *The Sopranos*, and sometimes in considerable detail. The characters recall favorite scenes and motifs of the trilogy, discuss the interpretation of various turns, and sometimes even chide one another for insufficiently scholarly knowledge of the films. Indeed, the mobsters are so thoroughly familiar with the *Godfather* movies that, in conversation, they frequently refer simply to "one," "two," or "three," and—even without any explanatory context—assume that the numerals will be understood as referring to the three parts of Coppola's trilogy. Clearly, the *Godfather* trilogy has a kind of authority for Tony and his associates that is matched not only by no other movies, but by no other texts of any sort, up to and including the Bible, Machiavelli's *The Prince* (whose author Paulie refers to as "Prince Machabelli," with the "ch" given a soft pronunciation), and Sun Tzu's *The Art of War*. Such written texts have a certain prestige for the mobsters, owing either to the mobsters' religious heritage or to their vocation. But Tony and his fellows (though not his wife and daughter) live in a post-literate condition—Tony once tells Dr. Melfi that reading always puts him to sleep—and cinema serves as the new established writ, with the three *Godfather* films serving, so to speak, as the three testaments of the mob's Bible.[44]

It is, of course, a commonplace that real-life American mobsters, since the 1930s, have frequently modeled themselves on their counterparts in the movies. In a line of work where lethal violence is usual and where formal sanctions and legal guarantees ultimately backed by the armed might of the state are unavailable, the projection of a compelling, authoritative personal style is vitally important, sometimes literally making the difference between life and death. For the gangsters of the 1930s, valuable materials for the construction of such self-presentation could be found in the performances of James Cagney, Edward G. Robinson, Paul Muni, and George Raft. More recently, Marlon Brando's portrayal of Don Vito Corleone is said to have influenced the personal styles of two generations of real-life Mafiosi. Yet this imitation of art by life is *not* what is being represented in *The Sopranos*. As we have seen, Chase's characters live in a world far more akin to the blue-collar street of *GoodFellas* than to the quasi-aristocratic mansions of the Corleones. There is little that they can take directly into their own lives from Coppola's films; and Tony's own style owes nothing to Brando-as-Vito. On the only occasion (in "All Happy Families...," season 5, episode 4) that Tony is addressed as "Godfather," Vito's favorite appellation for himself, it is by a disgruntled subordinate whose intention—which is immediately clear to the viewer and to Tony himself—is to mock.

For the Soprano mobsters, the authority of Coppola's trilogy is not as a model but rather as a kind of lost utopia. Though the Corleones, as we have seen, are not immune to the physical violence on which their enterprise depends, they personally encounter it more seldom than Tony and his colleagues do. The Corleones seem in control of things to an extent that the Sopranos almost never do, and rarely need to get their own hands dirty as Chase's characters do in nearly every episode. Moreover, even the wealthiest characters in the television series—such as Tony himself and several of his counterparts in the New York mob—never enjoy the easy dignity and elegance of Coppola's characters, with their expensively but tastefully decorated family seats and their chauffeured luxury cars. It is quite explicable why Chase's characters, unlike their creator, should be so much more absorbed by the *Godfather* films than by *GoodFellas*. Tony and his fellows all know Scorsese's film, but have little reason to dwell on it: for all they could encounter there is a lifeworld too much like their own. In Coppola's trilogy, by contrast, they can find a kind of meaning and richness of life that their own existence sorely lacks.

Television against film

For all the various debts, however, that *The Sopranos* owes to the mob movie and especially to *GoodFellas* and the *Godfather* trilogy, we cannot understand the television series without grasping how fundamentally Chase's series is structured *against* Scorsese's and Coppola's films. Chase's respect for his cinematic precursors is, to be sure, profound. But part of the real genius of the series is to understand that television cannot merely emulate cinema without consigning itself to mediocrity—without becoming "second-rate film," in Alfred Shaughnessy's phrase. The formal resources of the two media are in crucial ways fundamentally different, and *The Sopranos* could not attain an aesthetic stature comparable to that of the greatest mob films without using its own specifically televisual capabilities to do what cinema cannot do. A sly, implicit declaration of televisual independence from cinema is provided by the fact that the film-within-the-series—*Cleaver*, a combination of the mob and the horror movie in whose making several of the characters (most notably Christopher) are involved during season 6 of *The Sopranos*—is obviously of abysmal aesthetic quality. The direct-to-DVD production is a very long way from being worthy of a Coppola or a Scorsese.

In the remainder of this chapter, I will concentrate on three major aspects of the deconstruction that Chase's series performs on the mob movie, particularly on *GoodFellas* and the *Godfather* trilogy: the elegy for the Mafia as an evidently dying institution that is, however, by no means quite dead yet; the exploration of psychotherapy and the resources of talking; and the transformations of the American family. Each of these themes corresponds to one of the three major settings (or group of settings) that largely define *The Sopranos*. The drama of the Mafia is enacted primarily in those places where Tony and his colleagues do business: the Bada Bing! of course, but also Satriale's Pork Store (which seems to be second only to the Bing as a hang-out and headquarters for Tony and his subordinates), and a wide variety of other more-or-less public places, including bars, restaurants, construction sites, hotels, and highways and street corners of different kinds. The drama of psychotherapy, by contrast, takes place in the most private of all spaces: the therapist's consulting room, where Tony and Dr. Melfi (rarely joined by Tony's wife Carmela [Edie Falco]) try to fathom Tony's psyche, especially the potentially dangerous panic attacks to which he is subject. Finally, the family story is acted out mainly in a setting much less public than the Bing but not completely private in the way that Dr. Melfi's office is: the Sopranos' upscale family home, where the series frequently takes on elements of the domestic sitcom that, it is said, Chase at one point planned his series to be.

It should be stressed that these three settings, with their attendant dramas, are by no means hermetically sealed off from one another: quite the contrary. However hard Tony tries to compartmentalize his life—to keep the dirty and not infrequently deadly details of his business out of his home, and to keep his therapy even more secret than any of his criminal schemes—the different dimensions of his life, and of the series, are constantly bleeding (sometimes literally) into one another. Indeed, this totalizing portrayal of the mobster's life, this stress on surprising and unwanted interrelations, should itself be considered one element of the deconstruction of the mob film that *The Sopranos* performs. A film may show sensational moments when borders are transgressed, as when Michael and Kay's cozy, luxurious, and apparently well-guarded bedroom is machine-gunned in the second *Godfather* film. But a television series like *The Sopranos*, with roughly 86 hours to develop its plots and subplots, can more amply and concretely show how such transgression becomes woven into the fabric of everyday life.

The decline (but not fall) of the Mafia

By the time that *The Sopranos* first appeared on American television screens, the real-life Mafia was in a serious state of decline. It was caused partly by a new aggressiveness and efficiency on the part of federal prosecutors, who, armed from 1970 onward with the Racketeer Influenced and Corrupt Organizations Act, and with the Witness Protection program, were finding it easier than ever before to secure convictions and extended prison terms in the fight against organized crime. RICO (the acronym has often been taken as an allusion to *Little Caesar*, in which the gangster protagonist, played by Edward G. Robinson, is named Rico) enabled pre-trial seizure of assets, sometimes making it difficult for indicted Mafiosi to afford an expensive legal defense. Even more important, RICO provided for much longer terms of imprisonment than gangsters had usually faced in the past. Sentences of multiple decades kept Mafia kingpins off the streets, while the threat of such sentences gave prosecutors a powerful weapon to break the Mafia's famous *omertà*, or code of silence, and to coerce lower-level mobsters into turning state's evidence. It was, after all, one thing to keep your mouth shut and to go to prison for three or four years, trusting that your family would be looked after and that your position within the mob would be enhanced upon release. It was something else entirely to face the possibility of spending the rest of your life behind bars. Moreover, the most powerful incentive against co-operating with the authorities—the overwhelming probability that one would be murdered for doing so—was significantly weakened by the Witness Protection program, which allowed the federal government to set up new residences and legal identities for their co-operating witnesses and to offer them at least some measure of physical protection for life. It is no wonder that RICO and Witness Protection figure prominently in the regular anxieties of Tony and his colleagues.

Overall, however, the efforts of law enforcement have doubtless been less important in weakening the Mafia than certain long-range trends in US society and economy. The primary recruitment base of the Mafia was always the urban male Italian-American working class; and, in the early years of the American Mafia, it provided (like the priesthood and big-city machine politics) one of the relatively few alternatives to a life of factory work or other ill-paid manual labor. As Italian-Americans (like other Catholic and Jewish immigrant groups) became better educated and more prosperous—as university educations became available to them and success in the professions and in "legitimate" businesses moved increasingly within their reach—the appeal of a career in organized crime was bound to wane. Dr. Melfi is a perfect example of an educated Italian-American whose life and family intersect at no point with the Mafia (until she takes on Tony as a patient). During the most candid conversation that Tony ever has with his daughter Meadow (Jamie-Lynn Sigler) about how he makes his money (in "College," episode 5 of season 1), he attempts somewhat to excuse his involvement with organized crime by maintaining that, in his day, Italian-Americans did not have many options. Meadow teases him, and undermines her father's self-serving rationalization, by replying with the name of a famously law-abiding, respectable, and distinguished Italian-American who would seem to be more than a full generation *older* than Tony: Governor Mario Cuomo of New York.[45]

The increasing corporatization and globalization of American capital have also played a part in eroding the power of the traditional Mafia, with its dependence on the small-business culture of old-fashioned urban neighborhoods. This point is dramatized in one of the most memorable humorous turns in the entirety of *The Sopranos*. In "Johnny Cakes" (season 6, part 1, episode 8), two minor members of Tony's organization are making their rounds collecting protection money from the local merchants, and arrive at a new shop in the neighborhood, which turns out to be (evidently) a Starbucks. The mobsters introduce themselves to the manager and, in their usual mock-friendly way, explain their business. But the manager, a young and fiercely articulate African-American, is unmoved. He explains that he has no discretion to lift money out of the till; all expenditures are monitored by computer and must be authorized in advance by corporate headquarters in Seattle. When asked how the corporate bosses would feel if someone tossed a brick through the shop's main window, he replies, "They've got, like, ten thousand stores in North America—I don't think they'd feel anything". The threats immediately escalate to include physical violence against him personally. But the manager, with the exasperated air of someone explaining a simple point to an obtuse child, can only reiterate that "every last fucking coffee bean is in the computer and has to be accounted for". The corporation can easily replace him at any time with another, equally dispensable employee. Defeated, the Mafiosi leave, one sadly commenting to the other, "It's over for the little guy".

And so it seems to be. The increasing bureaucratization of the American economy and the American polity is a major factor in foreclosing the traditional Mafia lifeworld in which an ordinary young man from the working-class street (like Henry Hill in *GoodFellas*) might hope, even without much formal education, to find profitable employment—and the chance, perhaps, of extremely profitable employment—through his own innate toughness, shrewdness, and sense of initiative. Tony himself, indeed, is almost a stereotypical Horatio Alger success story. The trajectory of his personal financial position—an arc not exactly from rags to riches but from polyester to riches, as it were—is illustrated many times in many ways. For instance, every time we see the luxurious home where Tony lives with his wife and two children (and it is featured in nearly every episode, even without counting the unchanging opening credit sequence, in which Tony drives home from New York City), we are bound to be impressed, especially if we recall, by contrast, the very modest dwelling in which he was raised. In addition to his spacious and well-appointed home (which his envious, bitter mother sarcastically but almost accurately calls a "mansion"), Tony enjoys a wide variety of luxury goods, for which, despite his blue-collar background and manner, he has developed a sometimes knowledgeable taste: for example, meals in gourmet restaurants, single-malt Scotch, expensive wine (Tony once acutely comments that wine shipped in wooden cases rather than in cardboard boxes tends to be of the highest quality), state-of-the-art titanium golf clubs, the furs and jewelry that he gives to Carmela (often as peace offerings for his countless infidelities), and a large motorized pleasure boat of which he is particularly fond (the elegant craft is useful for some business purposes too, such as the disposing of dead bodies). Though Tony never reaches the fully haute-bourgeois heights of a Don Vito Corleone, and though his personal style and manner are extremely different, he resembles Don Vito in being, in his own way, a living embodiment of the American Dream.

Yet Tony, as Christopher, especially, is anxiously aware, is unlikely to have many successors. In the pilot episode ("The Sopranos," season 1, episode 1), during his very first therapy session with Dr. Melfi, Tony himself confesses his sense of ennui and depression at having arrived during the declining years of the Mafia (though of course he never explicitly names the latter as such). He even expresses envy of his own late father, who was in the same line of work. "Johnny Boy" Soprano (Joseph Siravo) never personally attained as much success as his son has achieved, but nonetheless "had it better," as Tony maintains, in being part of an enterprise still at peak vigor and vitality. Professionally and materially, Tony is doing just fine for the time being. But, as he becomes more and more acutely aware throughout the following seasons, he seems to have less and less to look forward to, beyond the probability of ending his days either in federal prison or as the victim of a mob hit. There is, so to speak, jam today throughout the Mafia, and there will be jam tomorrow, and probably next week as well. But the prospects for jam next year are becoming increasingly cloudy. Whereas cinema is perfectly suited to representing punctiform catastrophe (as when the climax of *GoodFellas* dramatizes the sudden collapse of the neighborhood criminal organization to which Henry Hill has belonged), the much more gradual pace of *The Sopranos*, with its 86 episodes and its elaborate interweaving of multivarious plots and subplots, captures this sense of glacial decline, this prospect of a slow, unsensational, but ineluctable winding-down of energy, with a force and plausibility that film could hardly match.

From the viewpoint of any given individual, the future is most meaningfully represented, perhaps, by one's own children; and the narratives of Tony's children have a particular importance for the way that the series understands the future of the Mafia. The two younger Sopranos—both major characters, in keeping with the family-drama and family-sitcom dimension of the series—are in most respects quite different from one another. Meadow (the elder of the two, and whose very name signals the extent to which Tony has moved beyond the traditional proletarian and petty-bourgeois cultural norms of his origins)[46] is very nearly the perfect kid. Tony's own favorite and something of a daddy's girl, Meadow is a bright, good-looking, hard-working, popular, outgoing straight-A student. She is one of those youngsters who seem to do everything well. Of course she is not wholly without problems—typically adolescent battles with her mother, some limited and fairly inconsequential experimentation with illegal drugs, a few misadventures in romance—but they are normal enough and cause no lasting harm. Meadow seems well poised to make an excellent life for herself, one that will permanently remove her from the milieu of organized crime from which her father has generally (though not invariably, as he once remarks with self-puzzlement to Dr. Melfi) tried to shield her. She leaves home to become a brilliant Ivy League undergraduate with plans for a medical career, preferably in pediatrics: thus precisely conforming, it appears, to the pattern of education and upward mobility that can lead young Italian-Americans into the mainstream of upper-middle-class American society and decisively away from the environs of the Mafia. Near the end of the series, after Meadow has changed her career goal from medicine to law, Tony muses with Dr. Melfi about how much he would have enjoyed having a "Dr. Soprano" in his family. There is a poignant echo here of the famous scene in the first *Godfather* film that we have discussed before, where Vito, chatting with Michael (Al Pacino) after his youngest and favorite son has become irrevocably committed to the Mafia life that his father never wanted for him, confesses that he had hoped Michael would become "Senator Corleone. Governor Corleone. Something".

Tony's son—Anthony Soprano Jr., or "A.J.," as he is usually known (Robert Iler)—traces a path very different from his sister's. If Meadow seems to do everything well, from academics to athletics to social life, A.J. struggles to find *anything* at which he is not hopeless. Physically unprepossessing and a terrible student (he eventually flunks out of a community college), A.J. spends his life emotionally and spiritually adrift, unclear even in his own mind as to what he wants from the world. Most goals as he does occasionally manage to formulate (like becoming a CIA agent in the War on Terror, or the personal helicopter pilot for a billionaire mogul like Donald Trump) are mere fantasy. A suicide attempt fails only because he is incompetent even at trying to drown himself in the family swimming pool. At one point (in "The Army of One," season 3, episode 13), Tony decides, against Carmela's strong inclinations, to straighten out A.J. by sending him to a ferociously demanding military school. But this plan has to be cancelled when A.J. turns out to suffer from the same kind of violent panic attacks that originally led Tony to seek therapy with Dr. Melfi (and that had afflicted his own father before him). Like Vito Corleone, Tony might well not have wanted his son to follow in his own footsteps even if his son had been capable of doing so. But it is obvious to Tony that A.J. could not survive half a day in the line of work in which he himself, as the mob boss of northern New Jersey, has achieved such success.

In keeping with the basic theme of the series that the Mafia is dying but by no means dead yet, both Meadow and A.J. wind up, however, rather closer to the mob than the viewer has had reason to expect prior to the final episode ("Made in America," season 6, part 2, episode 9). Upon completing law school, Meadow, it transpires, plans to join a Mafia-connected law firm, where she will defend (for a remarkably high salary) people much like her father.

Engaging in just the same sort of bad-faith rationalization that she has earlier punctured in Tony, Meadow (who has always professed strongly liberal political and social views) presents her intended career as a kind of civil-rights law. But the mob defense bar is, of course, the safe, elegant, (comparatively) respectable, and (usually) legal way to make big money from organized crime. The apple has not fallen so very far from the tree after all. As for A.J., in the final episode he begins to display unwonted interest and energy in a business career. As the series ends, he is engaged, with crucial help from his father, in prosperous and promising work in mob-connected sectors of the nightclub and film (!) industries. Neither Soprano child becomes a full-fledged gangster (Meadow would probably have been prevented by her sex from doing so anyway), but both are embarked on trajectories that show there is still real—albeit diminishing—life in the Mafia yet.

The *very* end of *The Sopranos* suggests, though, that the future, at least from Tony's particular viewpoint, will be even darker than what we might have expected before this point. Not only is Tony on the verge of being indicted on major RICO charges that could send him to prison for decades, but in the final scene of the final episode, as Tony and his family are preparing to enjoy a pleasant supper together in a favorite restaurant, something even more dire happens. Though exactly *what* happens when the screen unexpectedly goes black and silent—never again to be filled with anything but the final credits of the series— remains slightly ambiguous, it is possible to infer the *dénouement* of *The Sopranos* with tolerable confidence. The cut (*not*, as is often mistakenly said, fade) to black presumably signifies sudden death, a death that cannot possibly be Tony's own, since the viewpoint from which the cut occurs is one from which Tony is visible in medium shot immediately prior to the cut; and the basic rules of televisual (or cinematic) syntax require that the viewpoint of the final shot immediately before the cut be the viewpoint from which everything goes black. A close examination of the camera angles of the scene suggests that this viewpoint is probably Meadow's, who is just entering the restaurant to join her parents and her brother. Apparently, she is hit by a bullet aimed at the back of Tony's head by one of the suspicious-looking characters we have seen earlier in the restaurant.

Not only, then, is the Mafia dying, and not only do its death spasms possibly include life imprisonment for the series protagonist. Even worse, Tony has lost his treasured daughter, the most valued human being in the world to him; and the end of the series thus precisely "rhymes" with the end of the *Godfather* trilogy, when Mary Corleone (Sofia Coppola), as we have seen, dies from a bullet meant for her father, Michael, who had cherished *his* daughter above all else. In both multi-part works, one fundamental irony is the same: Vito and Michael and Tony have always maintained that their careers in organized crime have been undertaken primarily in order to provide for their families. Yet the shattering of family is the ultimate result in both *The Sopranos* and the *Godfather* films. For Coppola, the work of the Mafia goes on, to be sublimated into the "legitimate" business of global capital. For Chase, the Mafia itself will not very long outlive Meadow. Having "translated" the mob movie into a mob television series that records this decline, Chase thus implicitly suggests that we will not be needing mob movies for much longer.

Analyzing the Mafioso

The drama of therapy that takes place in Dr. Melfi's consulting room bears an interesting formal resemblance to the drama of organized crime that is mostly played out in more public spaces: for both psychotherapy and the Mafia are institutions on the decline but not yet completely fallen. To be sure, Jennifer Melfi is no strictly orthodox Freudian. She allows weekly sessions rather than insisting on the four- or five-times-a-week routine of full-fledged psychoanalysis; and she does not hesitate to prescribe the drugs that her medical degree authorizes her to dispense (for a while Tony becomes an avid consumer of Prozac). In addition, Dr. Melfi is a good deal more talkative than any completely strict Freudian could be, frequently engaging Tony in something like real conversation (though of course it is always different in crucial ways from any conversation that takes place outside the therapeutic situation). Like many real-life therapists today, Dr. Melfi seems not much concerned to define her methodology with precision or to engage in polemics on the relative merits of various therapeutic approaches. She is somewhat eclectic, apparently content to employ diverse techniques in ways that seem indicated for the particular patient of the hour.

Nonetheless, it is clear throughout the series that Dr. Melfi's practice is grounded in the humanistic tradition that descends principally from Freud. She finds that drugs can be useful for certain limited purposes, but she warns Tony not to overestimate their importance. For Dr. Melfi, real therapeutic progress comes not, mainly, from pharmacological manipulation of brain chemistry, but from the gains in self-knowledge attained when two people sit in a room together, talking and listening to one another. It is, indeed, impossible not to sense an eerie parallel between the way that Tony's enterprise is daily under assault by the FBI and other apparatuses of law enforcement, with their RICO predicates and their Witness Protection program, and (even though we see much less of it) the way that humanistic psychotherapy is under siege by the neurochemical reductionism of drug therapy backed by the enormous economic might of the pharmaceutical and insurance industries. This parallel helps to explain the curious affinity that Dr. Melfi seems to feel for someone as radically different from herself as Tony Soprano. It explains the correspondence between them—and James Gandolfini and Lorraine Bracco are, after all, in the technical terms of casting, the male and female leads of the series, clearly presented as such in the opening credits—much better, I think, than any supposed counter-transferential sexual attraction Jennifer might feel toward Tony (something for which there is hardly any evidence, especially after the first season), or any supposed thrill she may find, as a member of the law-abiding community, in vicariously participating in the imagined "freedom" of organized crime (for Dr. Melfi, treating Tony's symptoms, knows very well just how suffocating and unfree the world of the mob truly is).

Tony and Dr. Melfi also share a quest for knowledge of the self. This is Dr. Melfi's professional practice as a humanistic psychiatrist, and it is a quest to which Tony—despite initial and even to some degree continuing skepticism about the talking cure—devotes a good deal of his none too abundant free time. Indeed, so attached does Tony become to psychotherapy—despite the danger in which it places him when word of his therapy leaks out to his professional associates, danger that includes at least one actual (and nearly successful) plot to murder him—that, during one period when Jennifer Melfi is unavailable to him, he desperately searches for another psychiatrist willing to accept him as a patient. That *The Sopranos* offers what is almost certainly the most compelling and realistic portrayal of psychotherapy in the entirety of film or television is due not only to the high intelligence of the writing and acting but also to the sheer extent of the series, with its capacity for unhurried development of its themes over a period of months and years.

Most fictional representations of therapy, after all, tend to focus on sudden "breakthroughs," moments when the patient abruptly grasps certain long-repressed truths about the forces that have driven his or her unhappy behavior—and after which, it is usually suggested, the patient can move forward in a relatively untroubled way. In television and film, these breakthroughs often tend to occur, conveniently enough, shortly before the final credits. In actuality, of course, psychotherapy is a matter not of such isolated "eureka" moments, but of a long, difficult, gradual struggle in which even the best progress is bound to be accompanied by regressions, set-backs, wrong turns, and periods of stasis and blockage along the way. The very structure of Freudian repression—which is essentially an unconsciously willed forgetting of that which it would be unbearably painful to remember—guarantees that the patient's first responses to crucial advances in self-knowledge will be not to welcome these gains but furiously to resist them, and even, in many cases, to resist the entire therapeutic process.

Such is precisely what we see with Tony in Dr. Melfi's office. The temporal structure of the multi-season television series makes possible the representation of therapy as it actually unfolds over a period of years. Tony's acts of resistance are frequent, sometimes inclining him to have done with therapy and Dr. Melfi altogether, and, in at least one memorable instance, leading him to threaten the terrified Dr. Melfi with physical violence when she dares to help him learn more about his psychic history than he wishes to know ("I Dream of Jeannie Cusamano," season 1, episode 13). Yet Tony always returns, and does make genuine advances in self-knowledge. He makes progress in bringing his panic attacks under control when he comes to understand their origin, and their association with the Italian meats he loves, in a long-forgotten incident from his childhood, when he witnessed his father cutting off a butcher's finger as punishment for non-payment of a gambling debt ("Fortunate Son," season 3, episode 3). More because of increased self-knowledge than because of Prozac, Tony's bouts of depression also abate. Above all, perhaps, Tony comes to appreciate that his lifelong inability to please his mother, Livia, results less from his failings than from her own joylessness and her compulsion to harm those around her (a compulsion that extends even to Livia's connivance in a mob plot to murder Tony).[47]

The audience of *The Sopranos* shares the understanding that Tony gains of himself, and our extensive knowledge of Tony largely accounts for the sympathy that many viewers have been puzzled to feel for a character that they know perfectly well to be a professional criminal and a ruthless murderer. However vicious and numerous his crimes, it is difficult not to empathize with someone whose inner struggles and conundrums—and even whose dreams—we know as well as we do Tony's. Thanks mainly to the small dramas enacted in Dr. Melfi's office during episode after episode—and to her own crucial interventions as well as to Tony's free-associative musings—Tony Soprano possesses for the viewer a more extensive, complex, and concrete inner life than virtually any other character in the history of mob cinema and television.[48]

This emphasis on psychic interiority thus constitutes an important aspect of the deconstruction that *The Sopranos* performs of the Mafia movie. The early protagonists of the genre, like Rico Bandello in *Little Caesar* and Tom Powers (James Cagney) in *The Public Enemy*, are nearly cartoonish in their simplicity compared to Tony. Vito Corleone, for all his grave, weighty dignity, remains, insofar as the inner wellsprings of his actions are concerned, something of an enigma both to the audience and to the other characters in the first *Godfather* film. Henry Hill can talk directly to the viewer in voice-over through much of *GoodFellas* without letting us know very much of what really makes him tick beyond his lifelong and rather one-dimensional desire to be a gangster. Even Michael Corleone, probably the most three-dimensional character in mob cinema, often seems nearly as hard to understand as his father, especially in the first two *Godfather* films; and it is noteworthy that the scene in the third film where he most displays some inner psychic reality is the scene of his confession with Cardinal Lamberto (Raf Vallone). As Foucault would remind us, the Roman Catholic sacrament of confession as developed during and after the Counter-Reformation is the distant ancestor of the psychotherapeutic session.

Film, of course, lacks the technical resources for extensive psychological verisimilitude possessed by the novel and the television series. But the relative lack of such verisimilitude in the mob movie probably also owes something to our own disinclination to share the psychic life of amoral professional killers, our reluctance to accept that such sociopaths are after all human beings with whom we have more in common than we may like to think. Largely (though not entirely) in Dr. Melfi's consulting room, the 86 episodes of *The Sopranos* finally give us a Mafia killer whose humanity cannot be missed or denied. Like us, Tony Soprano is all too human.

The scenes in Dr. Melfi's office also deconstruct the mob movie in a more strictly formal way. For it is in these scenes that the series most emphatically makes clear its formal distance from cinema, and claims its properly televisual identity as "electronic theater," in Alfred Shaughnessy's felicitous term. If the therapist's consulting room is akin to the Catholic confessional in one way, it is akin to the naturalistic stage in another way. The consulting room, after all, is a box where human beings gather and do very little other than to talk at great length with one another. The dramas of therapy are precisely dramas of an enclosed room and thus have a deep affinity with the naturalist theater that Raymond Williams shows to be allied to television drama. If the consulting room seems less "dramatic" in any crude or obvious sense than the courtroom, say, or even the living room, that only makes the dramas that take place there *more* dramatic in the sense of being stagier, more literary, less cinematic, and more exclusively composed of talk. Films that deal with psychotherapy often attempt to compensate for the deficit of "action" in therapy by the use of flashbacks to the world outside the consulting room—Hitchcock's *Spellbound* (1945) is a famous example—and this device is not altogether absent in *The Sopranos*. Yet Chase's series consistently finds what happens in Dr. Melfi's office to be just as exciting as anything that happens anywhere else; and at this point the series is at its most radically televisual.[49]

It is worth noting that the (apparent) death of Meadow at the very end of *The Sopranos* has a formal parallel in the penultimate episode of the series ("The Blue Comet," season 6, part 2, episode 8), when Dr. Melfi finally severs for good her therapeutic relationship with Tony. Her own psychiatrist, Dr. Elliot Kupferberg (Peter Bogdanovich), has long taken a dim view of her being in a therapeutic relationship with Tony. Now, at a dinner party with Jennifer and several other therapists, he violates professional ethics by revealing to the whole company exactly what she has been up to: whereupon everyone gangs up on Jennifer, trying to convince her that no good can come of treating a sociopathic killer. Such people, they maintain, may actually become *more* dangerous after the experience of the consulting room, for they simply use the therapeutic situation to exercise and sharpen their skills as confidence men. Though Dr. Melfi resents both Dr. Kupferberg's unprofessional conduct and the general bullying (the latter of which, indeed, bears some stylistic similarity to the ethos of the Mafia itself), she soon decides that her colleagues are right. At her next session with Tony she announces that—for no very convincing reason that she is able to give—their relationship must be terminated. This turn of events is abrupt, if not quite so abrupt as the evident shooting of Meadow, and taken together they amount to the loss of two of the three most important women in Tony's life (Carmela, of course, is the third). Again there is an echo of the very end of the *Godfather* trilogy, when we are reminded that Michael has lost not only his daughter but also both of his wives (one to a bomb meant for him, the other through divorce). The future is bleak indeed.

The Mafioso at home

If *The Sopranos* represents the "translation" of the mob movie into the very different form of the television series—and the attendant deconstruction of the former—then one of the most important aspects of this translation and this deconstruction is the overdetermination of the Mafia story by perhaps the most durable and most thoroughly televisual of all television genres: the situation comedy. More specifically, Chase's series is haunted by the kind of family comedy in which the children are always getting into zany but ultimately harmless misadventures; in which the mother, a paragon of domestic efficiency and cheerful common sense, keeps the household on track; and, above all, in which the father, while choosing to imagine that he exercises firm patriarchal control, is again and again shown to be hilariously inept at managing his family, if also fundamentally good-hearted and loveable beneath his pretensions.

The paradigm of the type is probably Howard Lindsay and Russel Crouse's hugely popular naturalistic comic drama *Life with Father* (1939), which, with over three thousand performances, still holds the record as the longest running (nonmusical) play in Broadway history. Based on a 1936 book of autobiographical stories by Clarence Day, *Life with Father* was made into a very stagy and thus minimally cinematic film by Michael Curtiz in 1947 and then into a CBS television sitcom that ran from 1953 to 1955. Its influence has been enormous, helping to set the pattern for countless family sitcoms during the 1950s—the "classic" age of the genre—and after. *Father Knows Best*—which ran from 1954 to 1963, appearing at different times on all three US television networks—is perhaps the most widely remembered example from the Eisenhower era, though the frequent irony of the title (which ended with a question mark in the older radio version) is sometimes forgotten. The widely acclaimed current ABC sitcom *Modern Family* (2009–present) shows that, given a few adjustments, the old formula retains considerable vitality to this day. Perhaps no other genre in any medium has demonstrated a greater ability to show, if usually in idealized comic form, the everyday life of a family over an extended period of time.

The formula of the family sitcom is very much at work—sometimes just below the surface—in *The Sopranos*: and, by incorporating elements of this radically televisual genre, the series shows us a mobster's family life, and its intersections with his business life, to an extent that mob cinema can hardly approach. The series is almost certainly the funniest representation of mob life ever constructed, and much (though by no means all) of its humor is to be found within the Soprano family home that constitutes one of its major settings. Indeed, it should be noted again that the unchanging montage over the credits that opens every episode shows Tony driving home from New York City: a journey, that is to say, from that particular urban locale typical of the mob movie (like *GoodFellas* and much of the *Godfather* trilogy) to the kind of suburban family residence where the television sitcom has most abundantly flourished. Inside the spacious house at 633 Stag Trail Road, North Caldwell, New Jersey, Meadow and A.J. test the limits of parental authority in much the way that sitcom children have always done. Meanwhile, Carmela—despite the deep sadness, guilt, and greed that fundamentally define her character—can turn in a tolerably convincing performance as the domestic goddess whose level-headedness and concern for her family manage to keep the household machinery ticking over. Most of all, Tony often bears more than a passing resemblance to the comically represented patriarchs of *Life with Father* and its successors. He repeatedly attempts to impose a paternal authority that neither the viewer nor the members of his own family can recognize as such.

In one episode ("Nobody Knows Anything," season 1, episode 11), for instance, all four Sopranos are at breakfast one morning, and Meadow launches into a diatribe against the persecution of Bill Clinton during the Monica Lewinsky (or "Kazinksi," as A.J. misnames her) scandal—and, more generally, against the sexual repressiveness and prudery of the United States in comparison to many other countries. Tony—whose income derives in part from stripping, lap dancing, and prostitution, and who is compulsively unfaithful to Carmela— objects to this kind of talk in his home. "It's the '90s," Meadow replies. "Parents are *supposed* to discuss sex with their children". As if to settle the matter for good, Tony says, "Yeah, but that's where you're wrong. You see, out there it's the 1990s. But in this house it's 1954".

Is it merely a co-incidence that, reaching for a year at the heart of the 1950s, Tony happens to pick the one when *Father Knows Best*—the title of which is humorously echoed in the title of this episode—first appeared on American television screens? In any case, it is quite clear that, in the venerable sitcom tradition, the father of the Soprano household is failing to know best, or to know much of anything at all. "What's with him?" asks Meadow rhetorically and with confident superiority as Tony exits. Years later, in the final episode, Meadow explains to her father why she wants to be an attorney—and, as she sees it, a civil-rights attorney—by saying, "The state can crush the individual". Tony replies with two words that, in context, speak for the goofiness of all sitcom dads ever: "New Jersey?".

Of course, the generic tendency of the sitcom not only overdetermines the Mafia drama in *The Sopranos* but is also—and to an even greater degree—overdetermined by it. One way to understand this particular overdetermination is by considering the category of work. In the traditional family sitcom, work is not particularly prominent. The fathers nearly always have jobs—"Clare" Day Sr. in the various versions of *Life with Father* is a stockbroker, while Jim Anderson (famously played by Robert Young) in *Father Knows Best* is an insurance agent—but their work life stays mainly in the background. A family drama is almost necessarily home-centered, and sitcom dads are usually seen applying their energy not in the world of paid labor but to the running of their own households—in large part, of course, because their frequent domestic incompetence supplies much of the humor. The father's occupation may sometimes play a minor role in the narratives—as when Dr. Alex Stone (Carl Betz) on the ABC family sitcom *The Donna Reed Show* (1958–1966) makes use at home of his skills as a pediatrician—but to stress the world of work too much would tend to violate the generic integrity of the family sitcom. A few sitcoms, such as *The Dick Van Dyke Show* (CBS, 1961–1966) or, to some degree, *Bewitched* (ABC, 1964–1972), have, admittedly, managed to strike a balance between the family home and the workplace (though it should be noted that in these shows children are only very minor characters). But most workplace-centered television comedies, like *The Mary Tyler Moore Show* (CBS, 1970–1977), *Taxi* (ABC, NBC, 1978–1983), or *Cheers* (NBC, 1982–1993), have usually focused mainly on unmarried and childless protagonists.

To say that the world of Tony Soprano's work violates the sitcom aspect of the series is a considerable understatement. *The Sopranos,* after all, is not a sitcom but a Mafia drama with sitcom elements, and those elements are massively transformed by the deadly serious business of the mob that surrounds them. Here Daddy's business is not some anodyne office job, but such forms of illegal capitalism as loansharking and extortion, punctuated by the acts of aggravated assault and murder frequently required to keep the profits coming in. To some degree, the dimension of the series that features Tony and his immediate family—the dimension set mainly (though not entirely) in the house at 633 Stag Trail Road—does, so to speak, *want* to be a pure family sitcom; and this generic desire on the part of Chase's series precisely corresponds to Tony's personal desire to keep his work life and his home life in separate, water-tight compartments. But such separation proves impossible. It is annoying enough for Tony when his innumerable girlfriends call him on his home telephone (heterosexual promiscuity being almost an informal job requirement among his business associates, as overt homosexual desire is so taboo as to be, sometimes, a capital offense). This is not, needless to say, the sort of problem that ever bothers Jim Anderson. It is much worse than annoying when the violence integral to his work leaks into his domestic life, threatening the family whose welfare all of Tony's professional efforts are, as he likes to think, ultimately designed to serve.

For instance, in one narrative strand (during season 3), Meadow becomes romantically involved with the son of one of Tony's deceased friends—the boss, in fact, who until his death from cancer ran the criminal organization that Tony has now inherited. Tony at first approves of the relationship. But, as Jackie Aprile Jr. (Jason Cerbone) increasingly violates Tony's wishes by attempting to follow in his own late father's footsteps, and as his sociopathic tendencies spin more and more dangerously out of control, it becomes clear that, for a mobster like Tony, romance between one's daughter and the son of one's close friend is far from being the naturally appropriate connection that it would be for a genuine sitcom dad. Eventually, Tony finds it necessary to have young Jackie murdered, thus seriously traumatizing Meadow (even though she had already broken up with Jackie, and even though she seems not to suspect her father's hand in what is made to look like a street-level drug deal gone wrong). Tony's business violates the domestic tranquility of his family even more directly toward the end of the series, when a powerful New York crime syndicate declares all-out war against the Soprano organization, and the Sopranos are forced to vacate, temporarily, the home that has been so important as a setting for the series. The danger seems to be that, though Mafiosi do not deliberately target each other's wives and children, neither do they take any special pains to insure that wives and children will not be "collateral damage," as it were, from bullets or bombs. Few things are more basic to a family sitcom than the family home; and at this point, as the Sopranos are exiled from 633 Stag Trail Road, the sitcom elements of *The Sopranos* are almost completely crushed beneath the weight of the mob drama.

The same is of course even more emphatically true in the ultimate scene of the series, when Tony's line of work causes everything to go black for Meadow. It seems significant, indeed, that in this scene Meadow is a few minutes late entering the restaurant to join her family because of some trouble she has had parallel-parking her car outside. Chase's cameras spend a surprising amount of time showing her struggles to fit the car into the parking space, to no very obvious narrative point. But Meadow's automotive ineptness is just the kind of zany problem that any sitcom kid might experience. In a pure sitcom, her parking difficulties might well have been the subject for some jokes after she joined her family at their table inside the restaurant. In *The Sopranos*, of course, the *dénouement* of the scene is not a bit funny at all.

The end of the mob movie

Since *The Sopranos* began appearing on HBO in 1999, Hollywood has produced, so far as I am aware, not a single Mafia film of major interest—and certainly no film even remotely comparable in stature to the masterpieces by Coppola and Scorsese. Aesthetics is not a science that allows for such precise prediction as, say, astronomy, and it would be rash to proclaim, flatly, that we will never see great mob movies again. Yet the reconstitution of the mob movie after the deconstruction of the genre performed by *The Sopranos* would be a task requiring such massive ingenuity and originality that it is, at least, a little difficult to imagine how it might be accomplished. For *The Sopranos*, by using the specifically televisual resources of its own medium to show that which for the most part lies beyond the power of cinema to represent so well—the gradual dwindling of the Mafia's power, the psychic depths of the typical Mafioso, the everyday transgressing of the boundaries between work and home life for the mobster—has apparently, and at least for the time being, rendered the mob movie obsolete. When Tony Soprano relaxes after a hard day's work in front of his big-screen TV set to enjoy yet again the adventures of Rico Bandello or Tom Powers, he cannot know that he is observing the first major representatives of a character type of which he himself may well be the last.

In closing this chapter, however, it is worth noting that, since the end of *The Sopranos* in 2007, there has been, though no major mob film, yet a mob television series—also on HBO—that looks likely to rank as an important aesthetic achievement: Terence Winter's *Boardwalk Empire* (2010–present). Winter did extensive work on *The Sopranos* as a writer and producer, and his colleagues on *Boardwalk Empire* encompass over 100 other individuals with cast or crew credits on the earlier series—including Steve Buscemi, the star of *Boardwalk Empire*, who worked as both an actor and a director on *The Sopranos*, though not including David Chase himself.[50] (Martin Scorsese also has a credit on *Boardwalk Empire*, as a producer.) *Boardwalk Empire* is very clearly constructed in the wake of Chase's series, and with full self-conscious awareness of the fact. It manages to avoid direct competition with *The Sopranos* by the ingenious device of placing its action in the early 1920s, just as modern organized crime in the United States is beginning to take shape (and also, more incidentally but rather cleverly, by setting the action in southern rather than northern New Jersey). The central character is the political boss Enoch "Nucky" Thompson (Buscemi), a fictionalized version of the real-life Atlantic City Republican Party leader Nucky Johnson. Thompson is no stranger to crime (most prominently bootlegging), but, as it begins, the series makes clear that the significantly bloodier and more ruthless gangsters who lay the real foundations of the modern American Mafia—Al Capone, Charlie "Lucky" Luciano, Meyer Lansky—are young men just embarking on their careers. As *The Sopranos* is about the decline of the mob, so *Boardwalk Empire* is about its birth. If *The Sopranos* foreshadows the inevitable death of the Mafia, *Boardwalk Empire* takes that death for granted, perhaps, as it performs a historical archeology of the Mafia that looks likely to prove far more painstaking and detailed than anything that cinema can offer.

SECTION II

Noir and its Discontents

Marxism, cinema, and some dialectics of film noir and science fiction

Deflation and inflation

Consider four crucial moments from four well-known movies:

1. A gravely wounded insurance salesman settles behind his desk, and, speaking into a Dictaphone, confesses to murder: "I killed him for money, and for a woman," he says. "And I didn't get the money, and I didn't get the woman".
2. A criminal mastermind, having organized and led a major heist, stands ready to board an airplane with his girlfriend and make his final getaway. But in his haste he has stuffed the stolen money into a rickety suitcase, and, as the suitcase is being loaded onto the plane, it comes apart and the money flies off in all directions in the high winds of the runway. Not only has his profit been suddenly reduced to zero—or rather to less than zero, since the heist was quite expensive to organize and execute—but he knows that the likelihood of capture by the police has suddenly risen to near certainty.
3. A space alien who is physically indistinguishable from human beings, and who has been mortally wounded by a senseless act of earthly violence, emerges temporarily revived from his spaceship and proceeds, calmly and with complete authority, to explain to a group of scientists and soldiers that unprecedented opportunities await humanity if it learns how to behave peacefully—but that, if humans threaten to extend their aggressive ways into outer space, then the earth will be destroyed by the robot police force established by the other inhabited planets.
4. An astronaut, having been sent on a mysterious mission to Jupiter and then having been diverted by even more mysterious forces to remote parts of the universe, winds up in an ornately furnished apartment, where he passes through the stages of life from young manhood to extreme old age and is reborn as the "Star Child" of evidently planetary scope and godlike powers.

The four films referred to are, respectively, Billy Wilder's *Double Indemnity* (1944), Stanley Kubrick's *The Killing* (1956), Robert Wise's *The Day the Earth Stood Still* (1951), and Kubrick's *2001: A Space Odyssey* (1968). The first two are instances of film noir, the second two of science-fiction cinema; and each may be taken as exemplary of its kind. *Double Indemnity* is the most widely praised single example of noir, and has attracted even higher accolades as well, such as Woody Allen's designation of it as "the greatest movie ever made".[51] Produced relatively early in the original cycle of classic Hollywood noir, Wilder's film was hugely influential on the genre, helping, for instance, to establish such common noir motifs as the use of voice-over narration and the centrality of the *femme fatale*. *The Killing* is not commonly ranked quite so high but is likely to appear on critics' lists of the ten or fifteen best examples of classic noir. It is also perhaps the most influential of all heist films, and its continuing vitality is illustrated by (for instance) the impact that its structure has had on such movies as *Reservoir Dogs* (1992) and (to a lesser degree) *Pulp Fiction* (1994) by Quentin Tarantino, regarded by many as the pre-eminent master of crime cinema of his generation. *The Day the Earth Stood Still* is probably the strongest instance of Hollywood science fiction in its original 1950s phase. Its influence on later cinema (e.g., in its montage of newscasts during the film's opening sequence) has extended even beyond science fiction. *2001*, as I have elsewhere argued at some length,[52] is something like the permanently definitive masterpiece of science-fiction cinema, with not only no rival but virtually no second.

The two noir scenes described above emphatically proclaim the films in which they are embedded to be *deflationary* in outlook. Walter Neff (Fred MacMurray) begins Wilder's film not only by confessing to murder but also by admitting that his intricate scheme of grand passion and grand larceny has resulted in complete failure, and will yield nothing but his own destruction. Perhaps most deflating of all for Walter, he now knows that the passion he felt for the stunningly beautiful Phyllis Dietrichson (Barbara Stanwyck), his partner in crime, was never requited, her apparent interest in him just a cynical pretense to cover her real, and entirely mercenary, motives.

The conclusion of *The Killing* is equally, if somewhat differently, deflationary. Johnny Clay (Sterling Hayden) is shrewder than Walter Neff, and his main problem is not that he misjudges his associates nor that he underestimates the investigating authorities—as Walter disastrously underestimates Barton Keyes (Edward G. Robinson), his best friend and the chief investigator for the insurance company that he and Phyllis attempt to defraud. But Johnny (like Doc Riedenschneider, the master criminal played by Sam Jaffe in John Huston's 1950 noir heist film *The Asphalt Jungle*, which had a powerful influence on Kubrick's movie) underestimates something more fundamental and more formidable: the power of sheer blind luck. His criminal scheme is smarter and more complex than Walter's, and, unlike Walter's, is designed to allow, to a certain degree, for unexpected mishaps along the way. But even Johnny Clay cannot plan for everything. In film noir as in the mob movie, crime can never be quite perfect (a point explicitly made by Barton Keyes in *Double Indemnity*). In *The Killing*, it is an intrinsically trivial factor, namely the flimsiness of a piece of luggage, that manages to undo all of Johnny's brilliant work. For *The Killing* as for *Double Indemnity*, life has less—much less—to offer than one might have imagined: "What's the difference?" asks Johnny with weary, defeated resignation in the film's final line.

In the science-fiction films, however, life offers much *more* than expected. The humanoid appearance of the alien Klaatu (Michael Rennie) allows him to mix undetected in the mundane affairs of Washington, DC, and so helps *The Day the Earth Stood Still* to provide some fine realistic satire of Cold War America during the Truman Administration.

The short-sightedness and corruption of much in American life are highlighted, and are condensed in the character of Tom Stevens (Hugh Marlowe), the boyfriend of the lead female character played by Patricia Neal, and a man consumed by petty egoistic motives (and also, like Walter Neff, an insurance salesman by trade). But the film ultimately dismisses Tom. Klaatu's closing speech makes clear that the global (and ultimately cosmic) humanitarian perspective of the scientist Jacob Barnhardt (played by Sam Jaffe and clearly modeled after Albert Einstein) is far more compelling and actual than Stevens's myopic greed. If the planet faces possible catastrophe, it also enjoys undreamed-of opportunities, as Klaatu invites humanity to save itself and to live in peaceful co-operation with extraterrestrial races of far greater intellectual and moral attainments.[53]

2001 is even more inflationary in outlook, even more insistent that reality is richer and more various than most people tend to assume. As the film begins its second major section, which is set in the year that provides the title, humanity has reached a crisis of banality, pettiness, corruption, and mortal danger. The crisis not only corresponds to the more primitive but structurally similar impasse represented in the film's first part, set during "the dawn of man," but is also reminiscent of the state of affairs that Klaatu and Professor Barnhardt find so distressing in *The Day the Earth Stood Still*. But Kubrick's film offers a transcendence that is even more extraordinary, visually and thematically, than that provided by Wise's. In *2001* the human race is not "merely" given the chance to join in something like an extraterrestrial version of the United Nations (in the latter's original Rooseveltian conception, before the corruptions of the Cold War set in). Humanity, in the person of the initially unremarkable astronaut Dave Bowman (Keir Dullea), actually takes a stride forward in physical and spiritual evolution, going "beyond the infinite," in Kubrick's phrase: that is, beyond all supernatural mystifications in order to arrive, in neo-Nietzschean fashion, at a material and secular state of superhumanity. Dave Bowman begins as an Everyman at the dawn of the twenty-first century—technically competent and physically efficient, but an intellectual, spiritual, and aesthetic nullity—and ends as a natural god.

The opposition between the inflationary and the deflationary suggested by these four films provides a cognitive axis along which the cinematic genres of science fiction and noir can be contrasted overall. Science fiction of course has its origins in literature, more specifically in British Romanticism, one of the most inflationary movements in cultural history. The most widely accepted and most plausible candidate to be the first major work of full-fledged science fiction remains Mary Shelley's *Frankenstein* (1818), which tackles the awesomely inflationary theme of the artificial creation of human life (and which was composed under the direct inspiration of Percy Shelley's poetry, commonly regarded as more than usually inflationary even by Romantic standards). This inflationary bent—this cognitive affirmation and aesthetic demonstration that, as the Marxist philosopher Ernst Bloch put it, reality is never merely itself but always means "reality *plus* the future within it" (emphasis added)[54]— becomes the principal (though not the only) tendency in the history of science fiction. It is particularly in evidence in the strongest works of the genre, from pioneering classics like H. G. Wells's *The Time Machine* (1895) and, even more, Olaf Stapledon's *Last and First Men*

(1930) and *Star Maker* (1937), through the main achievements of the 1960s and 1970s— probably the genre's most creative period, owing to such authors as Philip K. Dick, Ursula Le Guin, Samuel Delany, J. G. Ballard, Thomas Disch, Joanna Russ, and many others—to more recent triumphs like Kim Stanley Robinson's Mars trilogy (1993–1996) and China Miéville's Bas-Lag trilogy (2000–2004).

As *The Day the Earth Stood Still* and *2001* illustrate, science-fiction cinema continues this inflationary bent in those (relatively few) science-fiction films that are allied, in cognitive substance and aesthetic integrity, to the main current of literary science fiction. To be sure, most cinematic productions of the genre tend to degrade the latter through an anti-intellectual obsession with technique and spectacle; and, accordingly, the typical science-fiction movie tends to display a hypertrophy of special effects.[55] Yet something of the inflationary pressure of science fiction—expressed particularly in the visual dimension—can survive even such degradation. Steven Spielberg's *Close Encounters of the Third Kind* (1977), for example, marshals narrative and thematic resources that are nugatory by the standards even of relatively mediocre—let alone the best—literary science fiction. But the visual splendor of Spielberg's Mothership—surely cinema's most artfully designed and compelling space vehicle since *2001* itself—maintains, though in purely spectacular fashion, the properly science-fictional impulse to transcend the mundane and to imply a depth and richness of reality that go beyond any empirical norm. Even when limited by Spielberg's notorious conceptual banality, science fiction does not necessarily cease to insist, or at least to suggest, that we need not and should not settle for the familiar contingencies of everyday existence. The typical lifeworld of science fiction is (to adapt Shakespeare's well-known phrase from *The Tempest*, the play that marks his own nearest approach to science fiction) a brave new world.

Settling for the empirical mundane is, by contrast, precisely what film noir is all about. Like the American hard-boiled detective fiction pioneered by Dashiell Hammett and Raymond Chandler, from which film noir partly derives, noir is not, to be sure, invariably cynical. It does not necessarily insist that human beings are driven only by the basest motives, or that honesty and decency are unattainable. In *Double Indemnity*, for example, Barton Keyes displays even greater acumen and toughness than the gangster anti-heroes like Rico Bandello for which Edward G. Robinson was most famous, while also adhering to a rigorous, if mostly unspoken, code of honor: in a manner strikingly similar, indeed, to that of the ideal detective celebrated in Chandler's influential (and exactly contemporary) manifesto, "The Simple Art of Murder" (1944).

Even so, if noir men (and, more rarely, women) are capable of honor, it is a difficult and rare achievement. In general, the most widely and reliably operative human motives in film noir turn out to be the most obvious, familiar, and selfish ones, mainly greed and lust; and, despite the labyrinthine complexity of many noir plots, the lifeworld of noir is fundamentally simple, usually boiling down to a Hobbesian *bellum omnium contra omnes*, a war of each against each and of all against all. This war leaves a distressingly small margin for human freedom, as people are repeatedly shown to be driven by lust, greed, and other such forces that are all but impossible to resist even when their dangers are at least partly understood. Walter Neff, for example, advances steadily toward his doom in the San Quentin death chamber even while always knowing, at heart, that involvement with Phyllis can lead to nothing but disaster. If not always cynical, noir is deeply pessimistic about human possibility and human happiness in a way that recalls the deflationary determinism of Freud: whose immense popularity in the United States during the heyday of classic noir forms an important part of the intellectual background of the genre. If you are doing as well as Barton Keyes—engaged, functional, decent, truthful, and, if not particularly happy, at least not consumed by crippling misery—then, by noir or by psychoanalytic standards, you are probably doing about as well as human beings can reasonably hope to do. Of the characters in the science-fiction films discussed above, the only one who could be a character in film noir is Tom Stevens. A convenient index of the distance between the two genres is provided by the fact that, in *The Day the Earth Stood Still*, Tom is utterly contemptible, hardly worthy even of living in the same solar system as Klaatu and Professor Barnhardt. In noir he would be no worse than average, and perhaps even a little better.

On the Marxist dialectic

The opposition between the deflationary perspective of noir and the inflationary perspective of science fiction recalls a dialectical tension at the heart of Marxism. For Marxism is both inflationary and deflationary at once. The deflationary dimension is represented by the attempt to destroy all illusions necessary or useful to the preservation of class society in general and of capitalism in particular. Such demystification is perhaps most familiar in the form of ideology-critique, that is, the exposure of those networks of habit and belief that capitalist societies generate and that in turn help to sustain the oppressive practices of capitalism by inhibiting the development of socialist ideas and attitudes. But the demystifying moment of Marxism is not limited to the attack on ideology. It also includes the exposure of those illusions structurally intrinsic to the actual economic mechanisms of the capitalist mode of production. One central instance is the way that the formally free contract between employer and employee conceals the coercive threat of homelessness and starvation that is always, if often implicitly, aimed at those who may consider declining the employer's deal. Another example is the way that the production of surplus-value and the concomitant structure of the wage-relation make it appear that the worker is paid for the entire working day, even though wages compensate the worker for only a fraction of his or her actual labor time. In the spheres of both culture and of political economy, the deflation of capitalist illusions is an indispensable part of the Marxist project.

But Marxism ultimately aims at the positive project of human liberation and self-realization, rather than only at the negative task of destroying capitalism and other forms of class and other oppression. For this reason, the deflationary moment of Marxism, however necessary, can never be sufficient. Marxism is inflationary as well, insisting that, despite the fact that class oppression is nearly coterminous with the history of the human race, it need not always be so. The overthrow of capitalism, for Marxism, need not result merely in the substitution of one ruling class (or ruling elite) for another, as the overthrow of feudalism (or the advent of Stalinism) did. It can instead be the prelude to genuine solidarity, to the radically democratic self-organization of the human race, allowing all individuals the maximum possible fulfillment of their creative potentialities: as mankind leaps, in Engels's well-known words, from the realm of necessity to the realm of freedom.

Even in *Capital*—not only Marx's most important work but also his most elaborately deflationary—Marx provides positive glimpses of the liberated classless future that beckons as a concrete possibility after the supersession of the capitalist property relations that the three volumes of his masterwork expose. In an important passage in Volume Three, for example, Marx defines the socialist freedom that can be attained when capitalism has been overthrown but scarcity not yet eliminated—"that socialized man, the associated producers, govern the human metabolism with nature in a rational way, bringing it under their collective control instead of being dominated by it as a blind power; accomplishing it with the least expenditure of energy and in conditions most worthy and appropriate for their human nature"—and then goes on to offer a briefer hint of the world of achieved communism and material abundance that may lie even further in the future: "[t]he *true* realm of freedom, the development of human powers as an end in itself" (emphasis added).[56] For Marxism, visionary transcendence is the necessary completion of astringent demystification.

Clearly, I am suggesting a certain homology between the two sides of Marxism and the antithetical cinematic genres of film noir and science fiction. But the matter is too complex to allow for any neat quadripartite symmetry. Quantitatively, the work of Marxism is overwhelmingly on the deflationary side; and this deflationary work aims to produce detailed scientific (which means always provisional) knowledge of the real world. To say that such strenuous investigation into the workings of economic, political, and cultural processes is far beyond the ability of film noir is not to condemn the latter but to acknowledge a vast *generic* difference. Patently, *Double Indemnity* is a very different *kind* of achievement from *Capital*. Yet film noir can be understood as producing what the Althusserian tradition might call a figurative analogue of deflationary Marxist knowledge. For example, the typical noir stress on greed is, strictly in itself, a matter of little concern to Marxist historical analysis. The principle, central to Marxist thought, of the ultimately determining role of the economy is a structural and transpersonal category that has no direct or necessary connection to the avarice (or other moral failings) of individuals. But noir representations of individual greed may allegorically *gesture toward*—though they do not actually produce—the kind of knowledge discoverable through conceptual application of Marx's principle of the economy as determinant in the last instance of human affairs. There is an aesthetic and affective link— even though not a fully cognitive one—between, on the one hand, Walter Neff's discovery that Phyllis Dietrichson cared nothing for him and everything for a big insurance claim, and, on the other hand, the analysis (to pick one out of countless examples) that reveals the armed opposition by Britain and France to the invasion of Belgium at the beginning of the First World War to have been based less on human sympathy for a small, violated nation than on the fear that the continued economic exploitation of their own empires might be threatened by German expansionism.

This relationship between film noir and Marxist deflation is not precisely parallel to that between science-fiction cinema and Marxist inflation. For science fiction may provide something more and something richer than a mere analogue of what the inflationary side of Marxism offers. This is partly because this inflationary side is itself fragmentary and impalpable compared to Marxist demystification. It is, after all, impossible to produce the same sort of exacting detailed knowledge about the potential future as about the actual past and present: and so it is that the moments of inflationary positivity in the Marx-Engels oeuvre, while fascinating and important, amount to a series of brief, sometimes ambiguous passages scattered throughout tens of thousands of pages of mainly deflationary scientific analysis. Since, furthermore, the future is strictly unknowable, attempts to comprehend it must be largely speculative. In this way, the cinematic and literary resources of science fiction, involving the development of fictional characters within an imaginary narrative framework, may sometimes be more useful than expository statements. *The Day the Earth Stood Still* cannot *fully* convey what it might feel like to live in the kind of interplanetary co-operative association offered to humanity at film's end. But Klaatu's unsentimental compassion, along with his authoritative and completely uncynical knowledgeability, provides a suggestive clue to the ethos of achieved human solidarity.

It should be stressed that inflationary and deflationary perspectives do not only combine in Marxism but form a genuine dialectic: each animates and concretizes the other. The production of deflationary Marxist knowledge, even at its most technical and recondite, is thoroughly *political*—and even moral—in orientation. Marxism, indeed, works to dismantle the conventional bourgeois dichotomy between fact and value: so that, for instance, Marx's central analytic discovery of the secret of profit in the structure of surplus-value not only provides scientific knowledge of capitalist production but shows the latter to be based on a certain practice that is quite highly charged morally, namely *theft*. Since the ethical unacceptability of practices integral to capitalist (and other class) societies is an inescapable conclusion of Marxist analysis, the latter necessarily implies some positive transcendence of the actual to be mandatory. Conversely, Marxist transcendence must be solidly based on a scientific understanding of the actual. The positive visions of Marxism must be utopian in the Blochian sense of offering some partial but genuine prefiguration of an unalienated classless future, without being utopian in the bad sense that Marx and Engels stigmatized with regard to the "utopian socialists"—whose schemes they criticized for being based on wishful thinking rather than on an accurate understanding of capitalist reality. If the deflationary side of Marxism is necessarily moral and political, the inflationary side is necessarily scientific.

Ultra-noir and utopia: On *Dark City*

Does this dialectic within Marxism have a counterpart in any aesthetic dialectic between science-fiction cinema and film noir? I think that it does, and that the dialectic between noir and science fiction is to be found above all in Alex Proyas's all too neglected masterpiece, *Dark City* (1998).[57] But the interaction of the two genres has a history before Proyas, one that might be traced as far back as Fritz Lang's seminal film, *Metropolis* (1926)—which has exercised a huge influence on *both* science fiction and film noir. Not only is *Metropolis* the first great example of science-fiction cinema, but it is also, though not an actual instance of noir, perhaps the most influential single production of German Expressionism, whose attitudes and techniques were to prove so important for the noir directors (not least Lang himself, who in his Hollywood phase made many noir movies.) Two later films that mix science fiction with noir, and that were clearly made under the influence of Lang's dark, brooding vision of the ominous city, are Jean-Luc Godard's *Alphaville* (1965) and Ridley Scott's *Blade Runner* (1982). Both point directly toward *Dark City*.

Alphaville is probably the first important film to combine noir and science fiction directly; but its method of composition is more that of pastiche than of the dialectic. The film relates how the hard-boiled secret agent Lemmy Caution (Eddie Constantine) travels—by car, wearing a trench coat and carrying an automatic pistol—across millions of miles of outer space to the totalitarian city of Alphaville, which is ruled by a new kind of supercomputer. After various noirish adventures, Lemmy finally assassinates Professor Von Braun (Howard Vernon), Alphaville's top computer scientist, and flees with his new girlfriend, the professor's beautiful daughter Natasha (Anna Karina).

As can be readily gathered even from this quick summary, in *Alphaville* noir and science fiction are not dialectically synthesized but instead (as Dr. Samuel Johnson might have put it) yoked together by violence. The result is a hilariously self-conscious triumph of pastiche, which not only jumbles together motifs from earlier science-fiction cinema and from classic Hollywood noir but also incorporates all manner of other cultural fragments, drawn (for instance) from the Dick Tracy comic strip and the Heckel-and-Jeckel cartoons as well as from such loftier sources as Dante, Shakespeare, Pascal, Baudelaire, and T. S. Eliot. Again and again the film rejoices in the deliberate absurdity of its own juxtapositions. For instance, at the end, as Lemmy and Natasha make their getaway (in a white Ford Galaxy!), Lemmy comments, in properly noirish voice-over, "A night drive across intersidereal space and we'd be home"—as though travel between star systems were like taking a spin on the Los Angeles freeways. The detail that two generations of overearnest science-fiction fans have identified as the film's chief "mistake"—the use of the term *light-year* as a unit of time (and later of computing power) rather than of distance—is of course not really a mistake at all. "Light year" is used as a comically generic signifier of scientificity, one that Godard gleefully pastes together with all the others in his thoroughly postmodern collage.

Blade Runner makes a more genuinely dialectical attempt to meld noir with science fiction.[58] The protagonist Rick Deckard (Harrison Ford) is a typically hard-boiled noir hero—directly modeled, at least in large part, after the Humphrey Bogart characters in *The Maltese Falcon* (John Huston, 1941) and *The Big Sleep* (Howard Hawks, 1946)—and his professional assignment to eliminate several out-of-control androids provides occasion for a series of noirish adventures that suggest a fairly bleak view of human nature and possibility: not least his encounters with two highly sexualized and extremely dangerous android *femmes fatales* played by Joanna Cassidy and Daryl Hannah. It is, however, in its setting in the Los Angeles of 2019 that *Blade Runner* is at its most powerfully deflationary. Scott's city is dark, both chromatically and otherwise, and presents us with an environment that is futuristic and high-tech yet also rainy, decaying, garbage-littered, and lethal. The earth is increasingly inhabited by the dregs of humanity, most of those with the resources to emigrate off-world having done so; and the determinant power of corporate capital and the efficacy of cynical economic motives are growing. Given the exaggeration, through futuristic science-fictional means, of classically deflationary noir motifs, *Blade Runner* might be described as *ultra*-noir.

Yet the dialectical complexity of the film is such that its fusion of science fiction with noir works not only to intensify the latter but also to open up some antithetical inflationary and utopian possibilities. In several particulars—the evidently sincere love, for instance, that the android leader Roy Batty (Rutger Hauer) expresses for the "pleasure model" Pris (Daryl Hannah), or the apparently reciprocated love that the android Rachael (Sean Young) feels for Deckard—the "replicants" (as the film calls them) that Deckard is charged with eliminating seem disturbingly human. Like *Frankenstein* (and, ironically, unlike *Do Androids Dream of Electric Sheep?* [1968], Philip K. Dick's science-fiction novel on which Scott's film is very loosely based), *Blade Runner* thus works to expand the category of humanity itself, suggesting it to be more capacious and less easily defined than common sense would suppose. When Roy Batty utters a dying speech of sublime poetic intensity—a speech that draws upon specifically science-fictional images ("attack ships on fire off the shoulder of Orion") to achieve a Shelleyan visionary force—new possibilities that transcend any simple human/android dichotomy are clearly in sight. This inflationary theme reaches its height in the movie's most hotly debated element, the hint that Deckard himself may be an android.

Dark City clearly owes much to *Blade Runner* (as well as to *Metropolis* directly), but offers, I think, the most thoroughgoing dialectic of noir and science fiction yet achieved. As in *Blade Runner*—but more systematically—an ultra-noir quality is here achieved through science-fictional means. Perhaps no two-word phrase could more strongly suggest the world of noir than "dark city" (which is, indeed, the title of William Dieterle's 1950 film noir starring Charlton Heston); and Proyas's visual depiction of the night-time metropolis with abundant use of shadows and of sharp, diagonal camera angles—techniques that classic noir inherited from German Expressionism—conveys the quintessentially noir sense of alienation, disorientation, and claustrophobic entrapment. Yet here the entrapment is taken to a science-fictional extreme and rendered terrifyingly literal.[59] As the protagonist John Murdoch (Rufus Sewell) and the viewer gradually discover, the dark city is always and everywhere dark. It is both perpetual and completely self-contained, in the sense that no means of urban transport seems capable of taking one beyond the city limits. Indeed, no one can even remember ever actually seeing the daylight. "There is nothing beyond the city," as the strategically named Dr. Daniel Poe Schreber (Kiefer Sutherland) at one point tells Murdoch. The metropolis at night is typically the "world" of classic film noir, but here it is the world in a precisely literal sense. For it eventually transpires that the city is not located anywhere on earth but is an immense starship hurtling through outer space. The scene in which Murdoch and the police detective Frank Bumstead (William Hurt) break through a brick wall and find the starry vastness of space on the other side is a narrative and visual masterstroke: at once utterly surprising and yet suddenly making sense of so much that had been mysterious in the film to that point.

Science-fictional means achieve a similarly ultra-noir effect in the film's presentation of human character. If the typical noir protagonist is a man driven by transpersonal forces like greed and lust, and equipped with only a limited grasp of his own motivations and an even more limited ability to determine his own fate, Murdoch is that protagonist raised to a higher power. As the film opens, Murdoch finds himself without memories—for memory is, of course, the indispensable pre-condition for human will or freedom—and wanted by the police in connection with a series of sadistic sex-murders about which he knows nothing. He also finds himself involved in a troubled marriage with a woman who claims to be his adulterous wife (Jennifer Connelly) but whom he cannot recognize. The explanation turns out to be that the city is under the control of a weird cabal of alien beings known as the Strangers, who are conducting experiments on the inhabitants in an attempt to learn about the human soul. The Strangers are constantly wiping out the memories of their captives and replacing them with new memories, so that they can observe how humans behave in a variety of circumstances. The deflationary determinism of noir is thus rendered technological and, indeed, apparently irresistible. It is noteworthy that the Strangers' programming (or "imprinting," as the Strangers themselves call it) of their human subjects is achieved with old-fashioned hypodermic syringes that are frighteningly large and look extremely painful. Though the archaic hardware does not seem entirely coherent, logically, with the advanced technical achievements of the Strangers (who can travel through outer space and also "tune," i.e., shape the material world by thought alone), the hypos serve a vital cinematic function as visual signifiers of the Strangers' brutal and oppressive rule.

As an ultra-noir production, then, *Dark City* is deflationary and deterministic in ways that allegorize aspects of both Freudian and Marxist materialism. A psychoanalytic note is explicitly sounded by Dr. Schreber's name, which combines the subject of one of Freud's most important case-histories with the American author who made groundbreaking contributions to science fiction, crime fiction, and horror fiction. Moreover, the way that the humans of the city are controlled by fluids directly injected into their heads recalls the psychoanalytic determinism that Freud himself always believed would eventually be grounded in the chemistry and biology of the brain. Similarly, the relation between the humans and the Strangers in the dark city provides a quasi-Marxist figure of class oppression. Indeed, the Strangers—with their unruffled sense of absolute superiority, their accents of icy and affectless detachment vis-à-vis their human captives, and their total lack of moral scruple when it comes to manipulating those under their control—amount to a brilliant satiric caricature (or perhaps a thoroughly realistic depiction) of a ruling class. The most memorable of the Strangers is their evident leader, Mr. Book, played by Ian Richardson. It is noteworthy that Richardson borrows heavily for his performance from one of his own finest roles, his then-recent portrayal of Francis Urquhart, the monstrously reactionary and repressive Tory prime minister in the *House of Cards* trilogy of three BBC television miniseries (1990–1995).

Yet *Dark City* as a science-fiction film not only raises film noir to a higher power but also—again as with *Blade Runner*, though again with greater emphasis and rigor—dialectically produces a powerfully inflationary and utopian theme that is the very antithesis of noir. For much of the film, it appears that a utopian alternative to noir actuality may be provided by Shell Beach, a seaside resort that Murdoch remembers as home. It is visually the opposite of the dark city—bright, sunny, and colorful rather than shadowy and monochromatic—and characters besides Murdoch recall it as a place of happiness and pleasure. A taxi driver, for example, remembers Shell Beach as the spot where he and his wife spent their honeymoon, and he thinks he knows right where it is. But, when pressed by Murdoch to describe *exactly* how to drive there, he finds he cannot. It turns out that nobody knows how to get to Shell Beach—for example, the place is clearly marked on a subway map of the city, but it is impossible to find a train that actually goes there—and that its utopian promise is as illusory as Marx and Engels maintained the schemes of the utopian socialists to be. For the memories of Shell Beach are false memories: not only in the narrative and diegetic sense that they have been imprinted on the humans by the Strangers, but also in the larger philosophic sense that no object of mere nostalgia can possess the strongest sort of utopian value. Utopia, as Ernst Bloch insisted, is necessarily geared to the future. It is no accident that the visual details of Shell Beach (displayed on postcards and the like) suggest a vacation resort of the American 1950s: which is not only the decade when someone of Murdoch's age in 1998 would have been a child but also the privileged image of social harmony for reactionary American ideology since the late 1960s. Such mere regression cannot provide escape from the dark city.

What does offer escape—or rather inflationary transcendence—is transformative human labor and action. "The only place home exists is in your head," as the always shrewd if sometimes traitorous Dr. Schreber tells Murdoch at one point. Perhaps more than he himself quite understands, Schreber's words point to the impeccably Marxist-Blochian principle that home—"homeland" (*Heimat*), as Bloch himself puts it—can never be merely *recovered* but must be attained through the revolutionary work of social transformation that, as Marx himself insisted, necessarily begins in the human intellect and imagination. *Dark City* ultimately offers a figure of precisely such revolutionary transformation. About two-thirds of the way through the film, Murdoch, Bumstead, and Schreber finally establish some bonds of human solidarity. Bumstead ceases to regard Murdoch primarily as a murder suspect, and Schreber ends his traitorous collaboration with the Strangers. Together, the three rebel against the Strangers' oppressive rule. Aided by Schreber's inside knowledge of the Strangers and, even more, by Murdoch's ability to "tune"—a talent that the Strangers had been confident was reserved exclusively to themselves—the humans prevail. Human freedom is possible after all, and the determining power of the ruling class, which had seemed unassailable, is broken.

Dark City is thus, finally, and despite its noir or ultra-noir deflationary aspect, a work in the great inflationary tradition of Blake's *The Marriage of Heaven and Hell*, Shelley's *Prometheus Unbound*, and Beethoven's *Fidelio*: a story of fetters broken and freedom attained. This upward narrative curve can be traced even in the film's most technical details. Proyas constructs the earlier part of his movie mainly through an accumulation of discrete shots, with little tracking or panning: and the effect is one of stasis, entrapment, and determinism. But, as the humans assert themselves and move against the Strangers' tyranny, the cameras begin to move as well, and a contrasting effect of progressive flow is achieved. Speaking for humanity, Murdoch—who all along has been a kind of ordinary Everyman—announces his ability to "make this world anything I want it to be": and he suits his actions to his words. He succeeds in "tuning" an entire ocean, water being both the indispensable basis of human life and the substance to which the Strangers have the greatest aversion. The film ends in a gloriously bright and colorful oceanside scene that is as far from the visual style of noir as possible. The tableau recalls the pictures we have seen of Shell Beach. Yet the film is careful not to *identify* the two. Shell Beach was a mere regressive wish, but this is the real thing, the real product of human thought and action. We leave Murdoch to begin a love relationship with the Jennifer Connelly character, no longer burdened with the false memories of having been Murdoch's cheating wife. It is the sort of visionary, material transcendence that has always been what science fiction does best—and that has always, at least since the final lines of *The Communist Manifesto* (1848), also been the ultimate point of Marxism itself.

Noir, neo-noir, and the end of work: From *Double Indemnity* to *Body Heat*

Labor and business in *Double Indemnity*

B illy Wilder's *Double Indemnity* (1944) is among the earliest major instances of film noir, and it has long been among the most popular and successful as well: "the greatest movie ever made," in Woody Allen's hyperbolic formulation quoted above. Though the genre is too varied and complex for any particular film to be completely typical, it would be difficult, as I have already suggested, to name another that comes closer to providing a paradigm for noir. The three major characters, all sharply drawn and all superbly acted, are as integral to noir as any types one could name. There is the insurance salesman Walter Neff (Fred MacMurray): the type of the ordinary and reasonably genial Everyman, who is not intrinsically evil but who is led by lust, greed, weakness, and gullibility to commit an evil act that results in his own destruction. There is the bored housewife Phyllis Dietrichson (Barbara Stanwyck): the type of the dangerous (and often, as here, ice-blonde) seductress whose sexual irresistibility is counter-pointed by her absolute lack of honor, conscience, or emotional warmth. And there is the insurance investigator Barton Keyes (Edward G. Robinson): the type of the smart hard-boiled detective who moves with toughness and savvy through an amoral world while maintaining a personal code of honesty and compassion that he tries to camouflage beneath a gruff manner.[60]

The plot is relatively simple. Walter and Phyllis conspire to murder her rich, unsympathetic husband (Tom Powers) so that they can share both the pay-off from a large accident-insurance policy and (as far as Walter is concerned) the pleasures of romance with one another. It superficially seems like the perfect crime—and Walter's inside knowledge of the insurance business is crucial to making it work—but the whole thing soon falls apart, as Walter himself, with his better judgment, has always foreseen that it would. After one or two false starts, Keyes begins to solve the crime with remarkable speed; and so the noose starts to tighten around Phyllis and Walter. Meanwhile, Phyllis's cold nature and cynical motives become increasingly apparent to Walter, and the burning passion he felt for her cools. At the end, Phyllis lies dead in her mansion, shot by Walter, while he, shot by her, lies seriously wounded at the insurance company for which he works, waiting for the ambulance to provide the medical care that will restore him sufficiently to allow him to walk unaided into the San Quentin gas chamber.[61] Keyes, who normally takes great gusto in cracking a case, is left to survey the scene with unspeakable sadness. The fact that Walter's confession provides him with the final few details of the crime that he was unable to deduce for himself hardly compensates Keyes for the loss of the man who has been his best friend as well as his business associate. Throughout the film, Walter has been helping to light Keyes's cigars, but now, as the incapacitated Walter lies bleeding on the office floor, Keyes lights a cigarette for him. The film's final lines are almost unbearably significant:

Walter Neff: Know why you couldn't figure this one, Keyes? I'll tell you. 'Cause the guy you were looking for was too close. Right across the desk from you.
Barton Keyes: Closer than that, Walter.
Walter Neff: I love you, too.

Though Wilder made many romantic comedies (and co-authored all the screenplays), this is, I believe, the only film where the words *I love you* are uttered with full intent by any Wilder character.

My point, however, is not only that Walter's jocular but totally sincere expression of affection for Keyes—uttered here not for the first time in *Double Indemnity*—gives unusually explicit voice to the homoerotic feeling that many critics have noted to be characteristic of film noir. To be sure, Wilder's movie precisely fulfills the familiar noir pattern whereby the solid reliability of masculine friendship is contrasted with the dangers and unpredictability of heterosexual dalliance. *Double Indemnity* even places considerable stress on the lifelong bachelorhood of the early-middle-aged Walter and the late-middle-aged Keyes; and both are doing just fine until Walter, while always at heart knowing better, allows himself to fall for the delicious but poisonous feminine charms of Phyllis.

At least as important as the homoeroticism itself, however, is the fact that Walter and Keyes are not just men together but *co-workers* and business associates. It is no accident that the movie's final scene, where the mutual affection between the two is most overt, should take place (like the first substantial scene and many scenes thereafter) at the Los Angeles headquarters of the Pacific All Risk Insurance Company. For a shared participation in and loyalty to the firm has always provided not only the institutional context for the personal friendship but a good deal of its affective content as well. If there is something quasi-sexual between the two men, then the equivalent of a proposition or a marriage proposal comes when Keyes suggests that Walter is "too good" to remain a salesman and should instead become Keyes's own assistant in the claims department (an offer that Walter coyly declines). In a sense, indeed, Walter's worst sin is not so much the murder of both Dietrichsons—for the viewer cannot feel very sorry for either—as the betrayal of the company to which he and, even more, Keyes have devoted their lives.

I do not mean that Wilder himself particularly endorses corporate loyalty as an ethical ideal. The Austrian-born and -raised director is in many ways a late follower of German Expressionism; and, while never positively socialist, he tends to be skeptical of capitalist values. But he also understands the capitalist transformation and exploitation of labor to be a fact of enormous affective as well as economic weight. Wilder's most frequent shot is of rows of identical desks in a large corporate building. Variants occur not only at the Pacific All Risk but also at the headquarters of the New York insurance company in *The Apartment* (1960) and at the Berlin headquarters of Coca-Cola in *One Two Three* (1961). In each case, the shot is neo-Expressionist in tone (the Berlin setting of *One Two Three* has important political and aesthetic resonances), and suggests the alienating power of capitalism that renders the company big and the human beings who work there relatively small. But, as Wilder implicitly insists, such alienation is, after all, the ground of our psychic being as subjects of capitalist society. In all three films, the actions and emotional lives of the characters are inseparable from their involvement with the companies that employ them. It is worth noting that if most of Wilder's romantic comedies have always seemed insufficiently romantic to many tender-minded viewers, it is because Wilder is nearly always honest enough to insist that love is not really separable from labor and money. Perhaps money can't buy you love, but love is most assuredly *not* all you need. Most people also need a job, and everyone needs hard cash. Even in a comparatively minor Wilder film like *The Fortune Cookie* (1966), a man's yearning for the wife who left him cannot be addressed without insurance fraud and the practice of personal-injury law; and here the results of insurance fraud are less catastrophic than in *Double Indemnity*, but not painless or purely comic either.

Wilder also sees, however, that the reification of labor under capitalism does not necessarily preclude a dialectically antithetical utopian dimension that the film locates in the justified pride of the craftsman. Walter Neff and Barton Keyes are not just employees of the Pacific All Risk, but unusually talented employees, who take great pride and satisfaction in their work. Walter is consistently the firm's top salesman, and, when Keyes tries to bring him into the investigative side of the business, he insists, "*Nobody's* too good to be a salesman". Keyes himself seems to be virtually a legend in his field: "the best claim man on the Coast," as he is called in James M. Cain's 1936 novel on which the film is based.[62] The screenplay that Wilder co-authored with Raymond Chandler discards this particular line. But it expands Keyes's role and highlights his investigative genius even more emphatically than Cain's novel does. It makes clear, for instance, that the fearlessness with which Keyes can show elaborate disrespect for Mr. Norton (Richard Gaines), the company's imbecilic young president, is based on his being that rare employee whose superlative talent and value to the firm render him immune to the terrors of the pink slip. The hard-boiled detective fiction that (as the names of Cain and Chandler remind us) is so consequential for so much film noir leaves its greatest impact on *Double Indemnity* in the film's upholding of the ethic and pride of the jobholder. It is significant that the confession which Walter leaves for Keyes on wax recording cylinders is explicitly designated by him an "office memorandum". Even the title (inherited from Cain) ratifies the movie's insistent stress on work and enterprise. There are surely not many films that are called by an arcane technical term from the insurance (or any other) business.

From noir to neo-noir: The effacing of work in *Body Heat*

To some degree, Lawrence Kasdan might appear an appropriate candidate to have remade *Double Indemnity*. For Kasdan, like Wilder before him, is a versatile, commercially proficient screenwriter-director, with a string of hits in various genres. But the comparison is superficial. Wilder, though always commercial in intention and usually in success as well, is also one of the true artistic giants of Hollywood cinema: the maker not only of *Double Indemnity* but also of other classic masterpieces that followed, such as *Sunset Boulevard* (1950) and *Some Like It Hot* (1959)—not to mention lesser but still excellent films like *The Lost Weekend* (1945), *Stalag-17* (1953), *Witness for the Prosecution* (1957), *The Apartment*, and *One Two Three*, as well as later and to this day much underrated aesthetic (if not popular) triumphs like *The Private Life of Sherlock Holmes* (1970) and *The Front Page* (1974).

Kasdan, by contrast, is seldom more than a competent hack with an undeniable flair for box office. He is best known for such shallow "feel-good" schlock as *The Big Chill* (1983), *The Accidental Tourist* (1988), and *Grand Canyon* (1991). He has a pronounced imitative bent, which has not, in general, served him well artistically. *The Big Chill*, for example (whose very title, connoting death, is a shameless imitation of Chandler's *The Big Sleep* [1939]), is a not-quite-actionable plagiarism of John Sayles's pathbreaking *Return of the Secaucus 7* (1980)—and one, moreover, that manages to eliminate nearly every thoughtful or vital element in Sayles's movie. *Silverado* (1985) is a lifeless confection of Western motifs culled from dozens of earlier and mostly better movies. Kasdan's *Wyatt Earp* (1994), though surely the most ambitious film ever made about that classic American hero, is hopelessly clumsy and dull compared to such much superior precursor-films as John Ford's *My Darling Clementine* (1946) or John Sturges's *Gunfight at the O.K. Corral* (1957).

Yet in *Body Heat* (1981), his first film as a director, Kasdan manages to craft a masterpiece that, if hardly the equal of *Double Indemnity*, is nonetheless not unworthy of comparison with its great predecessor. Far from merely copying his betters like Sayles or Ford, Kasdan here establishes a genuinely *revisionary* relationship with Wilder in something like the strict Bloomian sense. In other words, the interest of *Body Heat* lies not only in the ways that Kasdan follows Wilder but, even more, in the ways that he swerves from the earlier director. Since it thus both accepts and radically modifies the patterns established by one of the major noir classics, *Body Heat* may be considered among the most purely and precisely *neo*-noir of all films.[63]

The storyline of *Body Heat* follows the basic trajectory of *Double Indemnity*, but with certain elements of the earlier film accentuated and certain others effaced. "I killed him for money, and for a woman," as Walter Neff confesses near the beginning of Wilder's film. "And I didn't get the money, and I didn't get the woman". Ned Racine (William Hurt), Kasdan's hapless protagonist, could repeat these sentences word for word. Ned, though like Walter not irredeemably evil, is even greedier, weaker, more lustful, and more gullible; and he falls even harder for Matty Walker (Kathleen Turner) than Walter falls for Phyllis. Matty herself is even more ravishingly beautiful than her counterpart (or, at least, the collapse of Hollywood's Production Code Administration between 1944 and 1981 allows the viewer to see a great deal more of Turner's beauty than of Stanwyck's). Amazingly, she manages to be even more cynical and ruthless as well. Her husband, likewise, is even more repellent than his predecessor. Whereas Tom Powers's Dietrichson is merely grumpy, tight-fisted, and self-absorbed, Richard Crenna skillfully plays the smooth, smiling Edmund Walker as having more than a hint of the genuinely evil about him.[64] One difference between the two films is the absence, in Kasdan's, of any character who fully corresponds to Barton Keyes—an important matter to which we will return. Another difference is that *Body Heat*, unlike *Double Indemnity*, does not end in death. Ned winds up in prison—evidently serving a life sentence for the first-degree murder of Edmund— while Matty gets away scot-free with the entirety of Edmund's large estate. In the movie's final scene, she is sunbathing on the beach in some unidentified tropical paradise. (The scene, with mountains in the background, looks as though it could be in Hawaii; but Matty is presumably shrewd enough to appreciate the wisdom of being farther removed from US law enforcement authorities.)

In the best-known critical contrast between the two films, Fredric Jameson celebrates *Body Heat* as a "postmodern" artifact in which the sense of temporality or historicity is self-consciously blurred.[65] *Double Indemnity* represents, in a comparatively straightforward way, the America of the 1930s (for Wilder maintains the prewar setting of Cain's 1936 novel, explicitly dating the action in 1938). But, says Jameson, the apparent 1981 "present" of Kasdan's film is compromised not only by the way that *Body Heat* self-consciously evokes its precursor—so that the spirit of the '30s maintains a ghostly presence in the later film—but also, and more ingeniously, by the ways that Kasdan's script and cameras manage to avoid any reference or image that would date the movie too precisely. This is a shrewd observation, and Jameson might have gone on to note that at some points the chronological signs in *Body Heat* are not just indeterminate but positively confusing. Perhaps the best example is the sequence in which Ned and Matty, during their adulterous transports in the Walkers' Florida mansion, must struggle against the brutal summer heat. Kasdan merely ignores the obvious fact that, at any time even vaguely around 1981, no Florida home of remotely comparable affluence would be without air conditioning.

But Jameson himself ignores the most important aspect of the relative ahistoricity in *Body Heat*: namely, the way that, as we will see, the film's weakened sense of history helps to make possible Kasdan's determined erasure of the whole problematic of labor, business, and economic activity that is so important for *Double Indemnity*. In the later film, there is nothing at all that corresponds to the Pacific All Risk Insurance Company, which in a certain sense might almost be considered the dominant "character" of the earlier film. Ned is an attorney, a small-town solo practitioner; and, whereas Walter Neff is an excellent salesman, Ned is a miserably incompetent lawyer—a point established in an early courtroom scene and later ratified by a key plot twist that depends on Ned's proven inability to accomplish so elementary a legal task as writing a valid will. But then, Ned—again emphatically unlike Walter—dislikes his job anyway. In an interesting exchange between Ned and Edmund over an apparently friendly dinner (where, however, the sense of unspoken tension and menace is unmistakable), the film considers the whole matter of work only to dismiss it.

Ned Racine: I don't like it [practicing law] much. [*to Matty:*] Call me Ned, will you?
Edmund Walker: What's to like? That's the way of the world. Most people despise their jobs.
Ned Racine: Do you?
Edmund Walker: No. No, I love it. But it's not a job.
Ned Racine: What is it exactly?

Edmund replies vaguely, but "it" turns out to be a large, shady network of financial and real-estate investments in which Edmund, it appears, serves as a front man for organized crime: something that, for Edmund and for the film, is decisively removed from the world of ordinary labor. Again the contrast is sharp with *Double Indemnity*, in which Dietrichson, straightforwardly enough, works (like the co-screenwriter Raymond Chandler during one period of his life) at a white-collar job in the oil industry.

Kasdan's retreat from the world of labor is perhaps most markedly displayed by the absence in the film of any character truly comparable to Edward G. Robinson's Barton Keyes, in whose personality the importance of work is most emphatically highlighted. One might argue, however, that the Keyes figure is not exactly eliminated in *Body Heat*, but merely split into two: that is, into the prosecuting attorney Peter Lowenstein (Ted Danson) and the police detective Oscar Grace (J. A. Preston). These men do indeed appear to be Ned's best friends, and the film stresses both the personal bond of friendship and the latter's homoerotic connotations. Lowenstein, for example, likes to prance around, at least when with Ned, in a stereotypically effeminate way, and at one point jokes that, though married, he derives his sexual pleasure mainly from listening to the stories of Ned's own conquests.[66] But, in contrast to Keyes, Lowenstein and Oscar are not Ned's actual colleagues—even though all three are, very broadly speaking, in much the same line of work—and the amount of attention that the film devotes to their professional labor is reduced to the absolute minimum needed for plot coherence. The one exception is a brief montage, entirely without dialogue, that shows Oscar going here and there, doing his work of detecting; in this sequence we can glimpse (barely) the ghost of the police procedural that *Body Heat* otherwise so carefully avoids being. Yet even this exception is not really so very exceptional. For Lowenstein informs Ned (and the viewer) that Oscar's unusually strenuous efforts are motivated not so much by the pride of the craftsman or the honor of the jobholder as by the more strictly personal desire to find evidence that may exculpate his good friend Ned in the case of Edmund Walker's murder.

The thing that mainly fills the space left vacant in *Body Heat* by the relative absence of work is—logically enough—leisure. Since Ned is an untalented lawyer who dislikes the practice of law, it is unsurprising that he seems to spend as much time as possible doing other things. Kasdan's cameras rarely find Ned attending to professional chores, but—even apart from his sexual trysts with Matty—again and again show him engaged in various leisure-time activities: driving around in his red convertible, having a drink in a bar, listening to a band at an outdoor concert, walking or jogging down the beach, enjoying some food in a restaurant, and enjoying some carnal pleasures with attractive, anonymous young women (anonymous, that is, for the film and, one suspects, for Ned too). It seems clear that he plans to use the fortune he expects to acquire from Edmund's death not in order to help improve his position within the legal profession but in order to abandon work altogether and thereafter to spend all his time, as it were, on vacation. Work is for Ned essentially a nuisance, a nuisance financially necessary but, he hopes, only temporarily so; and this hope, no less than his passion for Matty, drives him to commit murder. Once again the contrast with *Double Indemnity* is clear: for Walter's turn to crime springs partly from impulses that grow out of his *fascination* with his job. He has worked so long and so hard at trying to prevent fraud from being perpetrated against the Pacific All Risk that he eventually comes to wonder whether he could not work the opposite way and perpetrate the perfect fraud himself. In his confession, he makes clear that this rather technical interest in outwitting the system is a longer-standing motive than his lust for Phyllis or his greed for the big money.

The relative occlusion of work in *Body Heat* is related to the film's generic composition. Not only quintessentially neo-noir, it also belongs to a genre that, owing to the Production Code, did not and could not exist in commercial Hollywood cinema when Wilder (whose struggles with the Code are legendary) made *Double Indemnity*: namely, the sex film (or "soft-core porn" film), whose interest inheres largely in the opportunity to gaze at beautiful unclothed bodies, especially when engaged in sexual activity. Kasdan's film made Kathleen Turner a star practically overnight, and her spectacular face and figure were hardly less important for her stardom than her fine dramatic performance. William Hurt was already something of a star, but *Body Heat* greatly enhanced his stature; and his own amply displayed physical charms were in no small part responsible. Of course, it might be argued that the generic tendency of the sex film in *Body Heat* is itself thoroughly neo-noirish, in that it merely actualizes certain potentialities always present in classic noir but thwarted by Code censorship. After all, sexual themes are prominent in noir from the beginning, and no motif is more common than the gorgeous *femme fatale* like Phyllis Dietrichson. There is some truth to this idea, but the matter is also more complex.

Whether, if permitted by the censors, Wilder and the other makers of classic noir "would have" filmed such sumptuous sex scenes as Kasdan offers with Turner and Hurt is finally, like all other counter-historical questions, a moot point. The facts of the matter are that such scenes were impossible during the main cycle of noir, and that this comparative visual chasteness leaves considerable cinematic space for the concern with work and professional activity that is so particularly strong in *Double Indemnity*—but that is also fairly common throughout much other classic noir. Outstanding examples include a founding text like John Huston's *The Maltese Falcon* (1941), which hinges on the skill, standards, and professional code of honor that Sam Spade (Humphrey Bogart) displays as a private detective; Abraham Polonsky's *Force of Evil* (1948), which focuses on the shadowy terrain where the financial-services industry and organized crime merge; Nicholas Ray's *In a Lonely Place* (1950), in which the profession of the Hollywood screenwriter Dixon Steele (again, Humphrey Bogart) is crucial to the narrative in several different ways; and a late instance like Don Siegel's *The Killers* (1964), which treats contract killing as an occupation and career much like any other. When, however, Kasdan combines neo-noir with the sex film, offering up generous visual servings of spectacular lovemaking, the effect is to help repress the properly noirish concern with work and to introduce the alternative problematic of leisure—the dominance of which makes *Body Heat* contrast so strongly, as we have seen, with its precursor-film. For sex, as Ned Racine would probably agree, might be considered the ultimate leisure-time activity: both in the sense that sex (except when expressly motivated by the will to propagate) typically strives toward no practical goal beyond itself, no *telos* save for pleasure and love, and also in the sense that to savor the sort of expansive, unhurried lovemaking represented in *Body Heat* it greatly helps to have an economic position or routine that allows for a good deal of free time.

The valorization of leisure is thus virtually built into the sex film. This point can be usefully illustrated by contrasting Kasdan's movie with another major film of the 1980s, that neglected Brechtian masterpiece of American Marxist-feminist cinema, Lizzie Borden's *Working Girls* (1987). In a sense, this film, set in an upscale brothel, is about nothing *but* sex. The actresses (if not the actors) are uniformly quite attractive, and a considerable amount of bare skin and sexual action is on view. Yet *Working Girls* is by no means a sex film, and its pornographic value—its capacity to stimulate erotic desire—is almost nil. The reason is quite simply that here sex is *not* a leisure activity. Sex here is, precisely, *work*, at least for the prostitutes from whose viewpoint the film is constructed. Probably the most memorable single line of dialogue in *Working Girls* is the (almost-)parting shot that the protagonist, the Yale-educated lesbian hooker Molly (Louise Smith), delivers to her exploitative madam and boss (Ellen McElduff): "Lucy, have you ever heard of surplus-value?" Perhaps Lucy has, for she was once a working girl herself. But it is certain that *Body Heat* has never heard of surplus-value. How could it? Just as Ned aspires to be, the film is on vacation nearly the whole time.

The ring of FIRE

This vacation ethos that Kasdan's film shares with its protagonist is inseparable from the film's own "vacation" from history that Jameson identifies. In order more fully to understand the representation of work, leisure, and history in *Body Heat*, it is, however, necessary to historicize the film itself, especially vis-à-vis *Double Indemnity*. One might be tempted here to suggest a typically Jamesonian aesthetic periodization, for instance the "modernism" of classic noir as against the "postmodernism" of neo-noir. But a more concrete and useful way of exploring the terrain is to consider the earlier and the later films in relation to what remains the defining and bifurcating event of twentieth-century American (and not only American) culture and economy—namely, the Second World War—and also with regard to the later vicissitudes of postwar economic development.

As Walter Neff conveniently illustrates, *Double Indemnity* represents a world in which men still wear hats in public and in which a man might appropriately be dressed in a white shirt and a dark tie even while hurling a bowling ball down a lane. This small point of fashion neatly encapsulates the prewar big-city America of "real" (masculine) work, a world that today may be nostalgically viewed as more "authentic" than its postwar successor. It was a world in which the United States still enjoyed a predominantly manufacturing economy rather than the predominantly service economy that was to follow, a world where the "genuineness" of (largely) urban production had not yet yielded, on the balance sheets or in public consciousness, to the suburban and ex-urban preoccupation with consumption. While representing this world, however, Wilder's film also suggests its imminent decline. It is significant (even beyond the mere functioning of plot mechanics) that the business where the work ethic of Walter Neff and Barton Keyes features so prominently is not a traditional industrial or manufacturing firm but an *insurance* company, that is, an economic entity whose output is only ambiguously (or, arguably, not at all) productive in the strict Marxist sense. The postwar world in which the manipulation of FIRE (finance, insurance, and real estate) increasingly trumps the production of tangible things—the very world through which Edmund Walker moves so expertly—is thus already prefigured.

Furthermore, *Double Indemnity* is concerned, after all, not only with insurance but with insurance *fraud*. Indeed, the film stresses that such fraud is more-or-less routine—and not *only* to be found in such elaborately malevolent conspiracies as Walter and Phyllis's murder plot—by introducing the audience to Barton Keyes in a scene that shows us a much pettier instance of the same thing. The evidently penniless Sam Garlopis (Fortunio Bonanova), whose truck has been destroyed by fire, sits in Keyes's office, angrily demanding that all he wants is his money, that is, his claim on a car-insurance policy. Keyes, of course, is way ahead of him, and, having determined that Garlopis set the fire himself, replies that all Garlopis is going to get is the cops. But Keyes, though always tough, is never cruel. Having defeated the hapless policy-holder in the battle of wills, he does not actually call the police, but only insists that Garlopis sign a waiver on his claim before going on his way—after which Keyes rants to Walter for a while about the lunacy of selling insurance to such a man in the first place.

This emphasis on fraud figuratively suggests a certain instability in American capitalism, a surrounding climate of economic anxiety that is psychologically concretized, for instance, by the way that the threat of false claims is always disrupting Keyes's digestion and his sleep. Such anxiety and instability are, of course, precisely what one would expect to find in a film set during the Great Depression, from which the United States was just emerging when Wilder's movie was made. *Double Indemnity* is, in fact, a Depression film: not in the overwhelming and social-realist way typified by John Ford's somewhat earlier *The Grapes of Wrath* (1940), but not quite so subtly that this aspect of the film should have been overlooked to the degree that it seems to have been. True enough, the major characters are largely shielded from the worst ravages of contemporary capitalist upheaval: Walter and Keyes because they happen to hold jobs at which they are brilliantly accomplished and hence of great value to their employer, and the Dietrichsons because they are rich. Yet even the Dietrichsons are not completely insulated from the general economic anarchy. When Walter first drives up to their mansion, he is impressed, but guesses that the owner may well be having trouble paying for it; and, surely enough, we learn from Phyllis shortly thereafter that her husband is having serious cash-flow problems (which is why she prefers insurance fraud to simply killing Mr. Dietrichson for his estate). Much more typical of the general American lot than the wealthy Dietrichsons are certain of the film's minor characters, who serve to provide some socio-economic background: Sam Garlopis himself, for instance, who looks extremely unprosperous and who must, presumably, be in pretty desperate financial straits to try his hand at arson; or the irritable but relatively honest Nino Zachetti (Byron Barr), whose medical education has evidently been derailed at least in part by his inability to pay for it.

Double Indemnity, then, possesses a very fine sense of its own historical moment. Made during the Second World War, it represents the world of the "classic" prewar manufacture-based capitalism being thrown into such awful turbulence by the Great Depression, while also—in the choice of the insurance business as its own thematic focus—subtly and presciently looking ahead to the FIRE- and service-based capitalism that was to become increasingly important and eventually dominant after the war. Indeed, the keen historical self-awareness that the film displays is surely enabled, in large part, by its chronological location on the temporal cusp, so to speak, that the year 1944 amounts to. Though all times are of course times of transition, 1944—the year, it should be remembered, that saw the establishment of the Bretton Woods international monetary system that so crucially helped to stabilize postwar capitalism for a quarter century—remains as far-reachingly transitional a date in modern American history as any that one could easily name.

1981 is a very different historical moment. By the time that *Body Heat* hits the screens, the de-industrialization of the United States is well underway, and the nation's traditional manufacturing base is being increasingly ravaged by domestic undercapitalization and by the concomitant export of manufacturing jobs overseas and south of the border. Indeed, this process is just about to intensify yet further, as the newly elected Reagan Administration prepares a massive re-orientation of American tax, fiscal, and monetary policy to the greater glory of the bond market and the greater immiseration of labor (using the latter term in its precise Marxist sense, i.e., to refer *not* necessarily to "misery" in any colloquial or absolute sense but to a widening discrepancy in the standard of material consumption between those who produce surplus-value and those who extract it). The "long down-turn" in the US domestic economy can, of course, be traced back to the end of the spectacular postwar boom than ran aground by the late 1960s or early 1970s. Nixon's 1971 abrogation of the Bretton Woods agreement is often taken as a convenient temporal marker.[67] But, by the early 1980s, the ominous decline of the domestic American economy (for most Americans other than those in a position to enjoy the profits from FIRE and from certain large, low-waged service industries) had widely penetrated mass consciousness. In much popular imagination it was typified, for example, by the alarming crisis that had struck the US auto industry. During the postwar boom, Detroit had been home to America's signature manufacturing enterprise, a branch of industry in which the global dominance of the United States had seemed invulnerable. But now domestic auto-making was in a panic caused largely by grimly efficient competition from Japan. It might be added that, when *Body Heat* appeared, America's terrible economic malaise had recently been aggravated by the political and moral humiliations of the Iranian hostage crisis that began in 1979.

We are now in a position, then, to articulate the *fundamental* contrast between Wilder's film and Kasdan's—and to see that this contrast is a function not only of the strictly generic shift from classic noir to neo-noir but also, and relatedly, of the passage from one moment to another in the history of American capitalism. At the moment of *Double Indemnity*, history, despite the ravages of the Depression and the uncertainties of wartime, is still going *with* the United States: so that it is no surprise to find this American film possessing such a keen sense of its own position in the march of time. The American work ethic is alive and well, and work can be amply and properly rewarded. Despite the film's tragic ending for Walter and Phyllis—and, indirectly, for Keyes—there remains an underlying optimism condensed in the fact that the ending is in fact perfectly *happy* for the movie's largest "character," the Pacific All Risk Insurance Company. Such optimism seems well founded. It is reasonable to suppose that, in the parallel universe where the Pacific All Risk actually exists, the firm went on to grow mightily during the postwar boom and, even after the boom collapsed—by 1981, say—was continuing, as a member of the charmed ring of FIRE, to rake in profits that would have astounded the late Mr. Keyes and that even the ineptitude of the aging Mr. Norton could not spoil.

For most Americans, however, history is clearly going *against* their country by 1981; and *Body Heat* responds by turning its back on history. This is the deep logic of the deliberate "postmodern" fuzziness that the film adopts with relation to its own temporal setting. Since it is ultimately nothing other than human labor that makes human history, the retreat from history is at one with the larger retreat from work itself. In a society in which the ability to create actual wealth is steeply declining in relation to the manipulation of the paper profits of FIRE, labor becomes an increasingly uncongenial and marginal topic. Edmund Walker is, in a way, perfectly right to say that what he does in order to get money is "not a job". Wholly engaged, it seems, on the wilder illegal shores of FIRE, he does not hold a job in any sense that a traditional factory worker—or Sam Garlopis or Walter Neff or Barton Keyes—would understand the term.

What mainly distinguishes Matty and Ned from Edmund in this context is that, whereas Edmund's entrepreneurial intelligence appears to be razor-sharp, Matty's only conspicuous talent is for heartless seduction and murderous scheming; and poor Ned does not seem to possess any real talents at all. Both yearn only for leisure. Matty achieves it. The final shot of her on a sun-drenched beach is as pure and emphatic an image of leisure as a filmmaker could offer. Ned, less happily, winds up in prison, enduring an existence that amounts to a hideous parody of leisure. Ironically enough, though, it is while behind bars that Ned, evidently for the first time in his life, becomes genuinely engaged in some purposeful work. He suspects that Matty, whom the police believe to have been blown up in an explosion that she herself set, is actually alive and well; and he performs some quite creditable detective work (which even Keyes himself might have admired) to establish that this is true. But so what? It is, of course, too late. As he lies trapped in his tiny cell, like an animal in a cage, work—and everything else—have really ended for Ned Racine, the shining all-American anti-hero at the dawn of the Age of Reagan.

SECTION III

Empire and Gender in the John Wayne Western

Versions of the American imperium in three Westerns by John Ford

_____

American imperialism and the Western

Every so often, Americans notice that they are citizens of an imperial nation; and, for many, the discovery repeatedly has the effect of novelty and surprise. Shortly after the 2003 invasion of Iraq, for example, false nostalgia in the United States helped to produce a curious right/left coalition congealed around opposition to the Iraq War. Commentators from Patrick Buchanan, at one end of the political spectrum, to Gore Vidal, at the other, protested that Bush's Babylonian misadventure had rendered the country that they could personally remember as a non-imperial republic into an aggressive empire.

Whatever the polemical value of the Buchanan-Vidal position, the implied historical narrative on which it rests is about as false as anything can be. Between 1898 and 1899—a time well beyond the memory of any living American—US forces seized control of the Philippines and proceeded to occupy the country with a ferocity whose spirit can only be described as genocidal. If this was not an aggressively imperialist act, then no such thing as imperialism has ever existed on our planet. But then, what of the Mexican War of 1846–1848, when the United States attacked its southern neighbor and succeeded in taking and annexing an incredible *half million* square miles of Mexican territory—a massive land theft bitterly resented south of the Rio Grande to this day? What, for that matter, of the trade in African slaves initiated in the seventeenth century? Though this was not imperialism in the "classical," late-nineteenth-century sense (and neither was the Iraq War), the assault that the slave traders mounted on West Africa must count as one of the most destructive episodes of imperialist violence (in any more general sense) in all history. Marx himself, as we have seen, recognized such violence as fundamental to the primitive accumulation that enabled the take-off of capitalism itself. Whatever else may be said of imperialism, it is clearly (as H. Rap Brown would have phrased the matter) as American as cherry pie.

Furthermore, this is true not only in the diachronic sense that American imperialism is as old as America itself. It is true synchronically as well. Imperialism, far from being something heterogeneous to the original or "essential" American spirit (as the followers of Buchanan and Vidal like to imagine), has been an integral, indispensable part of the American project from the beginning. For there never could have been an "America"—in the sense of the set of predominantly white anglophone settler-colonies that eventually became the United States—without the dispossession, often by mass murder, of the indigenous population of the North American continent. This dispossession—one of the most lethal acts of primitive accumulation in world history—was the foundational act of the nation itself. It is also the enabling premise (whether explicitly or implicitly) of the Western as a film genre. Indeed, recalling the pertinent history is necessary in order to understand why the Western, despite its apparently regional name, is the most completely *national* artistic form in American culture. For the West has never, in fact, been a mere region of the country in the way that New England or the South are: simply because the whole country was once the West. If the Wild West, though empirically locatable in the area west of the Mississippi during the period just after the Civil War, has acquired a mythic status that seems to transcend mere chronology and geography, that is because *everything* was wild and western to the English settlers who first landed at Jamestown and at Plymouth Rock. What Theodore Roosevelt, the quintessential American imperialist, called the "winning" of the West was the building of the American nation.

In Raoul Walsh's cinematic epic of westward migration, *The Big Trail* (1930)—one of the finest of early Westerns—the wagon-train scout Breck Coleman (played by John Wayne in his first major role) gives a rousing speech to his fellow pilgrims in which the fundamentally national character of their journey is made quite explicit:

> We can't turn back! We're blazing a trail that started in England. Not even the storms of the sea could turn back those first settlers. And they carried it on further. They blazed it on through the wilderness of Kentucky. Famine, hunger, not even massacres could stop them. And now we've picked up the trail again. And nothing can stop us! Not even the snows of winter, nor the peaks of the highest mountains. We're building a nation, but we've got to suffer. No great trail was ever blazed without hardship. And you got to fight! That's life. And when you stop fighting, that's death. What are you going to do, lay down and die? Not in a thousand years! You're going on with me!

The one word in this oration that may seem ambiguous is *fight*. It could refer to the struggle against natural obstacles like mountains, snow, and stormy seas. Yet, especially given the reference to massacres, it must also connote the fight against the people who happened to have lived in the way of the big trail for at least as long as England itself even existed.

The Big Trail, in fact, takes an ambivalent attitude toward the American Indians.[68] On the one hand, the supremely heroic Coleman goes out of his way to describe the Indians as his friends, who have taught him everything he knows about exploring and surviving in the wilderness. Several scenes suggest that friendly diplomacy is the way that relations between the Indians and the white settlers ought to be conducted. On the other hand, nothing in the film is seen from an Indian point of view: an omission especially consequential during the scene of a terrifying and apparently unprovoked Indian attack on the wagon train, in which the Indians appear as bloodthirsty savages. The viewer may choose to reflect that the Indians are, in historical fact, defending their homeland against an invasion that has caused huge suffering to them and promises (truly) to cause still more. But nothing in Walsh's film encourages such reflection.

The racial and imperial concerns of this particular movie characterize the Western genre as a whole. In this chapter I will trace the varied representations of the nation-building American project in *Stagecoach* (1939), *The Searchers* (1956), and *The Man Who Shot Liberty Valance* (1962)—three films that I take to represent the very finest work of John Ford, who by all but unanimous agreement ranks as the pre-eminent maker of Westerns. It is hardly accidental that, like *The Big Trail*, all three films are dominated by the most formidable and definitive of Western stars, John Wayne.

Stagecoach: New Deal liberalism and the Wild West

Stagecoach has been so enthusiastically (and justly) celebrated as an outstanding masterpiece—for example, it is famously the film that Orson Welles watched over and over again (as he delighted to recount) in order to learn how to direct a movie—that its context within the Ford oeuvre has been somewhat neglected. It is the first of three movies that might be termed Ford's New Deal trilogy, the other two being *The Grapes of Wrath* (1940) and *How Green Was My Valley* (1941). Though Ford's political views changed a good deal throughout his life, and even at any given time were usually complex and sometimes contradictory, the evidence from both his movies and his off-screen activities during the 1930s and early 1940s pretty consistently suggests a staunchly left-wing liberal. He helped to found the Motion Picture Artists Committee to Aid Republican Spain (no easy commitment for a practicing Roman Catholic like Ford, since his church strongly backed Franco); and, well before America's entry into the Second World War, Ford, as a member of the Hollywood Anti-Nazi League, publicly attacked Hitler. Ford was also a founder and an active militant of the Screen Directors Guild: a stance of genuine solidarity, since it was much less renowned and more vulnerable directors who stood to gain the most from union representation, not an acknowledged giant of the movie industry like Ford. In a now famous 1937 letter to his nephew Bob Ford, who was fighting with the International Brigade in Spain, Ford explicitly defined his own politics: "*Politically*, I am a definite socialistic democrat—*always* left" (emphasis in original).[69] Ford was a first-generation American, and he often maintained that his Irish heritage, of which he was intensely proud, gave him a natural sympathy with the oppressed and a natural antipathy toward the powers that be.

Though there is no reason to doubt the sincerity and good faith of Ford's leftist sympathies, we should be wary of exaggerating his radicalism. He was a firm opponent of fascism and could be a scathing critic of capitalism. But the problems he saw in capitalism were of the sort soluble, for the most part, within the ameliorative measures of Franklin Roosevelt's New Deal—which Ford ardently supported and which was, of course, a project designed to *save*, not to overthrow, the American capitalist system. Indeed, it seems likely that Ford's own use of the term *socialistic* in the letter to his nephew reflects not considered socialist convictions but the mere fact that Roosevelt's right-wing enemies often falsely attributed socialist designs to the New Deal (and also the fact that some American socialists chose to believe, despite a lack of evidence, that the president was "really" on their side). *The Grapes of Wrath* is the most politically tendentious of Ford's films of this era and arguably the finest work he ever did outside the Western genre; and it does indeed indict the American economic system more graphically and emphatically than perhaps any other movie made, before or since, in a major Hollywood studio. But the remedies it seems to call for do not really go beyond the effective organization of labor and beneficent state intervention by a government committed to the social welfare of its citizens: precisely the agenda of the New Deal. Ford, despite his occasional pose of being a simple-hearted storyteller without artistic pretensions, was actually an artistic perfectionist as exacting, in his way, as Flaubert or Henry James; he sweated the smallest details of his films. It is thus surely significant that Grant Mitchell, the actor in *The Grapes of Wrath* who plays the director of the peaceful, progressive government camp where the Joads find temporary shelter from the stormy violence of American capitalism, is made up to bear a striking physical resemblance to FDR himself.

Stagecoach, with its more distant Wild West setting, is not politically programmatic in quite the same way as *The Grapes of Wrath* (or even as *How Green Was My Valley*, which is largely concerned with the necessity of trade unions in the coal-mining regions of Wales). But it operates within much the same left-liberal ideology. Though Ford did not invent the device of strangers (or relative strangers) thrown into intimate proximity with one another by the accident of being traveling companions, it would be hard to name anyone since Chaucer who has used the device better. Specifically, Ford uses it to portray a cross-section of American society and to show that authentic moral and affective values are radically at odds with normative social ones. The characters with the loftiest social pretensions are the wealthy banker Gatewood (Berton Churchill) and the patrician ex-Confederates Hatfield (John Carradine) and Mrs. Mallory (Louise Platt). Gatewood is a thief, while Hatfield is a card sharp and a murderer who shoots his victims in the back. Mrs. Mallory has not, evidently, committed any such felonies, but she displays an icy, snobbish, repressive personality, utterly lacking in warmth, tolerance, or laughter. By contrast, the friendliest people in the stagecoach, who consistently display not only good humor but also genuine human compassion and respect, are those lowest in the social hierarchy: the prostitute Dallas (Claire Trevor), the penniless drunkard Doc Boone (Thomas Mitchell), and the escaped convict, the Ringo Kid (John Wayne).

Nothing in the film reflects Ford's New Deal politics more clearly (though by inversion) than the arrogant and hypocritical speech that Gatewood sputters out as the stagecoach rolls along the road from Dry Forks to Apache Wells:

I don't know what the government has come to! Instead of protecting businessmen, it pokes its nose into business. Why, they're even talking now about having bank examiners—as if we bankers don't know how to run our own banks! By gone it, I actually have a letter from a popinjay official saying they were going to inspect my books. I have a slogan that should be blazoned on every newspaper in America: America for Americans!

The government must not interfere with business! Reduce taxes! Our national debt is something shocking—over one billion dollars a year. What this country needs is a businessman for president.

In 1939, such a tirade would have been instantly recognized as a polemic against the New Deal. Most of the words could have been (and conceivably really were) taken verbatim from a typical Republican journalist or politician of the time. The great irony, of course, is that Gatewood has a special reason to resent any inspection of his books: namely, that he has embezzled his bank's funds and has joined the stagecoach in order to flee with the remaining cash before being caught. In the character of Gatewood, Ford in effect suggests that the right-wing opponents of Roosevelt are no better than a pack of thieves.

An equally repellent instance of conservatism is provided by Hatfield, the son of a Southern judge, a former officer in the Confederate army, and a man obsessed by the traditional ideologies of gentility. Not only is he a killer and a cheat, but his code of gentlemanly behavior is entirely formal. It consists mainly of behaving with arrogant contempt toward everyone else, save only Mrs. Mallory, the daughter of his former commanding officer, whom he considers "a great lady". Even in her case, as we will see, he makes clear (not to her but to the camera) that his idea of chivalry includes the possibility of murdering the object of his devotion.

Diametrically opposed to him is the Ringo Kid, who is clearly Ford's idea of a *true*, or natural, gentleman (a role that proved a perfect fit for Wayne, who brings to the part a vividness by no means obvious in the script, where Ringo's lines are much fewer than most viewers, remembering Wayne's robust performance, tend to realize). Innocent of any code of gentility, Ringo displays spontaneous good cheer and courtesy toward everyone, especially Dallas. Whenever Hatfield (or the Marshal played by George Bancroft) demands some particular consideration for "the lady," that is, Mrs. Mallory—pointedly excluding Dallas from the category—Ringo demands that the same consideration be extended to "the *other* lady" as well. Many viewers of *Stagecoach* have assumed that Ringo (who has been in prison since the age of sixteen, and so is presumably unschooled in the ways of the world and especially in the ways of women) is too naïve to grasp Dallas's profession and the reasons she is thus despised by "proper" folk. Though the film permits this reading, Ford leaves the matter somewhat ambiguous, allowing the alternate, and I think more plausible, interpretation that Ringo is simply acting as any true gentleman would. He treats Dallas with courtesy and respect, and ignores the facts that might lead conventional snobs to do otherwise. When it is finally made inescapably obvious to him how she has been earning her living, he shows no surprise. Nor does his attitude toward her—and, specifically, his stated desire to marry her—change one bit.

More a moral fable than either *The Grapes of Wrath* or *How Green Was My Valley* (for both have strong elements of social documentary), *Stagecoach* ratifies its left-liberal and left-populist politics in its happy Hollywood ending. The characters, for the most part, get what they really deserve, not what their social and cultural capital (or lack thereof) would have led one, realistically, to expect. As the credits appear, Hatfield is dead, Gatewood is under arrest, and Ringo and Dallas are on their way to begin a happy married life together on Ringo's ranch, south of the Mexican border. From Ford's viewpoint, it is all as gratifying as the presidential election returns of 1936.

But there is also more to *Stagecoach* than that. Visually, the film is defined by its opposition between the "wide open spaces" for which Westerns have always been famous and the small, enclosed spaces of the stagecoach itself (surely one of the most claustrophobic settings in the history of cinema) and of several rooms in the way stations along the road in Dry Forks and Apache Wells. Indeed, the cinematography of interior space is perhaps the most formally innovative aspect of the film (an opinion one suspects was shared by Orson Welles, for the lighting and the camera-angles of the indoor scenes, especially those in the way station in Apache Wells, leave their mark on *Citizen Kane* [1941]). But the outdoor cinematography is hardly less impressive. *Stagecoach* is the first of the seven films that Ford partially shot in Monument Valley,[70] which he much later described as "the most complete, beautiful, and peaceful place on earth".[71] It is at any rate one of the world's great landscapes, but in 1939 it was little-known and almost inaccessible except to the Navajo Indians who lived there. Ford introduced it to a wide audience, and the spectacular photographic portrait of Monument Valley that he composes across all seven films reminds us that filmmakers are, in one of their aspects, the successors to the landscape painters of the nineteenth century. Not the least of *Stagecoach*'s distinctions is that rarely, if ever, has a film encompassed both inside and outside space with such visually stunning power.

The inner/outer dichotomy of the film *is*, however, a dichotomy, not a dialectic—and here we come to the most serious limitations of this masterpiece. No merely formal matter of cinematography, the inner/outer opposition of *Stagecoach* is most consequentially a political and racial opposition. It is in the inside scenes and among the inside characters that the New Deal moral drama plays out. Here we laugh at Gatewood's obnoxious Republican bluster, and here we are repelled by the snobbery (or worse) of Hatfield and Mrs. Mallory. Here we appreciate the increasing shrewdness, bravery, and professional skill of Doc Boone (who first appears as a standard comic drunk) and the courage and compassion that lurk beneath the extremely timid, mild manner of the humble whisky salesman Peacock (Donald Meek). Here we watch John Wayne as Ringo develop the heroic persona with which he was forever identified. Here we watch Dallas establish herself as the classic whore-with-a-heart-of-gold, as she forgives Mrs. Mallory's frequent expressions of contempt for her, and gladly wears herself out attending Mrs. Mallory in childbirth and taking care of the newborn infant afterward. What all these characters have in common, despite the class and moral (and gender) differences, is that they are all white.

To be sure, the actual history on which the genre of the Western is based makes for a powerful multiracial tendency. For the place is land mostly stolen from Mexico, and the time is the post-Civil-War era, when many freed black slaves migrated westward to become cowboys. *Stagecoach* registers the pressure of this multiculturalism through the Hispanic presence in the film. The Mexican Chris (played by the uncredited Chris-Pin Martin) is associated with the passengers in his role as manager of the way station in Apache Wells, and he is a sympathetic character, though mostly a comic one. The even more sympathetic if also laughable stagecoach driver Buck (Andy Devine) is even more closely associated with the passengers; and the film goes rather out of its way to inform us that he has taken his job in order to help support the vast Mexican family into which he has married. One can even imagine a sympathetic African-American character somehow associated with the passengers, especially since Ford was known for giving work to black actors long before this was a common Hollywood practice—though in fact no such character appears (as we will see, a character of this sort *is* found in *The Man Who Shot Liberty Valance*).

But there *is* an iron line of racial apartheid in the film, and it falls between the white passengers inside the stagecoach and the Apache Indians outside, in the wide open spaces of Monument Valley. Only to the degree that the deadly threat posed by the Indians—who, in contrast to the complex ambivalence of *The Big Trail*, are *never* seen as other than vicious savages—is not an immediate concern do the politically charged moral and interpersonal conflicts among the passengers claim our full attention. In somewhat the same way that modern Israel (whose affinities with the Wild West have often been remarked) has been described as a "democracy for Jews," but not, fully, for anyone else, so can *Stagecoach* be described as a drama of New Deal liberalism for whites and possibly, to some degree, for one or two other races also—but never for Indians.

It is, of course, toward the end of the film, when an army of Apache warriors attacks the stagecoach, that the white/Indian dichotomy is most fully apparent. But it has been suggested throughout the whole movie. The often forgotten opening scene has nothing to do with any of the stagecoach passengers, but is instead devoted to establishing that Apaches are on the warpath. The point is made with effective ominousness as a crucial telegraph message is interrupted by the cutting of the line after only one word has been transmitted: and that word is the name of the most feared (by whites) of all Indian warrior chiefs, Geronimo. The mood of impending danger (for whites and because of Indians) thus hangs over the entire film, sometimes overt and sometimes merely understood, but never quite forgotten. The conflicts and contrasts among the passengers on which the film's New Deal liberalism is based appear in cinematic space which is, so to speak, "borrowed"—temporarily and insecurely—from the overarching narrative of threatened Indian attack against the whites. When the attack actually comes, the intra-white conflicts are immediately put aside: just as, two years after *Stagecoach* was released, the New Deal itself was put aside when the Japanese military attacked Pearl Harbor.

Indeed, like the attack of 7 December 1941, the attack by Geronimo's warriors has a special connotation of surprise and treachery: for it takes place just as the passengers are enjoying a toast to celebrate what they falsely believe to be their arrival, finally, in safe territory. Their mistake is made clear when a sudden loud thump reveals that an arrow has punctured Peacock's chest. That the meekest and most harmless of all the (adult) passengers should be the first to be wounded makes the Indian attack seem especially vicious, as does the care with which the camera reminds us that a newborn baby, Mrs. Mallory's daughter, is now among the threatened whites. Militant solidarity among the passengers is instantaneous, and all the men in (or on top of) the stagecoach capable of doing so fight gallantly against the nonwhite hordes. So transcendent is the anti-Indian cause that there is even a partial qualification of some of the moral criticism that the film had earlier leveled against the less admirable whites. Hatfield, for example, is partly redeemed. He dies not as poetic justice might have had it—shot down, say, by a fellow card sharp a trifle faster on the draw—but accepts death bravely after having fought well against the Apaches. Admittedly, it is during the attack that he prepares to murder the praying Mrs. Mallory, lest she suffer the proverbial "fate worse than death" at the hands of the Indians. But is his specifically racial horror at the prospect of a white woman being sexually violated by nonwhite men to be taken simply as an expression of the obnoxious bigotry that he has always displayed? Or is *this* particular bit of bigotry at least partly endorsed by the film itself, given the latter's general anti-Indian racism?

The New Deal liberalism of the film is ultimately circumscribed, then, by the necessarily racist premises of the "winning" of the West. Of course, *Stagecoach* remains one of the major classics of American liberalism, almost comparable, perhaps, to the greatest of all such classics, *Huckleberry Finn* (1885), whose final lines it echoes in its own closing, as Doc Boone observes that the fleeing Ringo and Dallas have been "saved from the blessings of civilization". Yet American liberalism is, so to speak, *American* liberalism: and there is a fearful honesty to the way that *Stagecoach*, for all its radically sympathetic New Dealism, does not attempt to conceal the deeply racist imperial project that, in one way or another, lies at the base of all things American.

The Searchers: Antinomies of white racism

Ford traveled a considerable political distance rightward between 1939 and 1956, when *The Searchers* was released. But so, of course, did America. The United States of 1939 was the country of Franklin Roosevelt, Eleanor Roosevelt, and the New Deal; the United States of 1956 was the country of Richard Nixon, J. Edgar Hoover, and, recently, Joseph McCarthy. Though Ford is too principled and complicated a figure to be considered a mere opportunist, it is nonetheless striking how the politics of the director more frequently celebrated than any other as the national laureate of American cinema did often seem to reflect the dominant ideologies of the nation at large. He was a left-liberal populist during the New Deal, a win-the-war patriot during the Second World War, and a conservative anti-Communist during the 1950s and after. To be sure, he never totally abandoned his old liberalism. He always opposed blacklisting—even, oddly enough, when he was a member of organizations expressly devoted to support of the Hollywood blacklist—and some of his last films, like the emphatically pro-Indian *Cheyenne Autumn* and the proto-feminist *7 Women* (1966), are perhaps his most politically progressive works after the New Deal trilogy. Yet, even as the 1950s gave way to the more left-leaning 1960s, Ford publicly supported Barry Goldwater,

Richard Nixon (who, as president, awarded Ford a Medal of Freedom), and (though with some private doubts) the Vietnam War.[72]

The political stance of *The Searchers* is not easy to categorize, though it is clearly nothing like New Deal liberalism. The later film is much darker and more tragic in its vision than *Stagecoach*, which features an upbeat ending and abundant comic relief. There is comparatively little occasion for laughter in *The Searchers*, which portrays a world in which humanity does not have much to laugh, or even smile, about. One index of the difference between Ford's two greatest Westerns to that point is the difference between the two John Wayne roles. Whereas the Ringo Kid is open, friendly, and generous-spirited, Ethan Edwards is bitter, repressed, and murderous (and the fact that Wayne played both roles to near-perfection ought to disturb the usual clichés about his supposedly narrow range as an actor). True enough, Ringo kills three men in the gunfight at the end of *Stagecoach*. But his action is about as sympathetic as a killing for private revenge can be. The Plummer brothers, whom he guns down in a fair fight (or rather a more than fair fight, since Ringo is one man taking on three), are the men who murdered his father and his brother and who sent him to prison on a frame-up. Ethan, by contrast, displays lethal impulses that shock some of the other characters as much as they do the viewer, and that go to the savage heart of American racism.

In *Stagecoach*, as we have seen, the fundamental American battle between white and Indian provides a kind of framing narrative, but intra-white tensions usually occupy the action on screen. In *The Searchers*, the racial and imperial conflict drives the main story and—especially after the Indian raid that takes place about twenty minutes into the film's two hours—is kept almost constantly in view. As in *Stagecoach*, the racial polarity between white and Indian largely corresponds to a cinematographic polarity between interior and exterior space. As in the earlier film, the wide open spaces of the outdoor realm are taken from Monument Valley, though *The Searchers* provides a much more thorough and detailed portrait of Ford's favorite location.

The inner/outer duality is stressed in the film's opening—one of the most justly celebrated opening sequences in the history of cinema—which begins in the darkness of the little house inhabited by Aaron and Martha Edwards and their three children. Almost immediately, Martha (Dorothy Jordan) opens the front door to reveal a spectacularly gorgeous, colorful view of Monument Valley, in which a lone distant figure can be seen approaching the house. Aaron (Walter Coy) comes up behind his wife, and, as he passes by her and looks into the distance, utters the film's first line of dialogue, terse but tremendously significant: "Ethan?" It is indeed his brother Ethan, who emerges from the outdoor vastness and finally crosses the threshold of the house, where he has come to pay a family visit.

At this point, then, the inside/outside dichotomy has not yet been racialized. It stands, instead, for the contrast between the snug, communal domestic harmony of the Aaron Edwards family in their hard-won but comfortable home, on the one hand, and, on the other hand, the isolated, rugged figure of Ethan Edwards, who—both at first and throughout the film—never seems quite comfortable in any indoor setting. Ethan, of course, is hardly a racial Other. He is Aaron's brother, tied to him in the closest of all blood relations. Even so, he brings a definite air of danger with him into the family's home. Ethan is a veteran of the Confederate army (the movie opens in 1868), and we soon learn that for him the Civil War has never really ended. He refuses to take any oath that might conflict with the oath he took to the Confederacy, and it is clear that the shiny new money he has with him has been stolen at gunpoint from the US government. Though Ethan perpetrates no physical violence while in his brother's house, many movements he makes, many facial expressions, and many tones of voice suggest a man who is more at home in the violent wildness of the great outdoors than in the peaceful domestic routine of the indoor world.

Ethan brings danger into Aaron's household in a subtler way too. Though Aaron may or may not have ever noticed, it soon becomes clear to the viewer that Ethan and Martha have long been deeply in love with one another. Their passion is never made explicit, and not a single line of dialogue is devoted to it. In a *tour de force* of directing on Ford's part and of acting on Wayne's and Jordan's parts, the feelings that Ethan and Martha have for one another and their implied history together are conveyed solely (but powerfully) by silent looks, glances, and light touches. Accordingly, much about the bond between them remains ambiguous. For instance, it is never certain whether or not their love has been physically consummated—a question, that, as we will see, becomes significant for the racial theme of *The Searchers*. It is also not completely clear why Martha has never left Aaron in order to be with Ethan—though, in the brief time we get to know her, she does seem to be the sort of woman who would sacrifice her own chance for erotic happiness rather than betray a good husband and abandon her innocent children. What *does* seem certain is that Martha and Ethan's attraction to one another has not abated during Ethan's long absence in the Civil War and its aftermath, and that it would require very little to re-ignite their passion with an explosive force that could blow apart the Aaron Edwards home.

Before anything of the sort can happen, however, that home is blown apart quite literally, and by a force very different from romantic passion: namely, the homicidal fury of Chief Scar (Henry Brandon) and his fellow Comanche warriors. The build-up to the Indian "murder raid" (Ethan's term), as seen from within the Aaron Edwards home, is another of Ford's masterstrokes. The tension at dusk within the house—where the parents understand the imminent threat but the children initially do not—becomes almost unbearable, until it is finally shattered by the shriek of terror uttered by the teenage daughter Lucy (Pippa Scott) when she suddenly understands her mother's insistence on not lighting a lamp. Moments later, in an outdoor shot, a chillingly quiet climax is reached when the younger daughter Debbie (Lana Wood) looks up from behind the gravestone where she has been hiding and sees Scar himself standing above her, his face covered with war paint. As in Greek tragedy, the actual physical violence of the raid is not directly shown. But, when the camera cuts back to the Aaron Edwards homestead, the house and its outbuildings are burning ruins, Martha and Aaron (and their son) have been slaughtered, and the two girls have been abducted. As with the Indian attacks on the wagon train in *The Big Trail* and on the stagecoach in *Stagecoach*, the film does not—at least at first—supply any hint that, in historical context,

Indian violence against white settlers was always basically defensive: structurally, that is, if not, in every instance, empirically. For the time being, Scar's raid appears merely as the wantonly cruel annihilation of the film's locus of innocent, lively domestic happiness.

It is at this point that the title of *The Searchers* becomes meaningful, as Ethan sets out on a five-year search for his kidnapped nieces. He is accompanied at first by an entire posse, but all but two of the others soon abandon the quest. Ethan, who would prefer to conduct the search single-handedly, is left with Brad Jorgensen (Harry Carey Jr.), the neighboring farm boy in love with Lucy (and whose parents' homestead succeeds the Aaron Edwards home as the film's chief site of peaceful indoor domesticity) and Martin Pawley, the adopted son of Aaron's household who thinks of Lucy and Debbie as his sisters. Brad, however, soon perishes, after Lucy is discovered, raped and killed, along the trail—so that the title really refers mainly to Ethan and Martin in their long journey looking for Debbie. As the search unfolds, the depth of Ethan's bitter hatred for Indians becomes increasingly clear, repelling both the viewer and Martin himself (who happens to be one-eighth Cherokee). Ethan's cold fury is first expressed during the first day of the search, when a slain member of Scar's raiding party is discovered in a shallow grave. Betraying no emotion, Ethan draws his revolver and shoots out the eyes of the corpse. Challenged to explain this apparently senseless act, Ethan explains, with the calm authority of an anthropologist, that in Comanche religion a dead man without eyes "can't enter the spirit-land" and is forced to "wander forever between the winds". For Ethan, death itself is insufficient punishment for Scar's Comanches.

As the five-year search continues, Ethan's anti-Indian zeal is expressed again and again. Indeed, the film makes crystal clear that his hatred extends far beyond the particular members of the raiding party who killed those closest to him. At one point, for instance, Ethan fires wantonly into a herd of buffalo—because, as he explains, the more buffalo he can kill now, the greater the chance that some Indians who depend on the beasts for sustenance will starve to death in the coming winter. The main expression of Ethan's deadly racial enmity, however, is that, as the years pass and Debbie (a pre-adolescent at the time of her kidnapping) reaches the age of overt sexuality, the object of his search shifts. He abandons his goal of rescuing Debbie and bringing her back to white civilization, and decides instead to find and murder her. Ethan reckons it as virtually certain that Debbie is living in a conjugal relationship with an Indian brave, and in his view a white woman in that position is no longer truly white, indeed—what comes to essentially the same thing for him—no longer truly human. Killing her would thus be, from Ethan's viewpoint, a sort of euthanasia.

Ethan is here morally at one with his fellow ex-Confederate Hatfield when, toward the end of *Stagecoach*, Hatfield prepares to kill Mrs. Mallory—though it might indeed be pointed out that Hatfield, at least, is concerned to prevent a genuinely violent rape, whereas what Ethan objects to is the presumably more-or-less consensual Indian marriage in which he assumes Debbie to be living. Yet in some ways the latter *is* just as much a rape as the former: not only in the strict etymological sense (Latin *rapere*, to seize and carry off by force—exactly what has happened to Debbie), but, more important, in the sense that patriarchal male outrage at rape has always had much less to do with the issue of female consent than with the objective "ruining" of a "pure" woman by inappropriate sexual contact, whether that contact be willingly entered into or not. In *The Searchers*, as often, the inappropriateness is entirely racial and racist in character. Increasingly horrified by Ethan's attitude, Martin insists on staying with him in order to prevent him from carrying out his murderous scheme. At one point, he actually places his own (part-Indian) body between Debbie (now played by the fully nubile Natalie Wood, Lana's older sister) and the barrel of Ethan's gun.

Ethan's racism, then, is breathtakingly vicious. The horror of a man driven by racial hate to murder his own niece is compounded if we reflect (in a speculation supported by what seem to be the facts of Debbie's age and the timing of Ethan's last visit before the Civil War to his brother's home) that, if Ethan and Martha did indeed ever allow their love to find sexual expression, then Debbie may actually be, biologically, Ethan's own daughter. It is clear enough that such virulent racism is integral to the imperial nation-building project that requires the slaughter or dispossession of an entire indigenous people. But what, precisely, is the attitude of *The Searchers* itself toward this racism?

In some ways, Ford takes pains to demonstrate the illogicality and incoherence of such racist ideology. For example, Ethan regards a white person raised by Indians as subhuman, and this view seems to be ratified by the evidently psychotic state of several white captives he sees who have recently been brought back to white society. Yet the older Debbie, when we finally meet her, is perfectly articulate and rational, and gives an admirably lucid explanation to Martin as to why, though she had once hoped for rescue, she now prefers to remain with the Comanches, whom she has come to regard as her own people. We see nothing in the least subhuman about her. Then too, Ford shows that whites can be just as bloodthirsty as Indians. The US Cavalry, who in *Stagecoach* appear only as heroic rescuers, are in *The Searchers* once shown as having senselessly slaughtered the inhabitants of an entire peaceful Indian village, the victims including an especially amiable Indian woman that Martin had inadvertently "married" in the course of the search. In deadly ferocity, white soldiers can be more than a match even for the warriors of Scar's raiding party against the Aaron Edwards home.

The most elaborate and interesting interrogation of Ethan's anti-Indian racism concerns Ethan's own connection with the Indians. In a stark refutation of the superficial liberal platitudes that would identify bigotry with ignorance and tolerance with understanding, Ethan, who hates the Indians with an intensity that far exceeds that of any other character in *The Searchers*, is also the only white character who displays any serious knowledge of Indian ways. He speaks the Comanches' language with a fluency that impresses Scar himself, and he repeatedly demonstrates himself to be knowledgeable of the whole range of Comanche culture and society, from religion, to marital customs, to military practices. Furthermore, Ethan's understanding of his enemies seems to be based not only on abstract knowledge but also on a kind of terrible personal affinity.

Though he is not, of course, an Indian by blood, Ethan *is* an Indian in the figurative sense that, in the overarching cinematographic duality of the film, he is, like the Indians, a creature of Monument Valley—of wildness and wide open spaces—rather than, like the other whites, of enclosed spaces and settled domesticity.

Indeed, the affinity between Ethan and Scar is made quite specific in the film's climax, the face-to-face meeting between them. It is not only that the two mortal foes evince a certain rough warrior's respect for one another. In addition, we learn that, just as Ethan's loved ones have been slaughtered by Comanche braves, so has Scar lost his two sons to white violence. The two men's mutual racial hatred describes a fearful symmetry. Yet, however compelling the parallel between Scar and Ethan may seem to the viewer, it does nothing to abate Ethan's bitterness. On the contrary, when Scar is killed, Ethan takes care to gouge out the chief's eyes with his knife, condemning him, according to Comanche belief, to an eternal limbo.

The Searchers does, then, seriously question the anti-Indian racism on which the American imperium is based. Despite Ford's general rightward drift between 1939 and 1956, this film, which features a murderous racist as its "hero" (at least in the sense of protagonist), is itself measurably *less* racist—and on this issue considerably more critical and progressive—than the New Dealish *Stagecoach*.

But the antiracist dimension of *The Searchers* is seriously limited by several factors. For one thing, Ethan is really the film's hero in something more than a technical and structural sense. Though the bitter hatred that consumes him is hardly an attractive trait in itself, it is at least partly offset by other qualities that Ethan also displays, notably awesome strength, competence, powers of endurance, and physical courage. These characteristics are of course integral to John Wayne's general heroic persona (they are shared by a character so different from Ethan as the Ringo Kid), and by 1956 this cinematic persona was one of the most powerful in Hollywood, transcending any single film and lending authority to any role that Wayne might take. Though many commentators, in a judgment that angered Wayne himself, have described Ethan as the movie's "villain"—reflecting, one suspects, the opinion that the critics would hold about a man like Ethan in real life—the film never truly represents him in quite this way. Instead, it almost teases us to wonder whether a man who is so strong and so right about so many things can be entirely wrong even in his racism. Furthermore, and on the more purely visual level, none of the elements in *The Searchers* that do question this racism ever rises to the level of cinematic power with which Scar's murder raid early in the film is presented. The Cavalry's slaughter of the Indian village, for example, is treated in a comparatively perfunctory fashion.

The antiracist tendencies of *The Searchers* are also blunted by the general collapse of the film's narrative and character structure at its end. Though Ford recovers magnificently in the very final scene (where the surviving white characters enter the Jorgensen home to re-establish happy domesticity, save for Ethan, who remains outdoors), the ending is in general one of the worst artistic blunders ever to disfigure one of the greatest of all cinematic masterpieces. The basic problem is that Ethan, when he finally gets his chance to murder

Debbie, declines to do so. Instead, he lifts her gently in his arms and lovingly tells her that he is taking her home. Since nothing that we know about Ethan prepares us for this reversal, and since not even a hasty, last-minute explanation is offered, the film's resolution rings somewhat false and hollow.[73] One suspects that extra-aesthetic institutional pressures were at work: not only the general Hollywood preference for a happy ending but also the fact that it was not commercially feasible in 1956 to represent John Wayne as transgressing dominant social norms so monstrously as to murder a young, beautiful white woman like Natalie Wood. Be that as it may, Ethan's unexplained and inexplicable abandonment of his central racist goal amounts to a sort of sleight-of-hand that, in effect, conjures Ethan's racism away. If Ethan were actually to kill Debbie (perhaps then to be overcome by remorse for the evil deed), the film at its conclusion would powerfully highlight its own genuinely antiracist elements. As the movie actually is, however, the falsely happy ending encourages the viewer to gloss over the undermining of racism that forms the most searching aspect of *The Searchers*.

In its complex ambivalence toward the Indians, *The Searchers* sharply contrasts with the taken-for-granted anti-Indian bias of *Stagecoach*. But the antiracist dimension of the later film is by no means sufficiently developed to pose any fundamental challenge to the imperial American project of white settlement in land genocidally expropriated from its original inhabitants. Indeed, *The Searchers* even features a patriotic nation-building speech by Mrs. Jorgensen (Olive Carey) that is somewhat reminiscent of Breck Coleman's in *The Big Trail*.

The Man Who Shot Liberty Valance: Invisible Indians

Nation-building is manifestly the central concern of Ford's last Western with John Wayne, *The Man Who Shot Liberty Valance*. But here the Indian question is engaged neither through the simple overt racism of *Stagecoach* nor the contradictory, sometimes self-questioning racism of *The Searchers*. Instead, we have to deal with what has been widely recognized (at least since Ralph Ellison published *Invisible Man* in 1952) as one of the most effective of all racist strategies: erasure. Thus, though I take *Liberty Valance* to be Ford's supreme masterpiece and in some ways the most nearly perfect instance of the entire Western genre, it can be considered here more briefly than the other two films. For, in the current context, its significance is much like the significance of Sherlock Holmes's dog that, famously, did not bark in the night.

One of the principal negative facts about *Liberty Valance* is that, despite Ford's profound love for Monument Valley, it figures nowhere in this film. In fact, *Liberty Valance* is notable for mostly avoiding the wide open spaces so important for Westerns generally. It is an atypical (though certainly not unprecedented) in-town Western, focusing on the streets and buildings of Shinbone. During the time present of the movie, Shinbone is a prosperous modern community with schools, churches, shops, and an extensive irrigation system. But it was still a rugged frontier outpost during the long flashback that occupies all but less than twenty minutes of the film's slightly more than two hours (it should be noted, though, that Tom Doniphon, the John Wayne character, unsurprisingly lives miles *outside* town, on his small isolated ranch). Most of the scenes of *Liberty Valance* are set indoors. But the absence of Monument Valley, and of the Indians for whom such outdoor settings constitute their "natural" home, does not mean that the theme of threatening wildness so important in *Stagecoach* and *The Searchers* is absent here. On the contrary, the battle between barbarism and civilization forms the central subject matter of *Liberty Valance*. But here it is an *intra-white* battle.

Interestingly, this battle is framed in terms that somewhat recall the left populism of *Stagecoach* (though the representation of class struggle in George Stevens's *Shane* [1953] is in most respects a closer comparison).[74] Standing for uncivilized wildness are the big ranching interests, who wish to keep the (unnamed) territory an open range for their cattle, and who enforce their will with hired gunslingers, most notably the pathologically sadistic Liberty Valance (Lee Marvin). On the side of civilization and civility are the ordinary people of Shinbone and its environs—the small farmers, the small ranchers, the shopkeepers, the few professional people—who are led and represented by the young lawyer Ransom Stoddard (James Stewart). Stoddard and Valance are thus the symbolic poles of the conflict, but no true confrontation between them is possible. Valance is no match for Stoddard's legal mind, but Stoddard is helpless before Valance's skill with firearms. This Gordian knot is cut, and the battle for civilization is won, when Doniphon—by personal temperament an untamed man of the gun like Valance, who however decides, for complex reasons, to choose the side of law and order—kills Valance, but in such a way that Stoddard gets credit for the deed. Stoddard is thus able to begin a successful political career, and some 30 years later he is still known by an adoring public as "the man who shot Liberty Valance".

The left populism of *Liberty Valance* is, to be sure, seriously qualified by the fact that Ransom Stoddard appears to become a reliable (and, eventually, corrupt) political ally of the railroad interests. Indeed, the film (which begins and ends with a shot of a moving train) explicitly credits the railroad with the main role in transforming Shinbone into the peaceful, affluent bourgeois community we see outside the long flashback. Needless to say, the railroad interests can hardly be seen as economically allied to the petty-bourgeois populists who evidently form Stoddard's mass political base. On the contrary, they own and control accumulations of capital compared to which even the greatest of the cattle barons are relatively minor economic players. The barons are locally powerful, but the railroad represents a genuinely *national* ruling class—and this national character is the real key to the film's politics. For *Liberty Valance*, true to the main spirit of the Western genre, is a film above all about nation-building. In the struggle between the big cattle ranchers and the ordinary people led by Stoddard, much is made of the fact that the former wish the territory to remain a territory, while the latter are strongly for statehood—though the economic logic behind this opposition of political strategies is never made clear. The triumph of law and order is also the triumph of statehood, enabling Stoddard to become the state's first governor, then one of its US senators, and finally, we are given to understand, a man who could have the vice-presidency of the United States for the asking. Though Stoddard's apparent (but only subtly suggested) corruption—and the fact, emphasized in the film's very title, that his illustrious career is founded on a lie—can be taken to imply some reservations about the American project, the dominant tone of *Liberty Valance* is nonetheless celebratory: the film affirms the economic *and* political growth of the United States.[75]

What, then, of the Indians at whose expense this growth necessarily takes place? They never appear in the film but are mentioned twice. The more significant of the two instances is found in the nominating speech by the newspaper editor Dutton Peabody (Edmond O'Brien) that helps to launch Ransom Stoddard's political career. Tracing the march of American civilization in which he sees Stoddard as the next great leader, Peabody invokes

> . . .the vast herd of buffalo and the savage Redskin roaming our beautiful territory with no law to trammel them except the law of survival—the law of the tomahawk and the bow and arrow. And then, with the westward march of our nation came the pioneer and the buffalo hunter, the adventurous and the bold. And the boldest of these were the cattlemen, who seized the wide-open range for their own personal domain—and *their* law was the law of the hired gun. But now, now today, have come the railroads and the people, the steady hardworking citizens—the homesteader, the shopkeeper, the builder of cities.

For Peabody, then—and for the film—the current struggle to supplant the rule of the gun with the rule of law comes decisively after an earlier transition *to* the gun from the tomahawk. Though the dispossession of the "savage Redskins" is no less necessary to the American imperium here than in *Stagecoach* or *The Searchers*, it has been achieved (in contrast to the earlier films) *before* the action of *Liberty Valance* begins.

The only other mention of Indians in the film is not without its own similarly grim significance. It is an apparently stray remark by a very minor character who praises Peabody's oratorical skills by saying that the editor can "talk the ears off a wooden Indian". The original American is no longer a feared and respected enemy like Geronimo or Chief Scar. Now he is just an inanimate piece of *kitsch* to decorate a cigar store.

This racism by erasure is all the more striking because, by the standards of 1962, *The Man Who Shot Liberty Valance* is strongly antiracist with respect to other nonwhite peoples. Andy Devine playing Marshal Link Appleyard—essentially the same cowardly but good-hearted and sympathetic comic character that Devine played 23 years earlier in *Stagecoach*—is again married into a large Mexican family; and in this film we actually see some of his Hispanic relatives, who include several notably smart and attractive children. Even more significant is the African-American character Pompey, Tom Doniphon's friend and dependent. Played by Woody Strode—the pre-eminent pioneer among black Western actors, who two years earlier had starred in Ford's emphatically pro-civil-rights Western *Sergeant Rutledge*— Pompey, while a loyal (but never servile) servant, radiates strength and dignity throughout the film. Indeed, he is the *only* character who invariably displays both strength and dignity, and so might almost be considered the real moral center of the film. It is worth noting that the movie carefully shows Pompey being excluded (like the women characters) from a political meeting, and that one scene—in a movie made, we should recall, two years before racial discrimination in public accommodations was outlawed by the Civil Rights Act of 1964—insists upon Pompey's right to be served in a bar. The movie also includes a nicely acid comment by Stoddard, who tells Pompey that *many* Americans forget the assertion, "All men are created equal," in the Declaration of Independence. But, of course, antiracism with regard to blacks is perfectly compatible, especially in a Western, with racism toward Indians: as *Sergeant Rutledge* itself also illustrates.

Conclusion

The foregoing analysis of the differing versions of anti-Indian racism in Ford's finest Westerns—which for me are the finest of all Westerns and among the finest of all films— should not, of course, be taken as a cynical "debunking" of his genius. On the personal level, actually, Ford's stance vis-à-vis the American Indians was by no means entirely dishonorable. In some moods, he regretted the sort of representations that this chapter has been concerned to analyze, and *Cheyenne Autumn* was expressly made as a kind of atonement. In other moods, Ford liked to compare his own record with that of the *bien-pensant* types who might express verbal sympathy for the plight of the Indians but who did nothing of concrete material benefit for them. Ford himself, by contrast, gave desperately needed work to the Navajos of Monument Valley, and sometimes supplied them with material sustenance even when he had no work to give. He was proud that the Navajos, for their part, made him an honorary member of their tribe, bestowing upon him the title, "Natani Nez," a Navajo phrase said to mean, "the tall leader"—an honor that Ford claimed to cherish more than all of his Oscars.

But, of course, the real point is not to judge Ford as a man but to understand the extremely various evidence that the Western—the most deeply American of all American art forms—supplies of the inescapable centrality of anti-Indian bigotry to the entire imperial American project. It is surely no accident that even the most radical and progressive Americans, who have taken up all sorts of other minority causes, from Palestine to East Timor, have very rarely, when not themselves of Indian heritage, adopted the Indian cause as their own. For this is a matter on which nearly every American— not just John Ford—whose ancestors have been in North America for four centuries or less necessarily has a bad conscience. No one is morally responsible for the actions of his or her ancestors, of course. But every non-Indian American, even the poorest and most oppressed, does continue to enjoy material benefits that ultimately derive from the murder and displacement of the continent's first inhabitants. The historic oppression of Irish-Americans, Italian-Americans, Jewish-Americans, Hispanic-Americans, and Asian-Americans has been comparatively (though *only* comparatively) contingent to the imperial nation-building project. Even the situation of the African-Americans is somewhat different. While the slave trade was indispensable to the development of Southern agriculture, it was not, perhaps, utterly necessary to the existence of something recognizably like the actually existing United States (though an America in which race-based chattel slavery never existed would certainly have been extremely different, in numerous ways large and small). But the dispossession of the American Indians is the absolute foundation on which the USA was built. In one of the ironies with which cultural history abounds, Americans—like John Ford—invented the Western to remind themselves (and the world) of what they otherwise try very hard to forget.

Post-heterosexuality: John Wayne and the construction of American masculinity

Gender and John Wayne

Perhaps no advanced industrialized nation is more occupied with the idea of masculinity than the United States; and there is certainly no place in American culture where the lineaments of the masculine ideal are ratified more definitively than in the Western film. More than a century after the closing of the frontier—and despite the decline, from the 1970s onward, of the Western from the position of dominance that it held in American popular culture throughout most of the twentieth century—the most solidly American masculine types remain Western icons: the cowboy, the rancher, the gunfighter, the frontier sheriff, the US Marshal, the Cavalry officer, even (with a different racial inflection) the bare-chested Indian warrior. The sexual content of such ideal masculinity, in quasi-"official" self-representation, is, of course, typically a robust, virile heterosexuality, with the privileged coupling normally that between brave men and beautiful, strong women. Many of the great Western films display this pattern, so that, for instance, Gary Cooper winds up with Grace Kelly in *High Noon* (Fred Zinnemann, 1952), and Burt Lancaster (it is strongly implied) winds up with Rhonda Fleming in *Gunfight at the O.K. Corral* (John Sturges, 1957).

But two generations or so of work by feminist critics and other scholars of gender studies—not to mention, on a more popular level, Jon Stewart's remarkable presentation at the 78th Academy Awards in 2006—have taught us that the normative heterosexuality of American macho, in the Western and elsewhere, is not necessarily to be taken at face value. Those texts that most insistently uphold the ideology of "compulsory heterosexuality" (Adrienne Rich's term) can contain reservoirs of barely subtextual homoerotic feeling: and not least in the traditional Hollywood Western (though also, as we have seen, in much film noir), as Stewart's brilliantly assembled series of film clips was designed to show. In many instances, the truth of American macho turns out to be an aversion to women, shading into a fear of feminine sexuality, and a concomitant emotional commitment to the "male bonding" of masculine friendship. A classic instance is *Shane* (George Stevens, 1953), in which Alan Ladd's eponymous hero not only looks slight and vaguely effeminate, but, of the married couple with whom he lodges, seems to prefer the ruggedly good-looking Joe Starrett (Van Heflin) to Starrett's lovely wife Marian (Jean Arthur), who clearly desires Shane. The real innovation of Ang Lee's 2005 masterpiece, *Brokeback Mountain* (which provided the occasion for Stewart's illustrated lecture), is not the representation of same-sex attraction but the overt and unapologetic centrality of such attraction to the film. Unlike the traditional Western, Lee's movie crosses the subtle but significant line that separates homoeroticism from homosexuality.

It seems to me, however, and will be the argument of this chapter, that *neither* overt heterosexuality *nor* covert homoeroticism is the chief connotation of the image of ideal American masculinity enshrined in the work of John Wayne: not only the most definitive of all Western stars but also the figure that still counts as the pre-eminent embodiment of what most American men (and many American women) feel that a man ought to be like. In thus invoking John Wayne, I do not, needless to say, mean the off-screen personality of the individual who was born Marion Morrison in Iowa in 1907 and who died in California in 1979. In much about this man—his loathing for horses, his fondness for luxury, his sartorial preference for suits or Hawaiian shirts over cowboy gear, his aspirations toward the Social Register, his almost obsessive concern with his own career, and, perhaps above all, his avoidance of military service—there was little enough of "John Wayne". John Wayne, in the only sense that really matters, was a myth in Roland Barthes's sense:[76] that is, a highly ideological cultural construction, one in whose shaping many directors, writers, producers, publicists, and others had a hand—though one in which the actor himself (along with John Ford, by far his greatest director) was surely pre-eminent.

It is remarkable how extraordinarily durable John Wayne has proved as the supreme American representation of manly toughness, courage, and competence. To take but one example: During the immediate aftermath of Hurricane Katrina—29 years after Wayne made his final film and 26 years after his death—the mayor of New Orleans could think of no more fitting compliment to pay the hard-nosed federal official who, finally, brought some efficiency and relief to the suffering city than to call him a "John Wayne dude". Something of Wayne's cultural significance is suggested when one reflects that Mayor Nagin could not conceivably have called General Honore a "Clark Gable dude" or a "James Stewart dude," still less a "Robert De Niro dude" or a "Tom Cruise dude"—and maybe not even a "Clint Eastwood dude". Many movie stars have been admired for many varieties of manliness. But no other has *defined* masculinity to the extent that John Wayne has.

Yet, however familiar Wayne (still, by some measures, the most popular movie star of all time) remains as the ideal type of masculinity, the specifically sexual character of Wayne's masculinity has not been widely understood. John Wayne as a cultural icon of the masculine is constructed, I maintain, so as to defuse a potentially fatal contradiction in the social exaltation of masculinity. On the one hand, if masculinity is to be socially normative—as it must be in any male-dominated civilization—then it must itself be thoroughly "normal" in character; and all same-sex erotic feeling and action have borne the stigma of abnormality (and often of effeminacy) ever since the anti-homosexual bigotry of the Book of Leviticus triumphed over the comparative tolerance of Greco-Roman paganism in the development of Christian (and later Islamic) society. Yet, on the other hand, active heterosexuality can never be fully masculine either. To act on heterosexual desire necessarily removes a man from the sphere of pure masculinity, shackling him to the feminine. For a man to want and to seek a woman is to confess that masculinity is incomplete; and a man actively desiring a woman thereby places himself—even if only in one specific department of life—under womanly power. Only sissies have anything to do with girls, as a high-school coach of my acquaintance used to instruct his young male charges.

The version of masculinity represented in the screen persona of John Wayne succeeds, however, in squaring this particular circle through what I call *post-heterosexuality*: a mythic ideal perhaps not wholly original with, or unique to, John Wayne, but—at least within modern American culture—one that is brought to its most compelling expression in Wayne's films. The typical John Wayne character carries no significant suggestion of same-sex eroticism, but is not sexually involved with women either. He is a man with a heterosexual *past*, who has outgrown that phase of existence and so is free to glory in his unalloyed masculinity without being suspected of the least abnormality. John Wayne as post-heterosexual may cast a friendly, approving eye on the heterosexual activity that frequently goes on around him, but he does so as if from above, in tranquil Olympian superiority. Sometimes, indeed, he helps to arrange the couplings of men and women a generation (or more) younger than himself. The young men are generally worthy types, but there is never the slightest doubt that none of them is remotely equal, as a man, to John Wayne himself.

In this chapter I will offer some supporting examples (and a few counter-examples) through a—necessarily quick—survey of the films that I take to be Wayne's finest Westerns. Though the stress on Wayne's Westerns is justified both by the fact that nearly all of his best work was done in that form and by the general historic importance of the Western for American culture and American masculinity, it is certainly true that films in other genres— notably the war movie—have also played a part in the construction of Wayne's screen manliness. Of particular importance here is the extremely influential *Sands of Iwo Jima* (Allan Dwan, 1949), for which Wayne won an Oscar nomination. Shortly after its release it became the semi-official movie of the US Marine Corps (a status it continues to hold); and it conferred an indelible aura of military glory on the actor who in real life declined the opportunity to serve his country in uniform. But—though the masculine toughness of Wayne's character, Sergeant Stryker, is beyond question—even this film seems haunted by the suspicion that Western modes of manliness are even more genuine than anything to be found in the Marines, and that the star has somehow strayed from his natural generic home: as is evidenced, for instance, by Stryker's rallying his men for action with the jarringly archaic call, "Saddle up!"

False starts

It may seem odd to describe Wayne's appearances in *The Big Trail* (Raoul Walsh, 1930) and *Stagecoach* (John Ford, 1939) as "false starts," and indeed they were not false starts in many senses (as we have seen in the previous chapter). Walsh's film, though relatively unsuccessful commercially in its own time (largely because of the advent of the Great Depression), is today ranked as one of the best early Westerns. It provided Wayne with his first great role, the heroic wagon-train scout Breck Coleman. *Stagecoach* is regarded, almost unanimously, as one of the finest Westerns ever made; and Wayne's performance as the (innocent and wrongfully convicted) escaped prisoner Ringo began his rise to permanent superstardom that was completed about a decade later. But both films were false starts in the sense that they did almost nothing to sculpt the post-heterosexual persona that would ultimately be of such decisive importance in the socio-cultural construction of John Wayne.

This is quite obviously true of *The Big Trail*. Here Wayne is both very young (the actor was 23 when the film was made, and Coleman looks no older) and stunningly good-looking, with a pure boyish handsomeness that faded from his features by the end of the decade. On both counts he would have made an unlikely post-heterosexual in *The Big Trail*, and Walsh's movie makes no effort to construct him as such. On the contrary, the reward for Coleman's almost superhuman courage, skill, strength, resourcefulness, and powers of endurance is to be united at film's end, in what one is meant to presume will be a lifetime of heterosexual bliss, with the gorgeous Southern belle Ruth Cameron (Marguerite Churchill), by far the prettiest girl in sight. It is perhaps worth noting that Breck does postpone his union with Ruth until he has tracked down and killed the murderers of the wolf-trapper who had been his best friend, even insisting upon the importance of his doing the deed personally: "I kill my own rats," he angrily replies to a suggestion that some judicial proceeding ought to handle the matter. In this posthumous tribute to masculine friendship, there is perhaps a whiff of "male bonding". But it is no more than (at most) a whiff; the trapper is dead before the film begins, and so nothing of the friendship appears on screen. The active heterosexuality of John Wayne as Breck Coleman is nearly unqualified.

The active heterosexuality of John Wayne as the Ringo Kid in *Stagecoach* is, in some ways, even more unqualified. Here too the narrative trajectory of Wayne's character ratifies the principle that, as Dryden famously put it, none but the brave deserve the fair. It is after single-handedly gunning down all three of the villainous Plummer brothers that Ringo rides off with his bride-to-be, the beautiful and kind-hearted prostitute Dallas (Claire Trevor). It is true that, as in *The Big Trail*, the John Wayne character insists that marriage plans must wait until his work of "frontier justice" (Breck Coleman's phrase) is complete. But, in *Stagecoach*, the motives for his vengeance are purely familial in nature (the Plummers murdered Ringo's father and brother long before the time present of the film), so that there is even less question than in *The Big Trail* of any "male bonding" that might call into question, however faintly, the hero's preference for the opposite sex. Indeed, far from being post-heterosexual, the Ringo Kid is just *beginning* his heterosexual career, and with great gusto. He has been in prison since the age of sixteen (having been framed by the Plummer brothers), and it is clear that his eager courtship of Dallas represents his first adventure in romance. If there is any element at all in *Stagecoach* that in any way foreshadows Wayne's later sexual persona, it can be found only in the physical features of Wayne's countenance. Wayne was 32 when the film hit the screens, and Ringo's own age is somewhat indeterminate. But the actor has here already lost the matinée-idol gorgeousness that he had displayed in *The Big Trail*. The features of the still youngish Ringo are already beginning to suggest the more mature, patriarchal image of John Wayne as post-heterosexual—though this insight is available, to be sure, only in retrospect.

The making of the post-heterosexual

Stagecoach made Wayne an authentic star, but during the late 1940s and early 1950s he completed a body of work that elevated him to the superstardom that he never lost. Several of these films are among not only his most popular but also his best: *Red River* (1948), *Fort Apache* (1948), *3 Godfathers* (1948), *She Wore a Yellow Ribbon* (1949), *Rio Grande* (1950), and *The Quiet Man* (1952). All of these half-dozen movies are Westerns (except for *The Quiet Man*, a romance and probably the finest film Wayne ever made outside the Western genre), and all are directed by John Ford (except for Howard Hawks's *Red River*). It is in the great Westerns of these years—made when the star, though only in his forties, was already looking the part of the rugged patriarch—that John Wayne's post-heterosexuality is definitively forged.

Given the overwhelming importance of Ford to Wayne's career, it is ironic that the key movie of this formative period, and thus, in some ways, of Wayne's whole oeuvre, is Hawks's *Red River*. *Red River* remains not only one of the strongest films in the genre but also the one that plays the central role in redefining the meaning of "John Wayne," and in which Wayne delivered his most searing performance to that point. Perhaps the most meaningful index of the film's greatness is the impact it had on John Ford himself. "I didn't know that the big son-of-a-bitch could *act*," as Ford has often been quoted as remarking to Hawks after seeing *Red River*.[77] Taken literally, the sentence is pure blarney: of course Ford knew very well that Wayne could act. But there seems little doubt that Ford did see a new dimension to Wayne's acting in Hawks's movie, and that Tom Dunson, Wayne's character in *Red River*, exercised a profound and vitalizing influence on Ford's best later work with the actor.

In Tom Dunson, John Wayne's post-heterosexuality is established with unforgettable force and tragic depth. As the film opens, Dunson, accompanied by his older sidekick Groot Nadine (Walter Brennan), is leaving a wagon train bound for California in order to head south to Texas and establish a cattle ranch. His beloved, a beautiful woman named Fen (Colleen Gray), begs to accompany him, using all of her considerable sexual charm in the effort. But he insists that his journey will be too difficult and dangerous—there have already been signs of hostile Indian activity in the vicinity—and that she should remain with the other pioneers on the wagon train. He promises to send for her later, but within hours the results of his decision prove terribly ironic. The wagon train is attacked by an Indian war party, and the travelers, Fen included, are slaughtered. Dunson and Groot, already a good many miles away, manage to escape unharmed. They soon come upon the young orphan Matt Garth (Mickey Kuhn as a boy but Montgomery Clift as the adult that Matt is during most of the movie), who is taken in and becomes Dunson's adoptive son. The household thus established, Dunson founds his cattle ranch, which over the years grows into a vast commercial empire.

Some have seen a touch of homoeroticism in this all-male household, but the film gives little actual support to such a reading. The relationship between Dunson and Matt is purely filial and develops in classically Oedipal fashion. As for Groot, his role is indeed in some ways a feminized one—for instance, he works as a cook, and at various times displays both "feminine" giddiness and "feminine" common sense—but, to the extent that he is to be seen as the "lady" of the house, the elderly Groot approximates not to Dunson's wife but to an older female relative who manages the labor of housekeeping, like Aunt Bea in *The Andy Griffith Show* (1960–1968). The film offers no evidence of same-sex attraction on Tom Dunson's part. Instead, it shows him to be a man strong enough to resist being mastered by his own heterosexual desires.

This strength is first displayed in Dunson's only scene with Fen. Desperately eager to come with him, she uses extremely suggestive remarks and gestures (as suggestive, probably, as Hollywood's Production Code of the time would allow) to indicate the pleasure that she could give him during the long nights at the ranch. Wayne plays the scene masterfully, making clear that he is mightily tempted but also that the force of his will is mightier yet. His post-heterosexuality is already foreshadowed. After Fen's death, it is irrevocably established, and becomes part and parcel of the awesome patriarchal strength that Wayne-as-Dunson displays throughout *Red River*. The power of his own heterosexual yearnings, glimpsed in the scene with Fen, becomes the measure of the even greater manly power that allows him to lead a celibate life. If Dunson is strong enough to triumph over himself in this way, he is strong enough for anything: most notably, for the unprecedented thousand-mile cattle drive up the Chisholm Trail to seek the market for beef that the Civil War has destroyed in Texas. Along the way Dunson's strength sometimes manifests itself in bitter fury and cruel tyranny—always the dark underside of strong masculinity—but of the strength itself there is never any doubt. It is highlighted most impressively, perhaps, in the Oedipal battle with Matt. Of all the actors who played son-figures opposite John Wayne, Montgomery Clift came closest to matching Wayne in masculine strength. Clift's rather proto-punk manly toughness (stylistically quite different from Wayne's persona, to be sure) and his refusal to be intimidated help to suggest just how awesome Wayne's even tougher version of masculinity must be.[78]

The rooting of Wayne's masculinity in his post-heterosexual character explains something that, on the strictly narrative level, the film leaves uncertain. Why has Dunson never found another woman to love? The reasonably good-looking and tremendously capable owner of one of the most successful ranches in Texas would not, one presumes, have been without erotic opportunities. Groot suggests that Fen was "the only woman [Dunson] ever wanted," and the film contains subtle hints that he may be leading a life of sexual self-denial out of remorse for having left Fen to be (presumably) raped and then killed by the Indians. But the fundamental reason that Dunson must remain single is that only by refusing to stoop to entanglement with the feminine can he maintain the supremely confident and self-sufficient masculinity that he exemplifies throughout the movie. Admittedly, he does at one point, while estranged from Matt, offer the sexy dance-hall girl Tess Millay (Joanne Dru) one half of everything he owns if she will bear him a son. But there is nothing of romance or sexual desire in the offer. It is a purely pragmatic ploy to replace Matt, and even as such is thoroughly ridiculous, as both Tess and Dunson see clearly enough. Later, after reconciling with Matt, Dunson makes clear that his real relation to Tess is not sexual but properly patriarchal in the strictest sense: "You'd better marry that girl, Matt," he says in one of the final lines of *Red River*. Matt agrees, and so from now on the Dunson home will include an actual woman. But she will be the daughter-in-law, not the wife, of the household. Tom Dunson will continue to preside in the unalloyed masculine strength of post-heterosexuality.

No other film of 1948–1952 displays John Wayne's post-heterosexuality quite so memorably as *Red River*. (Indeed, Wayne's other best film of the period is *The Quiet Man*, which, as an exuberantly heterosexual love story, constitutes the most memorable *exception* to Wayne's post-heterosexuality among all his films.) But Hawks's masterpiece is nicely complemented and in some ways counterpointed by Ford's so-called Cavalry trilogy, which is composed of *Fort Apache*, *She Wore a Yellow Ribbon*, and *Rio Grande*. Here Wayne is represented as post-heterosexual not in Tom Dunson's mode of Titanic or Ahab-like fury but in a far more relaxed, sympathetic way. Though the films were not originally planned as a trilogy, and though there is no single overarching narrative with a continuing set of dramatis personae, Wayne's character—named Captain Kirby York, Captain Nathan Brittles, and Lieutenant Colonel Kirby Yorke in the three movies respectively—is much the same person throughout. If Wayne is here considerably more likeable than as Tom Dunson, he is no less strong or manly; and his post-heterosexuality is no less important to his persona.

The character in *Fort Apache* who displays something like Dunson's bitter passion is not Kirby York but his commanding officer, Lieutenant Colonel Owen Thursday (Henry Fonda), a fictionalized version of George Custer. Thursday resents being posted by the War Department to an obscure Western command; despising Indians as mere savages, he feverishly dreams of a crushing military victory over them that will restore his career to glory. York, by contrast, seems at peace with himself. Respecting the Indians and sympathizing with their resistance to injustices inflicted by his own government, he works hard to find peaceful solutions to potential conflict. Interestingly, *both* men are post-heterosexual—and both draw strength from their pristine masculinity. Thursday is a widower whose only female companion is his beautiful daughter Philadelphia (Shirley Temple). He never displays any interest in other ladies. If he resembles Tom Dunson in his implacable stubbornness and his inclination toward petty (and not so petty) tyranny, he also matches Dunson in decisiveness and physical courage. His "last stand" against Cochise's warriors results from his own bigotry, catastrophically bad judgment, and refusal to heed York's sound advice. But he faces the consequences heroically, without a trace of weakness, self-pity, or cowardice.

Yet John Wayne as Captain York is even stronger, for his is the strength that feels no need to prove itself. Utterly confident of his ability to handle conflict, York is too wise to seek it. He feels a genuine bond with his fellow patriarch Cochise, and the Apache chief's concern for his young braves is matched by York's fatherly concern for the troops under his command. Sexually, York plays the precisely patriarchal role of superintending the heterosexual coupling

151

of young people. He begins encouraging romance between Philadelphia and the newly commissioned Lieutenant Michael O'Rourke (John Agar) almost from their (accidentally) simultaneous arrival at Fort Apache. Shouting desperate orders to O'Rourke during the climactic battle scene, he still finds time to add, "And marry that girl!". Wayne makes clear by the way he looks at Shirley Temple that York can feel Philadelphia's attractions himself. But he knows that active heterosexuality is not for him.

Kirby York blends so seamlessly into Nathan Brittles of *She Wore a Yellow Ribbon*—he is, indeed, even closer to Brittles than to Kirby Yorke of *Rio Grande*—that the two can almost be considered the same character. Like Captain York, Captain Brittles prefers to avoid fighting, but is totally brave and totally capable whenever a fight proves unavoidable. Also like York, Brittles regards young people with paternal beneficence. In the later film, the John Wayne character has a whole array of junior officers and NCOs under his wing: including the brilliant ex-Confederate scout Sergeant Tyree (Ben Johnson), the wealthy but not, ultimately, spoiled Lieutenant Ross Penell (Harry Carey Jr.), and his evident favorite, Lieutenant Flint Cohill (John Agar again). Indeed, so fond is Brittles of the young lieutenants, and so fatherly toward them ("I'm just old enough to be your father," Brittles once reminds Cohill), that the commanding officer, Major Allshard (George O'Brien), must, on one occasion, gently point out to Brittles that too much solicitude is not good for the junior officers. They must, Allshard points out, learn the rigors of combat for themselves, just as Allshard and Brittles did. As in *Fort Apache*, the John Wayne character also plays the patriarchal matchmaker, encouraging Flint Cohill's union with Major Allshard's niece Olivia Dandridge (Joanne Dru, looking considerably more respectable here than as Tess Millay)—while also respecting Ross Penell, the rival suitor for the young lady's favors.

She Wore a Yellow Ribbon differs from *Fort Apache*, however, in making the heterosexual past of the John Wayne character explicit and in generally treating the whole matter of his sexuality in much greater detail. Brittles is a widower. Making regular visits to his wife Mary's grave, he talks "to" her in the kind of relaxed, friendly tone that he might have used in casual dinner-table or bedroom conversation. His love for her is plain, but, at the same time, the objective effect of such an elaborate mourning ritual is necessarily to emphasize that the deceased is really and truly *gone*—and, with her, the actively heterosexual phase of Brittles's life. His post-heterosexuality is further stressed through an interesting analogy that the film constructs between Mary and Olivia. As Brittles is attending to the grave, a feminine silhouette suddenly falls across the tombstone, as though Mary, in an unexpected touch of Gothic, has miraculously returned to life. But it is actually Olivia, who has come to talk with Nathan. After she departs, he resumes the "conversation" with his dead wife, describing Olivia as a nice girl who "reminds me of you". The point here is that recognizing the similarity between the dead woman and the living one—and hence the abstract possibility of romance between Brittles and Olivia—only makes doubly clear the concrete inconceivability of such a thing actually taking place. Later, when Brittles finds Olivia wearing a yellow ribbon, the accepted sign that she loves someone in the Cavalry, he asks her who it is for (i.e., Cohill or Penell?). She flirtatiously replies, "Why, for you, of course, Captain Brittles". He laughs and says, "I'll make those young bucks jealous!"—the heartiness of his laughter signifying that he knows she is paying him a genuine compliment but not, of course, telling the literal truth. The master Cavalry officer is unflustered in his patriarchal and post-heterosexual masculinity.

Lieutenant Colonel Kirby Yorke of *Rio Grande* is slightly different in his own post-heterosexuality. For his wife Kathleen (Maureen O'Hara) is very much alive. But the couple have long been estranged from one another, and for reasons that directly involve the issues of masculine strength and duty. Kathleen comes from a wealthy Southern planter background, and during the Civil War her husband, as a US Army officer, found himself obliged to order that her family's plantation be burned to the ground. Fully aware that the result would be the end of any true marital relationship with his wife, Colonel (then Captain) Yorke did his duty as a man and a soldier, and completed the military operation. "It had to be done," as he says to his wife many years later. Maureen O'Hara's incomparable beauty—she may have been the most spectacularly good-looking actress in Hollywood at the time—serves as the most visible sign of how much Yorke has been willing to relinquish in order to be a real (and, necessarily, post-heterosexual) man.

During the time present of the film, Kathleen arrives at the fort where Kirby serves as commanding officer in order to retrieve their son Jefferson (Claude Jarman Jr.), who, having failed out of West Point, has enlisted in the Cavalry as a common trooper. (In *Rio Grande*, the son-figure to John Wayne is thus the character's *actual* son, though Harry Carey Jr. and Ben Johnson again play additional, figurative sons.) The sexual and emotional attraction between Kathleen and Kirby remains strong (stronger on her part, perhaps, than she had expected), and she offers to resume a real relationship with him if he will consent to their son's being relieved of his military commitments. He is sorely tempted, but again the masculine duty of the soldier must trump heterosexual desire: for to allow Jefferson to dishonor his freely taken oath would be a betrayal of Kirby Yorke's responsibilities as both a father and a commanding officer. As it turns out, Jefferson has no intention of leaving anyway, and at the end of the film he is receiving commendations for extraordinary valor during a dangerous mission. Might his happy success as a soldier—"Our boy did well," the wounded Kirby tells Kathleen—be matched by the happy reunion of his parents? It is easy to imagine how the film could have ended with the sort of overt romantic reconciliation conventional in Hollywood cinema. But this is precisely what Ford refuses to provide. We are left with the hint that the Yorkes *may* re-unite. It is, however, nothing more than a hint, and certainly nothing strong enough to cancel or even to seriously qualify the patriarchal post-heterosexuality of John Wayne.

It remains to consider *3 Godfathers*. Less renowned than *Red River* or any part of the Cavalry trilogy, this film about three outlaws who become the loving godfathers of an orphaned baby is somewhat marred by the excessive sentimentality that Orson Welles (though admiring Ford immensely) shrewdly identified as the director's most characteristic fault.[79] In terms of sheer visual beauty, however, *3 Godfathers* is perhaps the greatest of Ford's color films, rivaled mainly by *The Quiet Man*. Perhaps no other movie prior to *Lawrence of Arabia* (David Lean, 1962) offers such glorious views of desert landscape. The film also boasts an especially effective performance by John Wayne.

Wayne plays the cattle-rustler and bank-robber Robert Hightower, a merry, honest outlaw disinclined to harm anyone, and especially protective of his young partner, the Abilene Kid (Harry Carey Jr.). (The other partner in crime is Pedro "Pete" Fuerte [Pedro Armendáriz], who seems to be about Hightower's own age.) Wayne masters this semi-comic persona in the early part of the film, then modulates brilliantly into the anything but comic figure who successfully triumphs over all but insuperable hardship and agony as he crosses the burning Arizona desert with the baby. The journey becomes especially arduous after both of the other godfathers succumb to the environment's unendurable harshness, and at one point Hightower nearly gives up. But he presses on, and, after arriving back in civilization (willingly accepting the certainty of capture in order to get the baby to safety), he snaps back to his normal high-spirited self. In perhaps no other role does Wayne demonstrate greater strength, because here his strength is tested not against merely human adversaries but against the literally inhuman rigors of the Mojave Desert.

Though we know no facts of Hightower's past that indicate a specific narrative of post-heterosexuality—simply because we know no facts of his past at all—Wayne's post-heterosexual persona is very much in evidence and is integrally related to his masculine strength. Presumptively heterosexual by the laws of probability and the lack of evidence to the contrary, Hightower maintains his masculine toughness and displays no active interest in women. When the outlaws arrive in Welcome, Arizona, and Pedro begins to reminisce about a *señorita* he once knew there, Hightower brings things back to manly business by curtly remarking that they are in town to rob the bank, not to look up old friends. He behaves with the standard John Wayne patriarchal superiority toward the Abilene Kid, consistently addressing and referring to him affectionately as "Kid" or "the Kid". So far removed is Wayne's character from involvement with the feminine that, when the outlaws come upon the dying woman (Mildred Natwick) about to give birth in the middle of the desert, Hightower admits that, though an extremely "tough old bird" in his own estimation, he cannot face helping with the delivery. Pedro (who is perhaps assumed, as a nonwhite, to be more in touch with nature and femininity) handles the task instead. The only possible exception in the film to Wayne's post-heterosexuality is a very brief exchange at film's end that hints at possible future romance between Hightower and Ruby Latham (Dorothy Ford), the attractive young daughter of the president of the bank that Hightower and his colleagues had robbed at film's beginning. But the exchange lasts only a few seconds and is essentially a mistake; if there is going to be romance, then Hightower "ought" to preside over a coupling between Ruby and the Abilene Kid. But the Kid's death in the desert has foreclosed that possibility.

Ethan Edwards and Tom Doniphon

When John Ford came to make *The Searchers* (1956) and *The Man Who Shot Liberty Valance* (1962)—for me his finest achievements with John Wayne—he shaped his star actor much less in the image of the genial and calmly self-confident protagonists of *3 Godfathers* and the

Cavalry trilogy than in that of the bitter and furious Tom Dunson. This is especially true of *The Searchers*, where the post-heterosexuality of Ethan Edwards, like that of Dunson, has a tragic and ironic twist: one even crueler, indeed, than in *Red River*.

As we have seen, Ethan's heterosexual past has been with his sister-in-law Martha (Dorothy Jordan), the wife of his brother Aaron (Walter Coy). Like Fen in *Red River*, Martha is killed early in the film by savage Indians: in this case, in the "murder raid" (Ethan's term) by the Comanches who slaughter her, her husband, and their young son, and kidnap their two daughters. Whereas Dunson's loss is terrible but reasonably straightforward, Ethan's is equally terrible and the reverse of straightforward. Dunson, at least, was, we presume, able to enjoy an open and fulfilling love with Fen prior to their fateful parting. Ethan and Martha's love, by contrast, has been necessarily clandestine. Wayne and Jordan do a superb job of conveying, without a single line of dialogue beyond conventional pleasantries, the depth and tenderness of the feelings that their characters have for one another. What they also convey, however, is the intense frustration of having such feelings without being able to act on them or declare them openly. Even the viewer is kept somewhat in the dark. Though the film, as has been discussed in the preceding chapter, hints that Ethan and Martha's love may have been sexually consummated, we can never be sure.

After the murder raid, then, Ethan is post-heterosexual in the sense that his heterosexual career has ended—violently—before it could openly and properly begin. This intolerable psychological burden fuels the savage passion with which he conducts the search for his kidnapped nieces. He displays an anti-Indian hatred that, by comparison, makes Fonda's Owen Thursday look like a liberal and a tyrannical fury that makes Tom Dunson look like a nice guy.

Ethan's masculine strength and competence are as extreme as his bitterness. One relevant comparison here is with his two son-figures, who are both actively heterosexual and toward whom his attitude is far from benignly paternal in the Nathan Brittles way. One son-figure is (yet again) Harry Carey Jr., who plays the farm boy Brad Jorgensen in love with Ethan's older niece Lucy (Pippa Scott). Brad's infatuation is at one with essential weakness, and, when Lucy's raped and murdered body is discovered, he (in effect) commits suicide. Martin Pawley (Jeffrey Hunter), the adoptive son of the Aaron Edwards household, is tougher. Indeed, he is tough enough to stand up to Ethan at his most savage. After enough time passes for Ethan to reckon that his surviving niece Debbie (Lana Wood as a pre-adolescent girl, her older sister Natalie as a young woman) must be living in carnal relations with an Indian brave, he decides, as we have seen, that she is thus lost and should be killed rather than rescued; and Martin sticks with Ethan expressly to protect Debbie from him. Once Martin goes so far as to shield Debbie from Ethan's gunfire with his own body—an act of unquestionable physical courage that marks perhaps the only point in the film when Ethan particularly respects, though grudgingly, anything that anyone besides himself does. Still, even Martin is ultimately no match, as a man, for Ethan. At the end, when Debbie is brought back to white society (Ethan having inexplicably relented of his murderous intent), Martin rejoins his sweetheart Laurie Jorgensen (Vera Miles), Brad's sister; and all the main characters are united in the happy and relatively feminine domestic space of the Jorgensen household—all except Ethan, who remains in the more pristinely masculine environment of the great outdoors. His post-heterosexuality is for good, and—unlike John Wayne as a Cavalry officer—he is not sufficiently interested in erotic coupling even to play the part of the patriarchal matchmaker.

Tom Doniphon in *The Man Who Shot Liberty Valance* is closely related to Ethan and to Tom Dunson. Here, however, we see the process of the John Wayne character's *becoming* post-heterosexual in more detail than in any other film. Throughout most of the long flashback that comprises all but about twenty minutes of *Liberty Valance*, it seems, indeed, that Tom—the toughest guy around; even tougher, as he himself makes clear by both word and deed, than the widely feared and viciously sadistic gunfighter Liberty Valance (Lee Marvin)—is headed toward marriage with the prettiest girl in town, his sweetheart Hallie (Vera Miles). What happens to cancel these plans is nothing less than the building of the American nation.

Liberty Valance is usually, and appropriately, discussed as the tale of the (somewhat problematic) triumph in the American West of law-abiding civilization over gunslinging barbarism. Valance, as we have seen, embodies the latter, while the former is represented by the young lawyer Ransom Stoddard (James Stewart), who ultimately winds up as one of the most powerful politicians in the United States. Doniphon himself is best understood as constituting what Fredric Jameson has termed a "vanishing mediator," that is, a force from the old order that plays an indispensable role in the establishment of the new—but that must then necessarily vanish from the scene.[80] Belonging by temperament and talent to Valance's world of lawless gunfighting, Doniphon nonetheless slays Valance so that the new world of lawful bourgeois civility can be born; and, by allowing Stoddard to take public credit for the shooting of Valance, Doniphon enables Stoddard's political career as the champion of law and order to take off and flourish. In so doing, Doniphon necessarily provides for his own demise, for he now lacks any further meaningful role. Once not only the strongest but also the most popular and widely respected man in town, Doniphon ends his days in obscurity, squalor, and (it is implied) drunkenness, unknown except to one or two very old friends.

What has generally gone unnoticed in the discussion of this supremely great Western is that the social transition that Doniphon makes possible from barbarism to civilization is also the personal transition, for him, from heterosexuality to post-heterosexuality. Prior to Stoddard's arrival in town, everyone assumes that (despite what looks like a considerable age difference) Doniphon and Hallie are an obvious match. Expert at cooking and other domestic skills as well as physically beautiful, she is the most feminine woman around, as Tom is the most masculine man. In addition to his personal qualities of courage, strength, and competence, Tom is the owner of a modest but sufficient ranch and thus seems well-equipped to be a good provider as well as a good protector. He clearly desires her, and Hallie maintains just enough independence to be attractively spirited, in Doniphon's eyes and the viewer's. Yet Stoddard's entry onto the scene turns this apparently perfect couple into a sexual triangle. The attorney is hardly a macho man like Doniphon (or Valance). Indeed, the film repeatedly feminizes him, as he is shown, for instance, wearing an apron and serving food in a restaurant. Nonetheless, an attraction develops between Stoddard and Hallie, and she begins to care more for him than for Tom. Her choice is not inexplicable. After all, in the logic of the film, which the major characters seem to sense on some level, Stoddard is the future—he will eventually become a US senator—while Doniphon is the past.

As Doniphon sees this drama unfold, he naturally becomes jealous, and he begins to display something of the same bitter fury that characterizes Tom Dunson and Ethan Edwards. They lose their respective beloveds suddenly, in the primitive (and off-screen) violence of Indian attacks. But he must watch as he gradually loses *his* beloved to the progressive march of American civilization that Stoddard incarnates. He could, of course, be rid of his rival simply by doing nothing and allowing Valance to gun down Stoddard. But he seems to understand the futility of such a course. He knows that Hallie has come to prefer Stoddard, and, seeing which way the wind is blowing—on both the interpersonal and the national levels—he perhaps reckons that, even if Stoddard were to be eliminated, someone else like him would come along sooner or later. Perhaps, too, he loves Hallie so much that he wants her to have her own first choice. In any case, out of motives so complex that he himself does not appear to understand them fully, he shoots Valance from ambush, and thus makes possible the marriage of Stoddard and Hallie as well as the American nation-building that Stoddard's political career will exemplify. In so doing, he consigns himself to a life of unhappy post-heterosexuality. Yet the movie's larger resolution is not as happy as it may superficially appear. Just as the film does not allow us to forget that Stoddard's political career is founded on the lie that he was the man who shot Liberty Valance, so Hallie, even in late middle age and even after Doniphon's death, does not cease to remember, with yearning, her first and more masculine love: as is perhaps most memorably conveyed in the famous shot where Stoddard sees that Hallie has placed a cactus rose, which decades earlier had been the symbol of Doniphon's love for her, on top of Doniphon's cheap wooden coffin.

In Tom Doniphon, the typical John Wayne linkage between supreme masculinity and post-heterosexuality is thus presented in a partially proleptic and especially complex way. For Doniphon's status as the masculine ideal is most in evidence *before* he is actually set on the post-heterosexual path. At the same time, his masculinity is inseparable from those qualities of gunfighting prowess and rugged individualism that make that path inevitable for him.

Elder statesman of post-heterosexuality

The Man Who Shot Liberty Valance was not only Wayne's last Western (and, aside from the forgettable *Donovan's Reef* [1963], his last film) with John Ford. It was also the last great film in which he appears as what might be called the "classic" version of himself. After 1962, the persona established in the three major films of 1948 (*Red River*, *Fort Apache*, and *3 Godfathers*) appears to be creatively exhausted. It appears again only in things like, at best, Andrew McLaglen's mediocre *McLintock!* (1963)—though there largely stripped of the post-heterosexuality—and

McLaglen's equally mediocre *Chisum* (1970), and, at worst, such less-than-mediocre Westerns as *El Dorado* (1966) and *Rio Lobo* (1970), both directed by Howard Hawks. The actor himself, no longer guided by any particular director as he had been by Ford, seems to have realized that he was getting too old (and too heavy) to continue to do great work as "John Wayne" without some radical revision. It was such revision that produced Wayne's three late Westerns that deserve a place on any roster of his best: *True Grit* (Henry Hathaway, 1969), *Big Jake* (George Sherman, 1971), and *The Shootist* (Don Siegel, 1976).

True Grit, for which Wayne won his only Oscar, displays the *most* radical revision. His role here as the hard-drinking and disreputable Deputy US Marshal Rooster Cogburn has often been described as a brilliantly comic self-parody of his classic persona; and to a considerable degree this is so. Wayne is made up to appear even older and heavier than he actually was, and (to put it mildly) considerably less handsome as well; he also wears an eye-patch, supposedly having lost an eye in the Civil War. This deliberate de-glamorization of Wayne's face and body is matched by the change in his voice, which had been one of the most effectively melodic in Hollywood cinema. Here it is degraded by a harsh twang. In all these ways, Wayne in *True Grit* is well equipped to be a figure of low comedy in the venerable Shakespearian tradition; and this is precisely how the character of Rooster Cogburn functions throughout much of the film. Many of Ford's great Westerns had included such low comedy, but with Ford—as with Shakespeare—it was usually comic *relief*, performed on the margins of the main action by supporting players like Victor McLaglen. Wayne's Cogburn, indeed, owes something to McLaglen's persona in the Cavalry trilogy. But Cogburn is the starring role.

Yet the major revision that Wayne's image undergoes in *True Grit* should not blind us to the important elements of continuity. Rooster Cogburn may look comical and undignified compared to Nathan Brittles or Ethan Edwards, but he looks—and is—no less formidable. He may drink too much, but his reflexes are lightning-quick whenever they really have to be. Rooster cares more for money than John Wayne did in most of his earlier roles, and is less unwilling to shoot men without fairly calling them out. But he is, in the end, a hero who fights for the right. Challenged, in an early courtroom scene, to say how many men he has shot, he replies that he has never shot anyone he didn't have to shoot—a contention that the film generally supports. Indeed, the fact that Rooster Cogburn is, despite everything, ultimately the model of supreme masculinity that we expect John Wayne to be—strong and brave and equal to any crisis—is what really makes *True Grit* work. For a *purely* comic protagonist could not have successfully carried a John Wayne Western. In the film's climactic scene, Cogburn—reprising an earlier exploit that we have heard him brag about—takes his horse's reins in his teeth, and, firing a revolver with one hand and a rifle with the other, charges and defeats four armed outlaws. The scene's excellence depends on the fact that, as Garry Wills wrote in the best book about Wayne, it is fully "believable that *this* fat old drunk could face down an entire gang" (emphasis in original).[81] Though there are elements of Falstaff—surely the greatest character in the history of low comedy—in Rooster, Falstaff's cowardice is not among them.

With regard to Wayne's post-heterosexuality, Rooster is, again, in fundamental continuity with the persona created in 1948, but with comic twists. Rooster was once married but is clearly not at all heartbroken that his wife left him long ago. He lives in contented post-heterosexuality, spending as much time as possible chasing outlaws in the Indian Territory (where only federal law-enforcement officials have jurisdiction) and otherwise lodging happily enough with an elderly Chinese merchant and a cat. The main story-line of *True Grit* is set in motion when the young Mattie Ross (Kim Darby) hires Rooster to track down the man who murdered her beloved father; and their quest together displays Rooster's post-heterosexuality with a special and rather humorous emphasis. Though Darby was actually 22 (and a divorced mother) in 1969, Mattie—with her callow face, her hair cut very short, in tomboy fashion, and her breasts usually hidden beneath loose-fitting clothes—gives the general impression of being a smart, precocious pre-adolescent. Like a pre-adolescent, she displays not the slightest interest in romance. The film (unlike most of Wayne's) thus gives its star a female companion for almost the entirety of the action: but only in order to make clear, indeed almost *excessively* clear, that no erotic connection between them is possible, or even imaginable. Rooster appears old enough to be not just Mattie's father but her grandfather; and his post-heterosexuality dovetails neatly with her rather Huck-Finn-like innocence of sex.

A similar effect of sexlessness is achieved through opposite means in *Rooster Cogburn* (Stuart Millar, 1975), the much lesser but not unrewarding sequel to *True Grit*. Here again Rooster has a female companion during a dangerous and heroic mission. This time it is the prim, puritanical New England spinster Eula Goodnight (Katharine Hepburn). Eula makes clear that she has never had much use for men (except—as with Mattie—for her much-admired father); and, Hepburn having been 68 at the time of filming, she is in any case obviously well beyond what Hollywood norms regard as the age of overt female sexuality.

Jacob McCandles, the star's role in the much underrated *Big Jake*, is not a comic character in the manner of Rooster Cogburn, and is, indeed, closer to the classic 1948 persona of John Wayne. The film's construction almost suggests a retrospective consideration of Wayne's oeuvre. In plot, it is partly a remake of *The Searchers*—here the search is for Big Jake's grandson, kidnapped by an outlaw band demanding a million-dollar ransom—and Big Jake once echoes Ethan's signature line, "That'll be the day". The film also recalls *Rio Grande*, both in that its son-figures are represented by two of the Wayne character's actual sons (one of whom is played by *Wayne's* actual son) and in that the Wayne character is married but long separated and estranged from his wife, who is again played by Maureen O'Hara. In addition to O'Hara—always Wayne's favorite leading lady since their first work together in *Rio Grande*—John Agar, Harry Carey Jr., and Hank Worden provide familiar faces from many earlier John Wayne films. Also appearing are Bruce Cabot and Richard Boone, both of whom had been in movies with Wayne before, and the latter of whom here plays a villain that, though more restrained, owes something to Lee Marvin's Liberty Valance. In all these ways, *Big Jake* seems designed to give John Wayne fans more of what they always liked—an intention signaled nicely by the film's chief advertising slogan (itself based on a famous exchange from *Chisum*): "They wanted a ransom in gold. He gave 'em lead!"

The film (which Wayne himself, uncredited, helped Sherman to direct) *is*, however, deeply revisionist. Its revisionism is based mainly on its clear and self-conscious setting in a period when the classic John Wayne character has almost—though not quite—outlived his time. *Big Jake* repeatedly reminds us that it is set in 1909, and the film opens with a montage in historical-documentary style. The montage explains how refined and sophisticated America had become by 1909—Caruso was singing at the Met, the Barrymores were performing on stage, and the fat, comfortable Republican William Howard Taft was in the White House—but also makes clear that such urbanity was still found mainly in the East. West of the Mississippi, the Wild West, though dying, was not quite dead. John Wayne as Jacob McCandles is of course the personification of the Wild West, and of course it is he—not the US Army with its elaborate diplomatic procedures or the Texas Rangers with their new-fangled motorcars—who succeeds in defeating the outlaw gang and rescuing his grandson Little Jake (Ethan Wayne).

But both the film and Big Jake himself realize that this triumph is essentially a last hurrah. Jacob is necessarily becoming dependent on the modern technology he despises (in order to arrive promptly on the scene, he must travel by rail, not horseback), and he even wears glasses to help the fading eyesight that obliges him to delegate the sharpshooting work to his son Michael (Christopher Mitchum). The film succinctly encapsulates its double view of the John Wayne figure—that he is splendid, but fast becoming a splendid anachronism—in several scenes where strangers discover Big Jake's identity. They are awed by the name "Jacob McCandles," which clearly means to them everything that "John Wayne" *ought* to mean. But they are surprised to find him still walking around: "I thought you were [or "was"] dead," each of the strangers says. "Not hardly," he replies with understandable annoyance.

Jacob's near-superannuation coheres well with his post-heterosexuality. There is some talk—never exactly confirmed or denied—that his marriage broke up because of an *excess* of heterosexuality, in the sense that he could not keep his hands off numerous women who were not his wife. But during the time present of the film he is well beyond such things. He seems to live happily with his dog as his only companion (not unlike Rooster Cogburn with his cat), and the viewer is bound to agree with the honest, if tactless, remark by his son James (Patrick Wayne) that Big Jake gives the general impression of being anything but a ladies' man. James himself likes to pick up dance-hall girls when in town, while his father, with his superior masculinity, is happier picking a bar-room fight or shooting an outlaw.

One way that *Big Jake* differs from *Rio Grande* is that in the earlier film the Wayne and O'Hara characters spend a good deal of time together and (as we have seen) may just possibly re-unite "after" the final credits. But the estrangement of Jacob and Martha McCandles, who are on-screen together only briefly, near the film's beginning, seems almost certainly permanent. They have not lost all feeling for one another. Jacob carries Martha's picture in his watch-case, and it was Martha who insisted that Little Jake be named after his grandfather. But what seems to preclude any reconciliation is not so much Jake's possible past infidelities as the irreconcilable differences in the tastes and habits of these two equally strong-willed people. Martha likes to re-create as much European and East Coast culture as possible in her Southwestern mansion—all of which Jacob clearly finds effete and boring—while he is most at home on the range, in a world that she regards as vulgar and painful. Martha asks for Jacob's help in the rescue mission simply because the latter is, as she herself puts it, "a very harsh and unpleasant kind of business," which thus requires "an extremely harsh and unpleasant kind of man". But there is no suggestion that Martha (who once insists, "I have no husband!") wishes to allow such unpleasant harshness back into her own living-space, nor that Big Jake would wish to go there. The sons and the grandson will return to Martha's home, which is also their own. But the post-heterosexual Big Jake, like his predecessor Ethan Edwards, will undoubtedly remain in the masculine great outdoors.

The Shootist, Wayne's last film, is the finest of his late Westerns and arguably his only other film truly comparable in quality to *Red River* and the great John Ford Westerns. It stands to Wayne's films rather as *The Tempest* stands to Shakespeare's plays, and, as with *The Tempest*, even the most dogmatic formalist may find it hard to resist the lure of biographical interpretation. Here Wayne plays the legendary but aging gunfighter John Bernard Books, who, dying of prostate and colon cancer, chooses to end his life in one final gunfight, in which he rids the world of three dangerous villains. The parallel is clear with the situation of the actor, whose health was failing badly and who must have suspected (though he tried to deny the suspicion) that he was dying of the cancer that had cost him one lung almost two decades earlier. Surely Wayne, in some corner of his mind, guessed, correctly, that *The Shootist* would be his final movie? Having for decades played the most popular of screen heroes without displaying any particular off-screen bravery, Wayne ended his career on a note of genuine, real-life courage.

Like *Big Jake*, *The Shootist* stresses how the coming of modernity is fast rendering the classic John Wayne character obsolete. The film is set in Carson City, Nevada, in 1901, and people are just getting used to such innovations as motorcars, telephones, indoor plumbing, dry cleaning, and electric ceiling fans. The theme of modernization is diegetically emphasized by the city's marshal, one Walter Thibido (Harry Morgan), who, though no youngster himself, is an enthusiastically garrulous booster of social and technological progress, and who can't wait for Carson City to be rid of an anachronism like Books. As if to underscore that an era is ending, Books rides into town on the day the newspaper headlines proclaim the death of Queen Victoria, whom he greatly admires.

J. B. Books is, however, considerably more likeable than Jacob McCandles; if the latter is the descendant of Ethan Edwards, the former more closely resembles Nathan Brittles. He especially recalls Brittles in his paternal beneficence toward the last of Wayne's son-figures, Gillom Rogers (Ron Howard), the son of the landlady in whose boarding-house Books spends his final days. Books's relation to Gillom is, indeed, special among all the father-son relationships in Wayne's movies. Before *The Shootist*, the clear, if mainly implicit, message is nearly always that young men ought to grow up to be like the John Wayne character—or rather, as nearly like as possible, since genuinely to *equal* Wayne's masculinity is beyond reach. Gillom's own skills with firearms are considerable, and, idolizing Books, he seems for most of the film to be determined on a similar life. In the final scene, however, as Books lies dying on the floor, unable to speak, he signals with a nod of his head his approval of Gillom's sudden decision to *abandon* the way of the gun. More than Rooster Cogburn or Big Jake, Books clearly and unflinchingly accepts that history has overtaken him and his kind. In his final bit of acting, John Wayne, like Prospero, renounces his own magic.

A similar but more complex poignancy attends the representation of Books's post-heterosexuality. His history is a typical variation of the pattern that this chapter has been concerned to explore. He was once in love with the attractive *demimondaine* Serepta (Sheree North), but she left him—which turns out to be just as well, since the film shows Serepta to be a cold-hearted money-grubber. Books may visit the occasional whorehouse (more, one suspects, for the poker and whiskey downstairs than for the ladies upstairs), but he mostly lives his gunfighting life, as he says, in "the wild country," in post-heterosexual solitude.

But something happens when he arrives in Carson City and meets the widowed landlady Bond Rogers (Lauren Bacall). They seem an unlikely couple, and there is no question of love at first sight. On the contrary, Books hardly knows how to deal with a respectable woman, and Bond has a marked distaste for guns and gunfighters. Yet, in the brief time they get to know one another, each discovers the other to be more complicated and interesting—and more appealing—than either had supposed. Books begins to reveal, in his conversations with Bond, a vulnerability new to John Wayne's screen persona. He suggests that his life of masculine self-sufficiency has been a lonely one, and at one point describes himself as "a dying man, scared of the dark". Love between Books and Bond would clearly be a possibility—were it not for the fact that both know with certainty that they can have no future together, simply because Books has no future at all. So Books dies as he has lived, guns blazing and his post-heterosexuality intact. Even so, the film teases us to imagine an alternative ending in which Books is somehow cured of cancer, retires from gunfighting, and settles down to a more complex and satisfying heterosexual relationship with Bond Rogers than any he has imagined possible—and without losing (perhaps even with enhancing) his essential masculinity. Of course, such a story could not actually be told without exploding the ideological limits of the John Wayne Western. Still, the final instance of the genre does hint that maybe Wayne's powerfully mythic post-heterosexual macho is not, after all, necessarily the highest form of masculinity. But the continuing cultural currency of "John Wayne" proves that, whatever we may think or say, most of us have yet to learn that lesson.

Notes

1 Carl Freedman, *The Incomplete Projects: Marxism, Modernity, and the Politics of Culture* (Middletown, CT: Wesleyan University Press, 2002).

2 For example, the ideas in "Marxism Today" are always implicit and at certain points explicit in works of mine so different from one another as *Critical Theory and Science Fiction* (Hanover, NH: Wesleyan University Press, 2000)—a relatively technical work of literary theory—and *The Age of Nixon: A Study in Cultural Power* (Winchester, UK: Zero Books, 2012), a much more popular consideration of American electoral politics.

3 Stanley Aronowitz, "Film—The Art Form of Late Capitalism," *Social Text*, #1 (Winter 1979).

4 Some might question the designation of Stanley Kubrick as a Hollywood director, since most of his work was done outside Hollywood (and outside the United States altogether). But Kubrick (unlike Orson Welles, the other great American expatriate filmmaker) was careful to maintain a good working relationship with the Hollywood studios and their distribution system.

5 Outside the English-speaking world, the case for television is impressive too. For example, the full versions of such major masterpieces by Ingmar Bergman as *Scenes from a Marriage* (1973) and *Fanny and Alexander* (1984) were made not for the cinema but as miniseries for Swedish television.

6 The largest partial (or perhaps apparent) exception to this generalization is the work of Alfred Hitchcock, a giant in the history of crime cinema, whose films are generally taken to be dominated more by metaphysical than by social concerns. The absence of any sustained consideration of Hitchcock in this book is an omission that will, I hope, be made at least partially good by an article, on which I am currently working, about the film that I (like Hitchcock himself) take to be Hitchcock's finest: "American Civilization and Its Discontents: Nature, Society, and Sin in Hitchcock's *Shadow of a Doubt*".

7 Karl Marx, *Capital: A Critique of Political Economy*, Vol. 1, trans. Ben Fowkes (Harmondsworth: Penguin, 1976), p. 873. Further references will be given parenthetically by page number.

8 In Marx's original German, the term is *ursprüngliche Akkumulation*, which he offers as the translation of Adam Smith's "previous accumulation". But Marx's English translators have had good reason for rendering the term back into English as "primitive accumulation" (or, in at least one case, "original accumulation"), because Marx's concept is rather different from Smith's. For Smith, previous accumulation is an essentially peaceful operation, resulting from industriousness and frugality rather than from fraud and violence.

9 Jacques Derrida, *Of Grammatology*, trans. Gayatri Chakravorty Spivak (Baltimore: Johns Hopkins, 1976), p. 154. A further reference will be given parenthetically by page number.

10 All references to and quotations from the *Godfather* films are based on the boxed set of DVDs put out by Paramount Pictures in 2001.

11 Mario Puzo, *The Godfather* (New York: New American Library, 2002), p. 10.

12 Or perhaps one should say the OSS rather than its direct successor, the CIA, for the setting is just after the Second World War. But I mention the OSS/CIA advisedly, because Robert De Niro, 32 years after his brilliant performance as the young Vito Corleone in *The Godfather II*, directed *The Good Shepherd* (2006), which represents the CIA as, in essence, a WASP Mafia. A fruitful detailed analysis of *The Good Shepherd* (one of whose executive producers was Coppola) could be performed by reading the film as a sequel or self-conscious counterpart to the mob films of Coppola and of Martin Scorsese, to the success of which De Niro's acting made such an important contribution. Even the phrase, "the good shepherd" (Jesus's self-designation in John 10:11) is closely allied to "the godfather".

13 The allusion is to Fredric Jameson, "Reification and Utopia in Mass Culture," *Social Text*, #1 (Winter 1979), pp. 130–148. A reference will be given parenthetically by page number. Noteworthy examples of *Godfather* criticism written partly under Jameson's influence include Vera Dika, "The Representation of Ethnicity in *The Godfather*," and Glenn Man, "Ideology and Genre in the *Godfather* Films," both collected in Nick Browne, ed., *Francis Ford Coppola's* Godfather *Trilogy* (Cambridge: Cambridge University Press, 2000), pp. 76–108 and 109–132, respectively.

14 The reference is of course to *Apocalypse Now* (1979).

15 In fact, at just about the same time as the conference is taking place, Michael in Sicily witnesses a demonstration of communist workers—in a scene deleted from the film's final cut but available among the "bonus materials" of the boxed DVD set referred to above.

16 Pauline Kael, "The Current Cinema," *The New Yorker*, 18 March 1972, p. 138. No review of the film in 1972 displayed a grasp of its significance and stature better than Kael's did; her nearly essay-length piece is still worth reading in its entirety as an introduction to *The Godfather*. See, especially: "In *The Godfather* we see organized crime as an obscene symbolic extension of free enterprise and government policy, an extension of the worst in America— its feudal ruthlessness. Organized crime is not a rejection of Americanism, it's what we fear Americanism to be. It's our nightmare of the American system" (ibid.).

17 The filiations between Bertolucci and Coppola—who are almost exact contemporaries and have some claim to being the finest Italian director and the finest Italian-American director, respectively, of their generation—are worth exploring in detail. One important thing they share is the work of the brilliant cinematographer Vittorio Storaro, who has collaborated with each in a number of films: for example, with Bertolucci in *The Conformist* (1970), *Last Tango in Paris* (1972), *Novocento*, and *The Last Emperor* (1987), and with Coppola in *Apocalypse Now, One from the Heart* (1982), and *Tucker: The Man and His Dream* (1988).

18 Honoré de Balzac, *Old Goriot*, trans. Ellen Marriage (New York: Macmillan, 1913), p. 124.

19 My authority for this statement of Coppola's preference is an interview with him included in the DVD "bonus materials" referred to above. "The Death of Michael Corleone" is the title of the film's concluding "chapter" in the DVD format.

20 Jonathan Rosenbaum, "The Family That Preys Together," published on his website Jonathan Rosenbaum.com, 18 January 1991. See http://www.jonathanrosenbaum.com/?p=7367.

21 Of course, Michael cannot know that in 2011 Showtime would air Neil Jordan's historical dramatic series *The Borgias*, which is heavily influenced by the *Godfather* films.

22 Andreotti's place in Italian culture is nicely illustrated by a widely circulated joke. A political associate urges him to attend the funeral of an assassinated anti-Mafia judge: "The State must reply to the Mafia, and you are one of its top authorities!" Andreotti: "A top authority of which, do you mean?" The saying, "Power wears out those that don't have it" (*Il potere logora chi non ce l'ha*) is widely attributed to Andreotti, and, in *The Godfather III*, this sentence is whispered in Lucchesi's ear by the assassin, allied with Michael, who kills him. It is perhaps worth noting that *Il Divo* (2008), Paolo Sorrentino's remarkable biopic about Andreotti, is heavily influenced by Coppola's trilogy.

23 Michael's silent scream may be partly inspired by a storied moment in a famous production of Brecht's *Mother Courage* (1941) by the playwright's Berliner Ensemble in the 1950s. When Mother Courage learns of the death of her son Swiss Cheese, Helene Weigel, in the title role, opens her mouth wide and screams horribly, but with not a sound being heard. George Steiner's description of the moment—"It was silence which screamed and screamed through the whole theater so that the audience lowered its head as before a gust of wind" (*The Death of Tragedy* [New York: Hill & Wang, 1961], p. 354)—is a pretty good description of Pacino's soundless scream if one allows for the differences between theater and cinema. It has been suggested that Coppola may have intended (whether consciously or not) the scream to express his own grief for his son Gian-Carlo Coppola, who was killed in an accident in 1986.

24 To recall Beckett's own words: "[I]t [Joyce's influence on him] was an influence *ab contrario*. I realized that Joyce had gone as far as one could in the direction of knowing more, [being] in control of one's material. He was always *adding* to it; you only have to look at his proofs to see that. I realised that my own way was in impoverishment, in lack of knowledge and in taking away, in subtracting rather than in adding" (quoted in *Beckett Remembering, Remembering Beckett*, ed. James and Elizabeth Knowlson [New York: Arcade, 2006], p. 47). Of course, my analogy between Joyce/Beckett and Coppola/Scorsese as instances of influence *ab contrario* is, like all analogies, imperfect. Perhaps the most notable difference is that Beckett was a generation younger than Joyce and Joyce's protégé, whereas Coppola and Scorsese are peers.

25 For example, in one interview conducted shortly after *GoodFellas* was released, the filmmaker responded to this comment—"*The Godfather* is such an overpowering film that it shapes everybody's perception of the Mafia—including people in the Mafia"—by replying, "Oh, sure. I prefer *Godfather II* to *Godfather I*. I've always said it's like epic poetry, like *Morte d'Arthur*. My stuff is like some guy on the street-corner talking" (quoted in Gavin Smith, "Martin Scorsese Interviewed," *Martin Scorsese: Interviews*, ed. Peter Brunette [Jackson: University Press of Mississippi, 1999], p. 148).

26 All references to and quotations from *GoodFellas* are based on the two-disc "special edition" DVD set released by Warner Bros. in 2004.

27 I say the film is first-person "in a loose sense" because there is hardly such a thing as a *strictly* first-person film (as there are many strictly first-person novels). A film in which the

camera never showed anything not visible to the eyes of the protagonist would be almost unwatchable.

28   Quoted in Roger Ebert, *Scorsese by Ebert* (Chicago: University of Chicago Press, 2008), p. 199.

29   Robert Bolt, *A Man for All Seasons* (New York: Vintage, 1990), p. 158. Ellipsis in original.

30   Corey Robin, "The First Counter-revolutionary," *The Nation*, 19 October 2009; also available at http://www.thenation.com/article/first-counter-revolutionary?page=full.

31   Thomas Hobbes of Malmesbury, *Leviathan Or The Matter, Forme & Power of a Common-wealth Ecclesiasticall and Civill* (New York: Barnes & Noble, 2004), p. 77. Further references will be given parenthetically.

32   The reference is to Steven M. Sanders, "No Safe Haven: *Casino*, Friendship, and Egoism," in *The Philosophy of Martin Scorsese*, ed. Mark T. Conrad (Lexington: University Press of Kentucky, 2009), pp. 7–21.

33   In Nicholas Pileggi's *Wiseguy: Life in a Mafia Family* (New York: Pocket Books, 1987)—the journalistic account of the real-life Henry Hill on which Scorsese's film is based—Henry's boss Paul Vario (the model for Paulie in the movie) is represented as a kind of father-surrogate to Henry. It is significant that Scorsese almost completely eliminates any such family feeling from *GoodFellas*. A reference to Pileggi's volume (originally published in 1985) will be given parenthetically by page number.

34   Quoted in Patty Lou Floyd, *Backstairs with Upstairs, Downstairs* (New York: St. Martin's, 1988), p. 11.

35   All references to and quotations from *The Sopranos* are based on the seven boxed sets of DVDs released by HBO Home Video between 1999 and 2007.

36   This point of view is ably represented by the website of the abstract filmmaker Douglas Graves. See http://purecinema-celluloid.webs.com/. Jonathan Rosenbaum, though not in total agreement with the principles of pure cinema, has considerable sympathy for its aesthetic canons, and, evidently on this basis, ranks (in his *Movie Wars* [Chicago: A Capella, 2000], p. 99) Scorsese's *Kundun* (1998) above *Taxi Driver* (1976) and *Raging Bull* (1980)—a judgment that seems to me illustrative of the absurdity to which an overemphasis on the visual dimension of film can lead (not that *Kundun* is not an impressive and enjoyable film in its way).

37   Raymond Williams, *Television: Technology and Cultural Form* (New York: Schocken, 1975), p. 56.

38   The matter of scale largely (if perhaps not totally) accounts for the fact that those with a passionate devotion to a particular novel nearly always find any cinematic adaptation of it unsatisfactory: so much of the novel simply has to be left out. But such is not necessarily the case with a televisual adaptation. A useful test case here is the adaptation of Evelyn Waugh's *Brideshead Revisited* (1945) presented by Granada Television in 1981. The TV series, which faithfully reproduces the book in its entirety, requires eleven hours to do justice to a relatively simple novel of about 300 pages.

39   Nominally, there are six rather than seven seasons of *The Sopranos*, because Chase decided to designate the seventh season as "part two" of the sixth season.

40   In this context, it is interesting to note that, despite extensive work on such shows as *The Rockford Files* (1974–1980) and *Northern Exposure* (1990–1995), and some work

on *I'll Fly Away* (1991–1993)—all indisputably among the high points of broadcast television drama in the United States—Chase himself has said that, at least prior to *The Sopranos*, he greatly valued film over television: "All my life I wanted to do movies. I just resented every moment I spent in television. . . .[F]or me it was always cinema, cinema, cinema" (quoted in Bill Carter, "He Engineered a Mob Hit, And Now It's Time to Pay Up; Entering a 2nd Season, 'The Sopranos' Has a Hard Act to Follow," *The New York Times*, 11 January 2000, p. 90).

41 The reference is to an interview with Chase included as one of the special features in the HBO Home Video boxed set of the first season of *The Sopranos*.

42 See http://www.imdb.com/search/name?roles=tt0099685,tt0141842.

43 Christopher's inability to write even a decent English sentence involves a nice inside joke, since Michael Imperioli is an accomplished screenwriter, with five episodes of *The Sopranos* to his credit; he is, in fact, the only person to make an important contribution to the series as both actor and writer.

44 Cf. Alfred Auster, "*The Sopranos* and History," in *The Essential "Sopranos" Reader*, ed. David Lavery, Douglas L. Howard, and Paul Levinson (Lexington: University Press of Kentucky, 2011), p. 267: "*The Sopranos* uses *The Godfather* incessantly. For the mobsters, it is their *Niebelungen, Ramayana*, and Norse legends".

45 Cuomo experienced anti-Italian bigotry in his youth but went on to become a successful lawyer and a brilliant orator who served three terms as governor of New York, who was widely considered a potential presidential contender in the late 1980s and the early 1990s, and who has always been known for his cultivated, scholarly, distinctly un-thuggish demeanor. He was born in 1932. The various clues indicate that Tony was born in the 1950s, and closer to the end than to the beginning of the decade.

46 Cf. Ellen Willis, "Our Mobsters, Ourselves," in *This Thing of Ours: Investigating "The Sopranos"*, ed. David Lavery (New York: Columbia University Press, 2002), p. 3: "What 1950s gangster would. . . have a daughter named Meadow?"

47 Livia Soprano seems to be named, quite appropriately, after the famously murderous wife of the Roman emperor Augustus Caesar. It is probably no co-incidence that the Roman Livia is one of the most prominently featured characters in the BBC series *I, Claudius* (1976), one of the notable predecessors of *The Sopranos* in series television that is worthy of being compared to it.

48 Cf. James Harold, "A Moral Never-Never Land: Identifying with Tony Soprano," in *"The Sopranos" and Philosophy: I Kill Therefore I Am*, ed. Richard Greene and Peter Vernezze (Chicago: Open Court, 2004), p. 142: "Tony Soprano is a more fully-developed character than any other fictional gangster ever created, and we get to know him intimately".

49 Cf. Glen Creeber, "'TV Ruined the Movies': Television, Tarantino, and the Intimate World of *The Sopranos*," in *This Thing of Ours, op. cit.*, p. 127: "Tony's long-running battle with therapy implicitly parallels the narrative's own struggle with the personal requirements of television. Frustrated by the constant need to express his feelings, this Mafia boss is not simply resisting the contemporary preoccupation with self-analysis but also struggling to adapt to television's obsession with the *private* and *personal* dynamics of human experience" (emphasis in original).

50 See http://www.imdb.com/search/name?roles=tt0141842,tt0979432&sort=starmeter,asc& start=1.

51 Quoted in Cameron Crowe, *Conversations with Wilder* (New York: Knopf, 1999), p. 338.

52 See Carl Freedman, "On Kubrick's *2001*: Form and Ideology in Science-Fiction Cinema," in Freedman, *The Incomplete Projects, op. cit.*, pp. 91–112.

53 Since Klaatu and the forces behind him are, like Professor Barnhardt, so emphatically un-American—and since the film is so devastating in its portrayal of American social, political, and military life—it seems a bit incredible that the film could be read as Cold War propaganda, with Klaatu as a kind of veiled spokesman for a *Pax Americana*. But this interpretation of *The Day the Earth Stood Still* has been attempted, notably by Mark Jancovich, *Rational Fears: American Horror in the 1950s* (Manchester: Manchester University Press, 1996), pp. 41–46.

54 Ernst Bloch, "Marxism and Poetry," in Bloch, *The Utopian Function of Art and Literature: Selected Essays*, trans. Jack Zipes and Frank Mecklenburg (Cambridge, MA: MIT Press, 1988), p. 163.

55 See Freedman, *op. cit.*, for a detailed demonstration of this point.

56 Karl Marx, *Capital*, Vol. 3, trans. David Fernbach (New York: Vintage, 1981), p. 959.

57 All references to the film are based on the DVD issued by the New Line Platinum Series in 2001.

58 My comments on *Blade Runner* refer not to the original theatrical release but to the significantly different "director's cut" that Scott made available in 1992; in most discussion of this much-discussed film, the latter version is (I think rightly) considered definitive.

59 Mark Bould, *Film Noir: From Berlin to Sin City* (London: Wallflower, 2005), pp. 51–67, usefully emphasizes the importance of entrapment for classic noir.

60 All references to *Double Indemnity* are based on the two-disc DVD set issued by the Universal Legacy Series in 2006.

61 Wilder actually shot the gas-chamber sequence, and later described it as one of the two finest sequences he ever directed. Excluded from the film's final cut, it has evidently been lost. See Ed Sikov, *On Sunset Boulevard: The Life and Times of Billy Wilder* (New York: Hyperion, 1998), p. 210.

62 James M. Cain, *Double Indemnity* (New York: Random House, 1978), p. 63.

63 All references to *Body Heat* are based on the Warner Home Video DVD issued in 1997.

64 It may be no coincidence that Crenna had played Walter Neff in Jack Smight's undistinguished 1973 TV-movie remake of *Double Indemnity*, which attempts, very clumsily, to follow Wilder's original closely; it is (barely) worth watching for Lee J. Cobb's performance as Barton Keyes.

65 See Fredric Jameson, *Postmodernism, Or, The Cultural Logic of Late Capitalism* (Durham, NC: Duke, 1991), pp. 20–21.

66 Is this the truth of Sam Malone, Danson's Casanova-like character in the popular NBC sitcom *Cheers* (1982–1993), which Danson made almost immediately after *Body Heat*?

67 See Robert Brenner, "Uneven Development and the Long Downturn: The Advanced Capitalist Economies from Boom to Stagnation, 1950–1998," *New Left Review*, No. 229 (May/June 1998), for perhaps the most nearly definitive treatment to date of the global turbulence of postwar capitalism.

68 The (of course predominantly white) federal government of the United States invented the term *Native Americans*, which is today widely used by white people in the US. But every poll or study I have seen indicates that *American Indians* is the term overwhelmingly favored by the people thus designated; and I use it out of respect for their preference.

69 Quoted in Joseph McBride, *Searching for John Ford: A Life* (New York: St. Martin's, 2001), p. 271. This massive volume is the primary source for the biographical references in the current chapter.

70 The other six are *My Darling Clementine* (1946), *Fort Apache* (1948), *She Wore a Yellow Ribbon* (1949), *The Searchers, Sergeant Rutledge* (1960), and *Cheyenne Autumn* (1964).

71 Quoted in McBride, p. 288.

72 Nixon professed great admiration for Ford's work, and once claimed to have seen nearly *all* the director's films (Ford directed about 150, not counting his extensive filmmaking for the US military during World War II). In that case, one would like to know what Nixon made of Ford's excellent political drama *The Last Hurrah* (1958), one of the best scenes of which savagely mocks the young Nixon of the 1952 presidential campaign. What appears to have been Ford's final public political statement was uttered in 1973 on the occasion of his receiving the Medal of Freedom: "God bless Richard Nixon!"

73 A similarly illogical and infelicitous ending mars *Red River* (Howard Hawks, 1948)—a film that, as we will see, deeply influenced Ford's making of *The Searchers*, especially in the construction of the Ethan Edwards role for John Wayne. At the conclusion of Hawks's film, the logic of character and story suggest that Tom Dunson (Wayne) will kill (or at least attempt to kill) his adopted, and mutinous, son Matt Garth (Montgomery Clift), as he has promised to do. But he inexplicably chooses not to, and, as in *The Searchers*, a happy ending is thus forced against the grain of the movie as a whole.

74 For a deft analysis of the class politics of *Shane*, see Patrick McGee, *From* Shane *to* Kill Bill: *Rethinking the Western* (Oxford, UK: Blackwell, 2007), pp. 1–19.

75 One factor that prevents us from seeing Stoddard's corruption with full clarity is Stewart's dominant (though not invariable) film persona as a squeaky-clean type: a persona created most consequentially by his performance as Jefferson Smith, the passionate foe of political corruption in Frank Capra's *Mr. Smith Goes to Washington* (1939). That film was released in the same year as *Stagecoach* and shares something of the latter's New Deal liberalism.

76 See Roland Barthes, *Mythologies*, ed. and trans. Annette Lavers (New York: Hill & Wang, 1977). This work was originally published in French in 1957.

77 McBride, the best and most nearly definitive of Ford's biographers, accepts this anecdote as authentic. McBride also reports that Hawks, by his own testimony, deliberately imitated Ford's visual style in some scenes of *Red River*, and that Ford gave Hawks some assistance in editing the film. See McBride, *op. cit.*, pp. 459–460.

78 The Clash, the best of the classic punk bands, recognized the stylistic affinities between Clift and punk in "The Right Profile," their tribute to the actor, which explicitly mentions *Red River*. See their third album, *London Calling* (CBS Records, 1979).

79 Welles's comment, though specifically about *The Grapes of Wrath* (1940), succinctly describes the strengths and weaknesses of *3 Godfathers*: "Sentiment is Jack's [i.e., Ford's] vice. When he escapes it, you get a perfect kind of innocence". Quoted in McBride, p. 315.

80 For a full discussion of the concept, see Jameson's early essay, "The Vanishing Mediator; or, Max Weber as Storyteller" (1973), collected in his *The Ideologies of Theory: Essays 1971–1986, Volume Two: Syntax of History* (Minneapolis: University of Minnesota Press, 1988), pp. 3–34.

81 Garry Wills, *John Wayne's America* (New York: Simon & Schuster, 1997), p. 18. In my understanding of John Wayne (as of various other things), I must acknowledge a considerable general debt to Wills.

Index